Essays in Feminism

From the first appearance of the lead essay in this collection, "The Next Great Moment in History Is Theirs," published in 1969, Vivian Gornick established herself as one of the most respected voices in what was to become the new literature of contemporary feminism.

Speaking always for herself, always maintaining her independence while at the same time reflecting and commenting upon current feminist issues of concern, Ms. Gornick has become one of the most eagerly read writers in *The Village Voice*, *The New York Times* and numerous other periodicals.

With characteristic passion and a quick, penetrating intelligence, she dissects the culture that is at the root of female oppression, a culture that routinely defines woman in terms of her power to lure men, but rarely in the essential terms of the never ceasing human struggle to know *herself*.

This collection will stand as a permanent record of the evolution of one
(continued on back flap)

By Vivian Gornick:

The Romance of American Communism

In Search of Ali Mahmoud

Woman in Sexist Society
(edited with B. K. Moran)

(continued from front flap)

feminist's personal consciousness over the seven years that paralleled the renaissance of American Feminism. In such memorable pieces as "Feminist Writers: Hanging Ourselves on a Party Line," "Toward a Definition of the Female Sensibility," "The Conflict Between Love and Work," and "Why Do These Men Hate Women?" (on Mailer, Henry Miller, Bellow and others), Vivian Gornick has made a permanent contribution to both feminism and our understanding of society. These are essays to be read and reread for years to come, as both men and women begin to assimilate what we have all learned from the women's movement and begin to live with the new challenges, opportunities and problems with which it has presented us.

ESSAYS
==IN==
FEMINISM

Vivian Gornick

Harper & Row, Publishers
New York, Hagerstown, San Francisco, London

Grateful acknowledgment is made for permission to reprint:
"On Rereading Virginia Woolf" was originally published under the title "What Would Virginia Woolf Make of American Feminism in the 70's" from the April 27, 1978 issue of *The New York Times*. © 1978 by The New York Times Company. Reprinted by permission.

"The Woman and the Myth" by Margaret Fuller from the January 9, 1977 issue of *The New York Times*. © 1977 by The New York Times Company. Reprinted by permission.

Portions of this work originally appeared in *Life Special Report: Remarkable American Women, Ms Magazine, The New York Times Magazine,* and the *Village Voice.*

FIRST EDITION

Designed by Gloria Adelson

Library of Congress Cataloging in Publication Data

Gornick, Vivian.
  Essays in feminism.
  Includes index.
  1. Feminism—Addresses, essays, lectures. 2. Women
—Addresses, essays, lectures. I. Title.
HQ1154.G627 1978   301.41'2   77-6884
ISBN 0-06-011627-7
78 79 80 81 82 10 9 8 7 6 5 4 3 2 1

Contents

❧

Introduction

These pieces were written over a period of nine years. Nearly all of them appeared in the *Village Voice,* the New York weekly newspaper at which I worked for ten years. Although the pieces clearly reflect my own preoccupation with the growth of American feminism during the 1970s, many of them were written in the course of daily journalism, and I never thought that one day I would see them all side by side.

Rereading the pieces, often for the first time in five or six years, I was struck by the pamphleteering rush that characterizes most of them. I had forgotten how feminist insight burned in those early years; how, for me, everything, everywhere, suddenly flashed in the new light; and with what eagerness I climbed the barricades to plead, exhort, explain, command: *"Listen* to me, this is important, you must listen." How packed some of the sentences are! So much urgent feeling and pent-up energy and bad writing.

In this sense the collection taken as a whole seems to me a reflection of the manner in which American feminists—both as individuals and as a movement—have been coming of age in this past decade. For many of us the initial feminist understanding came as a kind of explosion: shattering, scattering, everything tumbling about, the old world within splintering even as the new one was collecting.

But there were moments of perfect, clarifying calm when the thing, as it were, was "grasped whole." And these moments were there from the very beginning, then lost, then recovered, again lost, again recovered, lurching forward in the unshapely manner of one proceeding through uncharted territory with a compass that works only intermittently.

Certainly one "moment of calm" was the early perception that feminist consciousness must be guarded against feminist dogma. I tried repeatedly to isolate the idea that contemporary feminism turned on self-knowledge even more than it turned on attacking the institutional nature of women's oppression: that out of an ever-deepening self-awareness would come, simultaneously, a more precise analysis of the political nature of our lives as well as a stronger weapon in the feminist arsenal necessary for the struggle that lay before us; and that for this awareness to flourish it was necessary to avoid the rhetorical "line," the "correct" analysis, the doctrinaire position: adopting ideological dogma meant losing the self-discovery that was the real promise of modern feminism.

When I look at the four pieces called "The Light of Liberation," "Lesbians and Women's Liberation," "Feminist Writers: Hanging Ourselves on a Party Line," and "The Women's Movement in Crisis" (written in 1970, 1971, and 1975), I see that this objection to the development of dogma in the women's movement has been a somewhat obsessive preoccupation of mine. And, indeed, I feel these last few years vindicate the obsession. The feminist perspective has grown immeasurably throughout American life because feminist consciousness has thrived and become ever more sophisticated whereas feminist dogma has shriveled and become ever more parochial.

Another preoccupation has had to do with the notion that contemporary feminism is bound up with a profound rereading of the culture; that, indeed, rereading the culture is what defines the feminist perspective. The essays "Toward a Definition of the Female Sensibility," "On Rereading Virginia Woolf," and "Female Narcissism as a Metaphor in Literature" were triggered by the excitement of "rereading" the books I'd grown up with, of suddenly seeing the universe within those books from another vantage point and realizing that there is a femaleness of experience that has been used as a metaphor for the human condition every bit as much as the maleness of experience has been used, and that that literature which *truly* mines women's experience is a powerful contribution to a revitalized and much enlarged understanding of why the world-making enterprise has taken shape as it has.

Concomitantly, I have felt that important attention must be paid to the lives of women we describe as "the brilliant exception." (Again, it came as a surprise to me—when I saw these pieces gathered together—how ardently I have felt that, and how often I have been drawn to examining the lives of gifted women living in times and places other than my own.)

The four essays on Dorothy Thompson, Rahel Varnhagen, Agnes Smedley, and Margaret Fuller are all instances of "rereading the culture," and I count them among the most focused pieces in the group. Here are four distinguished women whose lives, when we "reread" them, personify female outsidedness. Each was possessed of large artistic and intellectual talents, each lived intensely "in the world," and each conducted an isolated struggle for selfhood in a time and place when to pay concentrated attention to their lives as women *per se* was inconceivable.

Now, under the impetus of the feminist perspective, I could not *but* concentrate on them as women, and when I did I experienced the full dimension of their outsidedness, the contorted shape of their inner lives, and I came to see them—and all women like them—as part of a larger metaphor for a centuries-long struggle in pursuit of the conscious life.

In the strictest sense a number of these pieces are dated. Written in response to specific events—a local election, a university appointment, the production of a play—the immediate "point" has more often than not evaporated in the course of time. The specific circumstances described in "The Next Great Moment" now seem long ago and far away, and I wince at the naïveté of some of the things I said in that piece. The piece on consciousness raising, as well, now reads like journalistic melodrama, and the potential merger of Harvard and Radcliffe at the center of the piece on Matina Horner is an accomplished fact, one that has done away with the most overt forms of discrimination against women here described.

However, the condition to which these pieces speak is still very much the larger reality, and in this sense they—unhappily— remain pertinent. Female paralysis of will, the subject of "The Next Great Moment," will take generations to erase; that groping toward self-understanding at the heart of consciousness raising is still the wider experience; women now attend Harvard rather than Radcliffe, but the university is certainly still dominated by men making other men "leaders." In fact, rereading these pieces is a sobering reminder of how very little has changed in these eight or nine years, and how detailed, arduous, and generational an effort will be required to bring women to something that resembles social and political equality.

In the end, I think this collection is certainly uneven: Much of it feels like "bits and pieces." Some things are overwritten, some underwritten. And in general very little is carried to a satisfying wholeness of conclusion.

But the context in which the pieces stand is that of a personal and political apprenticeship—the self-education of an American feminist in the volatile decade of the 1970s—and so I disavow none of them. That apprenticeship, it seems to me, has turned on the straining effort to think clearly and consecutively about the larger meanings of women's lives. For me, that effort is in itself a metaphor for contemporary feminism. Thinking clearly is, I believe, the road to freedom. It was in the spirit of that feminist essential that I have tried to write.

The Next Great Moment
in History Is Theirs

One evening not too long ago at the home of a well-educated and extremely intelligent couple I know, I mentioned the women's liberation movement and was mildly astonished by the response the subject received. The man said, "Jesus, what *is* all that crap about?" The woman, a scientist who had given up ten working years to raise her children, said, "I can understand if these women want to work and are demanding equal pay. But why on earth do they want to have children, too?" To which the man rejoined, "Ah, they don't want kids. They're mostly a bunch of dykes, anyway."

Again: Having lunch with an erudite, liberal editor, trained in the humanist tradition, I was struck dumb by his reply to my mention of the women's liberation movement: "Ah shit, who the hell is oppressing them?"

And yet again: A college-educated housewife, fat and neurotic, announced with arch sweetness, "I'm sorry, I just don't *feel* oppressed."

Over and over again, in educated, thinking circles, one meets with a bizarre, almost determined ignorance of a fact of unrest that is growing daily, and that exists in formally organized bodies in nearly every major city and on dozens of campuses across America. The women of this country are gathering themselves into a sweat of civil revolt, and the general population seems totally unaware of what is happening; or, indeed, that anything is happening; or that there is a legitimate need behind what is happening. How is this possible? Why is it true? What relation is there between the peculiarly unalarmed, amused dismissal of the women's rights movement and the movement itself? Is this relation only coincidental, only the generally apathetic response of a society already benumbed by civil rights and student anarchy and unable to rise to yet one more protest movement, or is it more to the point in the case of women's rights; is it not, in fact, precisely the key to the entire case?

Almost invariably, when people set out to tell you there is no such thing as discrimination against women in this country, the first thing they hastily admit to is a *minor* degree of economic favoritism shown toward men. In fact, they will eagerly, almost gratefully, support the claim of economic inequity, as though that will keep the discussion within manageable bounds. Curious. But even on economic grounds or grounds of legal discrimination most people are dismally ignorant of the true proportions of the issue. They will grant that often a man will make as much as $100 more than a woman at the same job, and yes, it *is* often difficult for a woman to be hired when a man can be hired instead, but after all, that's really not *so* terrible.

This is closer to the facts:

Women in this country make 60 cents for every $1 a man makes.

Women do not share in the benefits of the fair-employment-practices laws because those laws do not specify "no discrimination on the basis of sex."

Women often rise in salary only to the point at which a man starts.

Women occupy, in great masses, the "household tasks" of industry. They are nurses but not doctors, secretaries but not executives, researchers but not writers, workers but not managers, bookkeepers but not promoters.

Women almost never occupy decision- or policy-making positions.

Women are almost nonexistent in government.

Women are subject to a set of "protective" laws that restrict their working hours, do not allow them to occupy many jobs in which the carrying of weights is involved, do not allow them to enter innumerable bars, restaurants, hotels, and other public places unescorted.

Women, despite one hundred years of reform, exist in the domestic and marriage laws of our country almost literally as appendages of their husbands. Did you know that rape by a husband is legal but that if a woman refuses to sleep with her husband she is subject to legal suit? Did you know that the word domicile in the law refers to the husband's domicile and that if a woman refuses to follow her husband to wherever he makes his home, legal suit can be brought against her to force her to do so? Did you know that in most states the law imposes severe legal disabilities on married women with regard to their personal and property rights? (As a feminist said to me: "The United Nations has defined servitude as necessarily involuntary, but women, ignorant of the law, put themselves into *voluntary* servitude.")

Perhaps, you will say, these observations are not so shocking. After all, women *are* weaker than men, they do need protection, what on earth is so terrible about being protected, for God's sake! And as for those laws, they're never invoked, no woman is dragged anywhere against her will; on the contrary, women's desires rule the middle-class household, and women can work at hundreds of jobs—in fact, a great deal of the wealth of the country is in their hands—and no woman ever goes hungry.

I agree. These observed facts of our national life are not so shocking. The laws and what accrues from them are not so terrible. It is what's behind the laws that is so terrible. It is not the letter of the law but the spirit determining the law that is terrible. It is not what is explicit but what is implicit in the law that is terrible. It is not the apparent condition but the actual condition of woman that is terrible.

"The woman's issue is the true barometer of social change," said a famous political theoretician. This was true one hundred years ago; it is no less true today. Women and blacks were and are, traditionally and perpetually, the great "outsiders" in Western culture, and their erratic swellings of outrage parallel each other in a number of ways that are both understandable and also extraordinary. A hundred years ago a great abolitionist force wrenched this country apart and changed its history forever; many, many radical men devoted a fever of life to wrecking a system in which men were bought and sold; many radical women worked toward the same end; the abolitionist movement contained women who came out of educated and liberal nineteenth-century families, women who considered themselves independent thinking beings. It was only when Elizabeth Cady Stanton and Lucretia Mott were not allowed to be seated at a World Anti-Slavery Conference held in the 1840s that the intellectual abolitionist women suddenly perceived that their own political existence resembled that of the blacks. They raised the issue with their radical men and were denounced furiously for introducing an insignificant and divisive issue, one that was sure to weaken the movement. Let's win this war first, they said, and then we'll see about women's rights. But the women had seen, in one swift visionary moment, to the very center of the truth about their own lives, and they knew that first was *now,* that there would never be a time when men would willingly address themselves to the question of female rights, that to strike out *now* for women's rights could do nothing but strengthen the issue of black civil rights because it called attention to all instances of rights denied in a nation that prided itself on rights for all.

Thus was born the original women's rights movement, which became known as the women's suffrage movement because the single great issue, of course, was legal political recognition. But it was never meant to begin and end with the vote, just as the abolitionist movement was never meant to begin and end with the vote. Somehow, though, that awful and passionate struggle for suffrage seemed to exhaust both the blacks and the women, especially the women, for when the vote finally came at the end of the Civil War, it was handed to black males—but not to women; the women had to go on fighting for sixty bitterly long years for suffrage. And then both blacks and women lay back panting, unable to catch their breath for generation upon generation.

The great civil rights movement for blacks in the 1950s and '60s is the second wind of that monumental first effort, necessary because the legislated political equality of the 1860s was never translated into actual equality. The reforms promised by law had never happened. The piece of paper meant nothing. Racism had never been legislated out of existence; in fact, its original virulence had remained virtually untouched, and, more important, the black in this country had never been able to shake off the slave mentality. He was born scared, he ran scared, he died scared; for one hundred years after legal emancipation, he lived as though it had never happened. Blacks and whites did not regard either themselves or each other differently, and so they in no way lived differently. In the 1950s and '60s the surging force behind the renewed civil rights effort has been the desire to eradicate this condition more than any other, to enable the American black to believe in himself as a whole, independent, expressive human being capable of fulfilling and protecting himself in the very best way he knows how. Today, after more than fifteen years of unremitting struggle, after a formidable array of reform laws legislated at the federal, state, and local level, after a concentration on black rights and black existence that has traumatized the nation, it is still not unfair to say that the psychology of defeat has not been lifted from black life. Still (aside from the continuance of crime, drugs, broken homes, and all the wretched rest of it), employers are able to say, "Sure, I'd love to hire one if I could find one who qualified," and while half the time this is simply not true, half the time it *is*, because black life is still marked by the "nigger mentality," the terrible inertia of spirit that accompanies the perhaps irrational but deeply felt conviction that no matter what one does, one is going to wind up a thirty-five-year-old busboy. This "nigger mentality" characterizes black lives. It also characterizes women's lives. And it is this, and this alone, that is behind the second wave of feminism now sweeping the country and paralleling precisely, exactly as it did one hundred years ago, the black rights movement. The fight for reform laws is just the beginning. What women are really after this time around is the utter eradication of the "nigger" in themselves.

Most women who feel "niggerized" have tales of overt oppression to tell. They feel they've been put down by their fathers, their brothers, their lovers, their bosses. They feel that in their families, in their sex lives, and in their jobs they have counted as nothing, they have been treated as second-class citizens, their minds have been deliberately stunted and their emotions warped. My own experience with the condition is a bit more subtle, and I do believe a bit closer to the true feminist point.

To begin with, let me tell a little story. Recently, I had lunch with a man I had known at school. He and his wife and I had all been friends at college; they had courted while we were in school and immediately upon graduation they got married. They were both talented art students, and it was assumed both would work in commercial art. But shortly after their marriage she became pregnant, and never did go to work. Within five years they had two children. At first I visited them often; their home was lovely, full of their mutual talent for atmosphere; the wife sparkled, the children flourished; he rose in the field of commercial art; I envied them both their self-containment, and she specially her apparently contented, settled state. But as I had remained single and life took me off in various other directions, we soon began to drift apart, and when I again met the husband we had not seen each other in many years. We spoke animatedly of what we had both been doing for quite a while. Then I asked about his wife. His face rearranged itself suddenly, but I couldn't quite tell how at first. He said she was fine, but it didn't sound right.

"What's wrong?" I asked. "Is she doing something you don't want her to do? Or the other way around?"

"No, no," he said hastily. "I want her to do whatever she wants to do. Anything. Anything that will make her happy. And get her off my back," he ended bluntly. I asked what he meant and he told me of his wife's restlessness of the last few years, of how sick she was of being a housewife, how useless she felt, and how she longed to go back to work.

"Well?" I asked, "did you object?"

"Of course not!" he replied vigorously. "Why the hell would I do that? She's a very talented woman, her children are half grown, she's got every right in the world to go to work."

"So?" I said.

"It's *her,*" he said bewilderedly. "She doesn't seem able to just go out and get a job."

"What do you mean?" I asked. But beneath the surface of my own puzzled response I more than half knew what was coming.

"Well, she's scared, I think. She's more talented than half the people who walk into my office asking for work, but do what I will she won't get a portfolio together and make the rounds. Also, she cries a lot lately. For no reason, if you know what I mean. And then, she can't seem to get up in the morning in time to get a babysitter and get out of the house. This is a woman who was always up at seven A.M. to feed everybody, get things going; busy, capable, doing ten things at once." He shook his head as though in a true quandary. "Oh well," he ended up, "I guess it doesn't really matter any more."

"Why not?" I asked.

His eyes came up and he looked levelly at me. "She's just become pregnant again."

I listened silently, but with what internal churning! Even though the external events of our lives were quite different, I felt as though this woman had been living inside my skin all these years, so close was I to the essential nature of her experience as I perceived it listening to her husband's woebegone tale. I had wandered about the world, I had gained another degree, I had married twice, I had written, taught, edited, I had no children. And yet I knew that in some fundamental sense we were the same woman. I understood exactly—but exactly—the kind of neurotic anxiety that had beset her, and that had ultimately defeated her; it was a neurosis I shared and had recognized in almost every woman I had ever known.

I was raised in an immigrant home where education was worshiped. As the entire American culture was somewhat mysterious to my parents, the educational possibilities of that world were equally unknown for both the boy and the girl in our family. Therefore, I grew up in the certainty that if my brother went to college, I too could go to college; and, indeed, he did, and I in my turn did too. We both read voraciously from early childhood on, and we were both encouraged to do so. We both had precocious and outspoken opinions, and neither of us was ever discouraged from uttering them. We both were exposed early to unionist radicalism, and neither of us met with opposition when, separately, we experimented with youthful political organizations. And yet somewhere along the line my brother and I managed to receive an utterly different education regarding ourselves and our own expectations from life. He was taught many things, but what he learned was the need to develop a kind of inner necessity. I was taught many things, but what I learned, ultimately, was that it was the prime vocation of my life to prepare myself for the love of a good man and the responsibilities of homemaking and motherhood. All the rest, the education, the books, the jobs, that was all very nice and, of course, why not? I was an intelligent girl, shouldn't I learn? *Make* something of myself! But, oh dolly, you'll see, in the end no woman could possibly be happy without a man to love and children to raise. What's more, came the heavy implication, if I *didn't* marry I would be considered an irredeemable failure.

How did I learn this? How? I have pondered this question a thousand times. Was it really that explicit? Was it laid out in lessons strategically planned and carefully executed? Was it spooned down my throat at regular intervals? No. It wasn't. I have come finally to understand that the lessons were implicit and they took place in a hundred different ways, in a continuous day-to-day exposure to an *attitude*, shared by all, about women, about what kind of creatures they were and what kind of lives they were meant to live; the lessons were administered not only by my parents but by the men and women, the boys and girls, all around me who, of course, had been made in the image of this attitude.

My mother would say to me when I was very young, as I studied at the kitchen table and she cooked, "How lucky you are to go to school! I wasn't so lucky. I had to go to work in the factory. I wanted so to be a nurse! But go be a nurse in Williamsburg in 1920! Maybe you'll be a nurse. . . ." I listened, I nodded, but somehow the message I got was that I was like her and I would one day be doing what she was now doing.

My brother was the "serious and steady" student, I the "erratic and undisciplined" one. When he studied, the house was silenced; when I studied, business as usual.

When I was fourteen and I came in flushed and disarrayed, my mother knew I'd been with a boy. Her fingers gripped my upper arm; her face, white and intent, bent over me: What did he do to you? *Where* did he do it? I was frightened to death. What was she so upset about? What could he do to me? I learned that I was the keeper of an incomparable treasure and it had to be guarded: it was meant to be a gift for my husband. (Later that year when I read *A Rage to Live* I knew without any instruction exactly what all those elliptical sentences were about.)

When I threw some hideous temper tantrum my mother would say, "What a little female you are!" (I have since seen many little boys throw the same tantrums and have noted with interest that they are not told they are little females.)

The girls on the street would talk forever about boys, clothes, movies, fights with their mothers. The thousand thoughts racing around in my head from the books I was reading remained secret, no one to share them with.

The boys would be gentler with the girls than with each other when we all played roughly, and our opinions were never considered seriously.

I grew up, I went to school, I came out, wandered again, taught in a desultory fashion, and at last! got married!

It was during my first marriage that I began to realize something was terribly wrong inside me, but it took me ten years to understand that I was suffering the classic female pathology. My husband, like all the men I have known, was a good man, a man who wanted my independence for me more than I wanted it for myself. He urged me to work, to do something, anything, that would make me happy; he knew that our pleasure in each other could be heightened only if I was a functioning human being too. Yes, yes! I said, and leaned back in the rocking chair with yet another novel. Somehow I couldn't do anything. I didn't really know where to start, what I wanted to do. Oh, I had always had a number of interests but they, through an inability on my part to stick with anything, had always been superficial; when I arrived at a difficult point in a subject, a job, an interest, I would simply drop it. Of course, what I really wanted to do was write, but that was an altogether ghastly agony and one I could never come to grips with. There seemed to be some terrible aimlessness at the very center of me, some paralyzing lack of will. My energy, which was abundant, was held in a trap of some sort; occasionally that useless energy would wake up roaring, demanding to be let out of its cage, and then I became "emotional"; I would have hysterical depressions, rage on and on about the meaninglessness of my life, force my husband into long psychoanalytic discussions about the source of my (our) trouble, end in a purging storm of tears, a determination to do "something," and six months later I was right back where I started. If my marriage had not dissolved, I am sure that I would still be in exactly that same peculiarly nightmarish position. But as it happened, the events of my life forced me out into the world, and repeatedly I had to come up against myself. I found this pattern of behavior manifesting itself in a hundred different circumstances; regardless of how things began, they always seemed to end in the same place. Oh, I worked, I advanced, in a sense, but only erratically and with superhuman effort. Always the battle was internal, and it was with a kind of paralyzing anxiety at the center of me that drained off my energy and retarded my capacity for intellectual concentration. It took me a long time to perceive that nearly every woman I knew exhibited the same symptoms, and when I did perceive it I became frightened. I thought, at first, that perhaps, indeed, we were all victims of some biological deficiency, that some vital ingredient had been deleted in the female of the species, that we were a physiological metaphor for human neurosis. It took me a long time to understand, with an understanding that is irrevocable, that we are the victims of culture, not biology.

Recently, I read a marvelous biography of Beatrice Webb, the English socialist. The book is full of vivid portraits, but the one that is fixed forever in my mind is that of Beatrice Webb's mother, Laurencina Potter. Laurencina Potter was a beautiful, intelligent, intellectually energetic woman of the middle nineteenth century. She knew twelve languages, spoke Latin and Greek better than half the classics-trained men who came to her home, and was interested in everything. Her marriage to wealthy and powerful Richard Potter was a love match, and she looked forward to a life of intellectual companionship, stimulating activity, lively participation. No sooner were they married than Richard installed her in a Victorian fortress in the country, surrounded her with servants and physical comfort, and started her off with the first of the eleven children she eventually bore. He went out into the world, bought and sold railroads, made important political connections, mingled in London society, increased his powers, and relished his life. She, meanwhile, languished. She sat in the country, staring at the four brocaded walls; her energy remained bottled up, her mind became useless, her will evaporated. The children became symbols of her enslavement, and, in consequence, she was a lousy mother; neurotic, self-absorbed, becoming increasingly colder and more withdrawn, increasingly more involved in taking her emotional temperature. She became, in short, the Victorian lady afflicted with indefinable maladies.

When I read of Laurencina's life I felt as though I was reading about the lives of most of the women I know, and it struck me that one hundred years ago sexual submission was all for a woman, and today sexual fulfillment is all for a woman, and the two are one and the same.

Most of the women I know are people of superior intelligence, developed emotions, and higher education. And yet our friendships, our conversations, our lives, are not marked by intellectual substance or emotional distance or objective concern. It is only briefly and insubstantially that I ever discuss books or politics or philosophical issues or abstractions of any kind with the women I know. Mainly, we discuss and are intimate about our Emotional Lives. Endlessly, endlessly, we go on and on about our emotional "problems" and "needs" and "relationships." And, of course, because we are all bright and well educated, we bring to bear on these sessions a formidable amount of sociology and psychology, literature and history, all hoked out so that it sounds as though these are serious conversations on serious subjects, when in fact they are caricatures, because they have no beginning, middle, end, or point. They go nowhere, they conclude nothing, they change nothing. They are elaborate descriptions in the ongoing soap opera that is our lives. It took me a long time to understand that we were talking about nothing; and it took me an even longer and harder time, traveling down that dark, narrow road in the mind, back, back to the time when I was a little girl sitting in the kitchen with my mother, to understand, at last, that the affliction was cultural not biological, that it was because we had never been taught to take ourselves seriously that I and all the women I knew had become parodies of "taking ourselves seriously."

The rallying cry of the black civil rights movement had always been "Give us back our manhood!" What exactly does that mean? Where is black manhood? How has it been taken from blacks? And how can it be retrieved? The answer lies in one word: responsibility; blacks have been deprived of the privilege of assuming responsibility, therefore, they have been deprived of manhood. Women have been deprived of exactly the same thing and in every real sense have thus been deprived of womanhood. We have never been prepared to assume responsibility; we have never been prepared to make demands upon ourselves; we have never been taught to expect the development of what is best in ourselves because no one has ever expected *anything* of us—or for us. Because no one has ever had any intention of turning over any serious work to us. Both we and the blacks lost the ballgame before we ever got up to play. In order to live you've got to have nerve, and we were stripped of our nerve before we began. Black is ugly and female is inferior. These are the primary lessons of our experience, and in these ways both blacks and women have been kept, not as functioning nationals, but rather as operating objects; oh, to be sure, blacks are *despised* objects, and women *protected* objects, but a human being who remains as a child throughout his or her adult life is an object, not a mature specimen, and the definition of a child is: one without responsibility.

At the very center of all human life is energy, psychic energy. It is the force of that energy that drives us, that surges continually up in us, that must repeatedly spend and renew itself in us, that must perpetually be reaching for something beyond itself in order to satisfy its own insatiable appetite. It is the imperative of that energy that has determined man's characteristic interest, problem solving. The modern ecologist attests to that driving need by demonstrating that in a time when all the real problems are solved, man makes up new ones in order to go on solving. He must have work, work that he considers real and serious, or he will die, he will simply shrivel up and die. That is the one certain characteristic of human beings. And it is the one characteristic, above all others, that the accidentally dominant white male asserts is not necessary to more than half the members of the race—that is, the female of the species. This assertion is, quite simply, a lie. Nothing more, nothing less. A lie. That energy is alive in every woman in the world. It lies trapped and dormant like a growing tumor, and at its center there is despair, hot, deep, wordless.

It is amazing to me that I have just written these words. To think that one hundred years after Nora slammed the door, and in a civilization and a century utterly converted to the fundamental insights of that exasperating genius Sigmund Freud, women could still be raised to believe that their basic makeup is determined not by the needs of their egos but by their peculiar childbearing properties and their so-called unique capacity for loving. No man worth his salt does not wish to be a husband and father; yet no man is raised to be a husband and father and no man would ever conceive of those relationships as instruments of his prime function in life. Yet every woman is raised, still, to believe that the fulfillment of these relationships is her prime function in life and, what's more, her instinctive choice.

The fact is that women have no special capacities for love, and when a culture reaches a level where its women have nothing to do but "love" (as occurred in the Victorian upper classes and as is occurring now in the American middle classes), they prove to be very bad at it. The modern American wife is not noted for her love of her husband or of her children; she is noted for her driving (or should I say driven?) domination of them. She displays an aberrant, aggressive ambition for her mate and for her offspring which can be explained only by the most vicious feelings toward the self. The reasons are obvious. The woman who must love for a living, the woman who has no self, no objective external reality to take her own measure by, no work to discipline her, no goal to provide the illusion of progress, no internal resources, no separate mental existence, is constitutionally incapable of the emotional distance that is one of the real requirements of love. She cannot separate herself from her husband and children because all the passionate and multiple needs of her being are centered on them. That's why women "take everything personally." It's all they've got to take. "Loving" must substitute for an entire range of feeling and interest. The man, who is not raised to be a husband and father specifically, and who simply loves as a single function of his existence, cannot understand her abnormal "emotionality" and concludes that this is the female nature. (Why shouldn't he? She does too.) But this is not so. It is a result of a psychology achieved by cultural attitudes that run so deep and have gone on for so long that they are mistaken for "nature" or "instinct."

A good example of what I mean are the multiple legends of our culture regarding motherhood. Let's use our heads for a moment. What on earth is holy about motherhood? I mean, why motherhood rather than fatherhood? If anything is holy, it is the consecration of sexual union. A man plants a seed in a woman; the seed matures and eventually is expelled by the woman; a child is born to both of them; each contributed the necessary parts to bring about procreation; each is responsible to and necessary to the child; to claim that the woman is more so than the man is simply not true; certainly it cannot be proved biologically or psychologically (please, no comparisons with baboons and penguins just now—I am sure I can supply fifty examples from nature to counter any assertion made on the subject); all that can be proved is that some *one* is necessary to the newborn baby; to have instilled in women the belief that their childbearing and housewifely obligations supersede all other needs, that indeed what they fundamentally *want* and need is to be wives and mothers as distinguished from being anything else, is to have accomplished an act of trickery, an act which has deprived women of the proper forms of expression alive in every talking creature, an act which has indeed mutilated their natural selves and deprived them of their womanhood, *whatever* that may be, deprived them of the right to say "I" and have it mean something. This understanding, grasped whole, is what underlies the current wave of feminism. It is felt by thousands of women today; it will be felt by millions tomorrow. You have only to examine briefly a fraction of the women's rights organizations already in existence to realize instantly that they form the nucleus of a genuine movement, complete with theoreticians, tacticians, agitators, manifestoes, journals, and thesis papers, running the entire political spectrum from conservative reform to visionary radicalism, and powered by an emotional conviction rooted in undeniable experience, and fed by a determination that is irreversible.

One of the oldest and stablest of the feminist organizations is NOW, the National Organization for Women. It was started in 1966 by a group of professional women headed by Mrs. Betty Friedan, author of *The Feminine Mystique,* the book that was the bringer of the word in 1963 to the new feminists. NOW has more than three thousand members and chapters in major cities and on many campuses all over the country, and its constitution was read, at its inception, into the Congressional Record. It has many men in its ranks and it works, avowedly within the system, to bring about the kind of reforms that will result in what it calls a "truly equal partnership between men and women" in this country. It is a true reform organization filled with intelligent, liberal, hard-working women devoted to the idea that America is a reformist democracy and ultimately will respond to the justice of their cause. They are currently hard at work on two major issues: repeal of the abortion laws and passage of the Equal Rights Amendment (for which feminists have been fighting since 1923), which would amend the constitution to provide that "equality of rights under the law shall not be denied or abridged by the United States or by any state on account of sex." When this amendment is passed, the employment and marriage laws of more than forty states will be affected. Also, in direct conjunction with the fight to have this amendment passed, NOW demands increased child-care facilities to be established by law on the same basis as parks, libraries, and public schools.

NOW's influence is growing by leaps and bounds. It is respon-

sible for the passage of many pieces of legislation meant to
wipe out discrimination against women, and certainly the size
and number of women's bureaus, women's units, women's com-
missions springing up in government agencies and legislative
bodies all over the country reflect its presence. Suddenly there
are presidential reports and gubernatorial conferences and congressional meetings—all leaping all over each other to discuss
the status of women. NOW, without a doubt, is the best-estab-
lished feminist group.

From NOW we move, at a shocking rate of speed, to the
left. In fact, it would appear that NOW is one of the few reformist
groups; that mainly the feminist groups are radical, both in structure and in aim. Some, truth to tell, strike a bizarre and puzzling
note. For instance, there is WITCH (Women's International Ter-
rorist Conspiracy from Hell), an offshoot of SDS, whose members burned their bras and organized against the Miss America
Pageant in a stirring demand that the commercially useful image
of female beauty be wiped out. There is Valerie Solanas and
her SCUM Manifesto, which claims that men are biologically defi-
cient and socially dangerous. Solanas's penetrating observation
on our national life was "If the atom bomb isn't dropped, this
society will hump itself to death." There is Cell 55. God knows
what they do.

There are the Redstockings, an interesting group that seems
to have evolved from direct action into what they call "consciousness raising." That means, essentially, that they get together
in a kind of group therapy session and the women reveal their
experiences and feelings to each other in an attempt to analyze
the femaleness of their psychology and their circumstances,
thereby increasing the invaluable weapon of self-understanding.

And, finally, there are the Feminists, without a doubt the most
fiercely radical and intellectually impressive of all the groups.
This organization was begun a year ago by a group of defectors
from NOW and various other feminist groups, in rebellion
against the repetition of the hierarchical structure of power in
these other groups. Their contention was: Women have always
been "led"; if they join the rank and file of a feminist organization, they are simply being led again. It will still be someone

else, even if only the officers of their own interest group, making the decisions, doing the planning, the executing, and so on. They determined to develop a leaderless society whose guiding principles was participation by lot. And that is precisely what they have done. The organization has no officers, every woman sooner or later performs every single task necessary to the life and aims of the organization, and the organization is willing to sacrifice efficiency temporarily in order that each woman may fully develop all the skills necessary to autonomous functioning. This working individualism is guarded fiercely by a set of rigid rules regarding attendance, behavior, duties, and loyalties.

The Feminists encourage extensive theorizing on the nature and function of a leaderless society, and this has led the organization to a bold and radical view of the future they wish to work for. The group never loses sight of the fact that its primary enemy is the male-female role system, which has ended in women being the oppressed and men being the oppressors. It looks forward to a time when this system will be completely eradicated: to prepare for this coming, it now denounces all the institutions that encourage the system—love, sex, and marriage. It has a quota on married women (only one-third of their number are permitted to be either married or living in a marriage-like situation). It flatly names all men as the enemy. It looks forward to a future in which the family as we know it will disappear, all births will be extrauterine, children will be raised by communal efforts, and women once and for all will cease to be the persecuted members of the race.

Although a lot of this is hard to take in raw doses, you realize that many of these ideas represent interesting and important turns of thought. First of all, these experiments with a leaderless society are being echoed everywhere: in student radicalism, in black civil rights, in hippie communes. They are part of a great radical lusting after self-determination that is beginning to overtake this country. This is true social revolution, and I believe that feminism, in order to accomplish its aims now, does need revolution, does need a complete overthrow of an old kind of thought and the introduction of a new kind of thought. Secondly, the Feminists are right: most of what men and women now are is determined by the "roles" they play, and love *is* an institution, full of ritualized gestures and positions, and often void of any recognizable naturalness. How, under the present ironbound social laws, can one know what is female nature and what is female role? (And that question speaks to the source of the whole female pain and confusion.) It *is* thrilling to contemplate a new world, brave or otherwise, in which men and women may free themselves of some of the crippling sexual poses that now circumscribe their lives, thus allowing them some open and equitable exchange of emotion, some release of the natural self that will be greeted with resentment from no one.

But the Feminists strike a wrong and rather hysterical note when they indicate that they don't believe there is a male or female nature, that all is role. I believe that is an utterly wrongheaded notion. Not only do I believe there is a genuine male or female nature in each of us, but I believe that what is most exciting about the new world that may be coming is the promise of stripping down to that nature, of the complementary elements in those natures meeting without anxiety, of our different biological tasks being performed without profit for one at the expense of the other.

The Feminists' position is extreme, and many of these pronouncements are chilling at first touch. But you quickly realize that this is the harsh, stripped-down language of revolution—that is, the language of icy "honesty," of narrow but penetrating vision. (As one Feminist said sweetly, quoting her favorite author, "In order to have a revolution, you must have a revolutionary theory.") And besides, you sue for thousands and hope to collect hundreds.

Many feminists, though, are appalled by the Feminists (the infighting in the movement is fierce), feel they are fascists, "superweak," annihilatingly single-minded, and involved in a power play no matter what they say; but then again you can find feminists who will carefully and at great length put down every single feminist group going. But there's one great thing about these women: if five feminists fall out with six groups, within half an hour they'll all find each other (probably somewhere on Bleecker Street), within forty-eight hours a new splinter faction will have announced its existence, and within two weeks the manifesto is being mailed out. It's the mark of a true movement.

Two extremely intelligent and winning feminists who are about to "emerge" as part of a new group are Shulamith Firestone, an ex-Redstocking, and Ann Koedt, and ex-Feminist, both members of the original radical group, New York Radical Women. They feel that none of the groups now going has the capacity to build a broad mass movement among the women of this country and they intend to start one that will. Both are dedicated to social revolution and agree with many of the ideas of many of the other radical groups. Each one, in her own words, comes equipped with "impeccable revolutionary credentials." They come out of the Chicago SDS and the New York civil rights movement. Interestingly enough, like many of the radical women in this movement, they were converted to feminism because in their participation in the New Left they met with intolerable female discrimination. ("Yeah, baby, comes the revolution . . . Meanwhile, you make the coffee and later I'll tell you where to hand out the leaflets.") And when they raised the issue of women's rights with their radical young men, they were greeted with furious denunciations of introducing divisive issues!

The intention of Firestone and Koedt is to start a group that will be radical in aim but much looser in structure than anything they've been involved with; it will be an action group, but everyone will also be encouraged to theorize, analyze, create; it will appeal to the broad base of educated women; on the other hand, it will not sound ferocious to the timid nonmilitant woman.

I mention these two in particular, but at this moment in New York, in Cambridge, in Chicago, in New Haven, in Washington, in San Francisco, in East Podunk—yes! believe it!—there are dozens like them preparing to do the same thing. They are gathering fire, and I do believe the next great moment in history is theirs. God knows, for my unborn daughter's sake, I hope so.

(November 1969)

A Feminist Magazine:
Radical Questions That
Reach the Mainstream

Notes from the Second Year: Major Writings of the Radical Feminists has been published in the form of a newsprint magazine, and is currently on the newsstands. It is the first overground publication of the radical feminist movement and, as such, is an important document.

Notes, according to its editorial statement, is meant to be "a radical feminist periodical in which to debate, a forum in which to present the proliferation of new ideas and to clarify the political issues that concern us . . . a movement periodical which (will) expand with the movement, reflect its growth accurately, and in time become a historical record, functioning politically much as did Stanton and Anthony's *Revolution* exactly a century ago." The decision to make this issue of *Notes* "public," so to speak, is a measure of how far the women's liberation movement has traveled since the 1968 underground publication of *Notes from the First Year*—in terms of both its own maturing self-confidence and its capacity to gain serious, establishment attention and aid (the magazine's printing was subsidized by the *New York Review of Books*). And, indeed, the decision to address all who would listen was a wise one on the part of all concerned. For although the journal is unmistakably a movement one (nearly every piece is presented as a position paper), its prose is mature enough and the issues it treats and the questions it raises wide enough and deep enough so that women who are even only slightly familiar with contemporary feminism will nevertheless respond as to a familiar rather than an esoteric document; *Notes from the Second Year* is written in a language that is there for all who are ready to avail themselves of it.

The periodical is divided into three major sections: "Women's Experience," "Theories of Radical Feminism," and "Founding a Radical Feminist Movement." In this manner, "road maps," as the editors say, of a broadly indicating nature are provided. Within each of these significantly named sections are contained the articles that illuminate both the issues of radical feminism and the spectrum of political concerns and attitudes within the radical feminist movement. A number of the pieces are underground classics, revised and here published together for the first time. The result is a remarkable gathering of thought which, even when it embraces contradictory elements, has the capacity to prick and sting and press and cause questions that simply will not go away unanswered to be raised repeatedly in the female mind that is being pried ever further open. . . . From "Female Liberation as the Basis for Social Revolution" to "The Politics of Housework" to "The Institution of Sexual Intercourse" to "Women and the Left" to "The Personal Is Political" to "Man-Hating" to "Sexual Politics: A Manifesto for Revolution," the mixture of radical thought here presented comes together to form a density of serious attention that will surely affect the daily increasing understanding of female liberation.

One of the most impressive pieces in the collection is Roxanne Dunbar's "Female Liberation as the Basis for Social Revolution." Dunbar, a movement theoretician, here works out her thesis that female oppression is more logically akin to a system of caste than to a system of slavery. The slave, she posits, is one who is denied humanity altogether, but only by virtue of having been adversely caught by the fortunes of war—that is, having been taken captive. In a caste system, those at the bottom of the caste ladder are considered *innately* inferior, and therein lies the peculiarly oppressive nature of the condition.

Instantly, one sees that she is dead right. The position of women in Western society is certainly analogous to a system that flourishes under the mythic conception that power is granted to the *innately* superior and withheld from the *innately* inferior. Dunbar drives her point home:

A further example of the importance to the higher castes of dominating human beings, not mere objects, is the way men view their sexual exploitation of women. It is not just the satisfaction of a man's private, individual, sexual urge which he fantasizes he will get from a woman he sees. In addition, and more central to his view of women, he visualizes himself taking her, dominating her through the sexual act; he sees her as the *human* evidence of his own power and prowess. Prostitution, however exploitative for the woman, can never serve this same purpose, just as wage labor, however exploitative to the wage slave, could not have served the same purpose in Southern society that black slaves served.

It is, however, the *essential* point of Dunbar's piece that this idea of caste oppression be understood thoroughly only so that women will clearly understand exactly what it is they are fighting:

A caste system provides rewards that are not entirely economic in the narrow sense. Caste is a way of making human relations "work," a way of freezing relationships, so that conflicts are minimal. A caste system is a *social system,* which is economically based. It is not a set of attitudes or just some mistaken ideas which must be understood and dispensed with because they are not really in the interest of the higher caste. No mere change in ideas will alter the caste system under which we live. The caste system does not exist just in the mind. Caste is deeply rooted in human history, dates to the division of labor by sex, and is the very basis of the present social system of the United States.

"The Politics of Housework," Pat Mainardi's now-famous analysis of the "triviality" of housework, is the polar opposite of Dunbar's piece. Instead of observing women's condition from a theoretical and historical position, this piece makes a detailed and remarkably effective examination of one of woman's most immediate and most defining experiences, housework, and demonstrates that rather than considering housework too trivial for them to do, on the contrary, men understood *in great detail* that housework is the true shitwork of this life, and what on earth will it profit them to see women liberated from the idea that it is their natural occupation? The most convincing aspect of the piece is Mainardi's sketch of her own husband, a liberal, edu-

cated, equal-partner type guy, as a man who supplies her with
the subtler forms of male evasion of housework and all the inescapable implications of that act.

Ti-Grace Atkinson's "The Institution of Sexual Intercourse"
deals with another of woman's most defining experiences: her
position in bed. Beginning with a definition of the word *institution*
as "any form of activity specified by a system of rules which
defines offices, roles, moves, penalties, defenses, and so on, and
which gives the activity its structure," Atkinson proceeds, at
white heat, to demonstrate that sexual intercourse as it is prac-
ticed today, under the influence of the sexual-role system, must
of necessity contribute to the oppression of women, and urges
that women learn to do without. Ann Koedt's classic "Myth of
the Vaginal Orgasm" also presents a startling and compelling
view of sex as an institution crucial to woman's oppressed state,
and Pamela Kearon's "Man-Hating" calls for making that word
as respectable as its counterpart, misogyny, so women can stop
choking on their rage and spit it out.

Carol Hanisch's piece, "The Personal Is Political," a paper
that explicates the principles of cultural awareness through the
examination of the self (otherwise known as consciousness raising) and invokes the pro-woman line, is very moving. Hanisch,
in this and other pieces, reveals herself as a dedicated revolutionary, a woman whose conversion from the left to feminism was
accompanied by much pain and genuine soul searching. Her
ultimate belief that women must work alone, that they cannot
work with men in the movement, is the outgrowth of much agonized thought and experience and, as such, is most persuasive
and reminiscent of the black civil rights movement's identical
experience.

The last section of *Notes from the Second Year* is devoted to
the various radical manifestoes: Kate Millett's "Sexual Politics:
A Manifesto for Revolution," the Feminists' Manifesto, Redstockings' Manifesto, and the Manifesto and Organizing Principles of New York Radical Feminists, whose founding members
are Shulamith Firestone and Ann Koedt, the editors of *Notes*.

Notes from the Second Year is, beyond doubt, a major contribution
to the literature of a political movement that is sweeping steadily
toward the center of American life.   *(1970)*

Boesman and Lena:
About Being a Woman

"I've been black, and I've been a woman, and believe me, being a woman is worse."

—Shirley Chisholm

Boesman and Lena, the newest work of the celebrated white South African playwright Athol Fugard to be performed in New York, is an extraordinary play, the kind of work in which a particularity of human experience becomes a metaphorical vessel for a vast amount of human feeling and history. The particularity of experience in Fugard's play to which I refer is not the condition of being a Cape colored—which Boesman and Lena, the title characters, spectacularly are—but rather that of being a woman. For the play is Lena's, and Lena is indisputably, first and foremost, a woman.

Boesman and Lena are two South African coloreds who spend their lives on the drifting, shifting, shambling, ambling, stumbling, mumbling, hungering, sweating, freezing, crazy, impenetrably lonely run. Boesman is strong and he can work. Lena is enduring and she can work; and yet, somehow, something always goes wrong (usually Boesman), and there they are again, with a box of corroded pots and pans on her head and a mattress and various bits of wood and metal on his back—walking. Somewhere out on the mud flats that surround the river Swartkops, which links up all these cities (Redhouse, Coegakop, Veeplass,

28

Missionvale, Kleinskool, Bethelsdorp, Swartkops, and Korsten),
they spend their lives madly veering toward, madly veering away
from, they wind up pitching a desperate camp, by turns cowed
and defiant, shivering at the prospect of regrouping.

When the play opens Lena is mad. Lost in a hallucination
of fatigue and startling hopelessness, she apparently has lost
her wits trying to remember the sequence of their wanderings:
"Let's see now. When were we at Redhouse? Before Missionvale?
After the dog died? Before Boesman blacked this eye? Just now?
Yesterday? Last month? Two years ago? When? Oh God, *when?*"
Boesman is infuriated by her lapsing reason, her endless talking
to herself, her frightening withdrawal. He threatens, he pleads,
he punishes, he cajoles. To each of his actions, she responds,
but her responses are rather like those of a half-dead body that
nevertheless twitches convulsively at the touch of an electric
prod. Boesman raises his arm threateningly, Lena cowers. He
taunts her, she taunts him back. He laughs with her, she softens.
He acts frightened, she becomes dignified. He rages that he
will leave her, she pleads desperately. Her responses are those
of a total reactor. She watches warily for his action, and then
she acts . . . all the while retreating into madness before our
eyes, while cunningly preserving her powers of recuperation.

Boesman and Lena are startlingly reminiscent of the two characters in *La Strada:* the wild man Zampano ("He's like a dog;
he wants to talk but all he can do is bark") and the girl whose
name I cannot remember but whose anxious, funny, expressive
face Giulietta Masina stamped indelibly upon my memory. They,
too, were the dreadfully cast off of the world, lurking in a wild,
peripheral existence at the edges of other people's lives, living
a grabbing, biting, violent, hand-to-mouth life of the spirit, the
woman taking on the added burden of being whipped daily not
only by the world but by Zampano as well; for beyond doubt
it was he, not the world, who was her immediate jailer and
tormentor.

In *Boesman and Lena* the condition is carried to the nth power,
held as it is under the powerful light of being black in a country
that unyieldingly holds black to be ahuman. Deprived as they
are, the equation of their despair is that much more exaggerated,

that much closer to the bone than is the despair of the two in *La Strada*—but the models are unmistakably the same. Between Boesman and the world is the road. Between Lena and the world is Boesman. "The landscape of my world is Boesman's back," she says with dead accuracy. In a life that is pressing down on both of them, pressing them into the ground, into their graves, their oppression is not yet equal, for she bears not only her own oppression but his as well. In the immediacy of her life it is Boesman, not the white world, who is the instrument of her destruction. When the world delivers a blow to Boesman, he turns and hurls one, twice as hard, at Lena.

Beaten black and blue, she muses on the quality of nightmare that has come to characterize his beatings: almost, there is the span of a lifetime between the time his arm is raised off her body, up into the air, down again onto her bruised flesh. What does he think in between hits? she wonders. And then in a flash of defiant agony she cries, "Why do you hit me? It's *my* life. Hit your own!" And, amazingly, he answers, "Then it doesn't hurt. I hit you. And you cry." Exactly. In an unspeakably dehumanizing life like the one they lead, it is not sufficient unto the cause that Boesman should mutilate himself; it will not provide the necessary sense of verification to simply stun one's own flesh. And then, Boesman does not want a partner. He does not want or need a woman who will walk arm in arm down the road with him. He wants and needs (oh how he *needs*, it is the need of his soul) a woman who will walk behind him; a woman who will relieve him of the load of curses and blows accumulating daily in his soul; a woman who for a moment, when his hand strikes flesh, will lift from him the enfeebling burden of powerlessness he labors under; a woman whose shriveled soul will be sacrificed to their common unwillingness to survive this life.

In a life that is not to be borne, a life that *must* end either in madness or suicide, it is Lena who assumes the burden of madness for both of them; it is Lena who allows Boesman the luxury of fury while taking on the necessity of annihilation herself. It is she who raves on and on, mixing up the past and the present, refusing the moment coherence, renouncing the cogency of chronology, refusing to remember—although she can remember every detail of the event—when or where their child died. Boesman lashes out at her dementia, but clearly it is tantamount to bloodletting for him; clearly, the scorn it induces in him reduces the pressure of his fear. And for this he *needs* her. Just as the white man needs him.

But then, after the long night whose events (full of pain, fear, and death) are a microcosm of their entire lives, Lena has had it. Boesman, running for his life from a black Kaffir whose dead body he has laid his hands on, demands that she follow him—and she refuses. She will go no longer with him. In a voice that is thrilling in its steadiness she says, "It's my life. I've held on *tight*. Now I'm letting it go. . . ."

Suddenly, the most amazing things begin to happen in this play, which Walter Kerr said has no movement (!!!) When Lena defies Boesman, when she stops holding on for dear life to her bits and pieces of a life, when she lets it all go, when she dies to her fears . . . on the very *instant*, Boesman's power over her comes to an abrupt end. Before our eyes, a slave dies and a person is resurrected. It is given to Lena, the woman, to embody the Christian-Freudian perception that one dies by drowning oneself in the sea of one's fears and is reborn with the power of self-possession.

Boesman, humbled by Lena's new majesty, capitulates utterly in a litany of penance; he recites the history of their wanderings, thus giving her back the life she has tried so hard to recall, the life he has been hoarding all this time. He tells her where they have just been, where they have come from, where their child died, when they were last in that same city. All, all. Now that it no longer matters he gives her all; but she understands, even as we do, that the litany is the plea of a really terrified man. And, of course, in her new strength she is infinitely merciful; she picks up her pots and pans and follows him on down the road, infinitely kind in her willingness to go on acting as though he is still her master.

It is a great play, and Ruby Dee gives the performance of her life. Every woman in New York should see it. *(July 1970)*

On the Progress of Feminism: The Light of Liberation Can Be Blinding

The women's movement has been under fire from the moment it drew its first breath. Its enemies and detractors are many, though often they pose, in their own minds, as supporters—"Yes, yes, there is much justification in what you are saying, but good God! those awful women you put on TV!" "Well, I'm willing to support you people, but you're just gonna have to do a lot better in the way of propaganda. That mimeographed Marxism. Jesus." "Look, I've always believed in women's liberation. I take my wife out to eat all the time. But my God, what's going on now is just incredible. These strident, man-hating bitches you people have for spokesmen." "You people." If I hear "you people" just once more.

Those who have responded with open fear and anger to the movement—no doubt out of the fullness of middle-class libertarianism—are too numerous to calculate properly on the sociological scale that will accurately place the many combinations of anxious self-interest they represent. (And, indeed, it is not now my intention either to castigate or to proselytize.) But there are many who declared themselves partisans from the start, many who claimed to see in the women's movement a hope of salvation denied elsewhere in the cultural politics that dominates our social passions, many who responded to the cause of justice for women with quick support and ready alliance who are now beginning to separate themselves from the movement. For many of those partisans—both men and women, but most especially the men— are striking out now, in boredom and irritation, at the many apparently unwholesome aspects of the movement. And in that quick partisanship and early souring lies an instructive tale, one that is crucial to both an increased understanding of and a re- newed faith in the movement that seeks to alter radically the psychic lives of men and women.

I have a story to tell, a story that contains all the dramatic elements involved in this significant play of life:

Recently, I was visiting old friends in Berkeley, a couple who are both radicals of many years' conviction, people who literally feel that the oppression of other people limits and corrodes their own lives. This conviction happens to be the best part of these people. Unlike many radicals whose radicalism is the worst part of them—that is, an arrogant excuse for mean-spirited and self-righteous behavior—in these people the disgust with capital- ism and the social inequities that follow from the system is nei- ther shallow nor fanatical: it has produced an extension of spirit- ual generosity, a disavowal of worldly accumulation without an absurdly false asceticism, and, more often than not, an emotion- ally developed desire to understand what the other person is all about. It was, in fact, this man and this woman who introduced me, two years ago, to women's liberation, and it was, at that time, the man's perceptiveness that I found most affecting. "I am just now beginning to understand," he had said softly, "that my wife's oppression has forced *me* into certain molds of behav- ior, and all of a sudden I see a whole world of behavior that has been denied me." The woman had become an active member of a women's collective (that is, a group of women who meet regularly to talk, and also to plan women's liberation actions), the man helped organize demonstrations and had started a coup- les' group.

Now it was two years later. I had seen them only once in the intervening time, and we were naturally anxious to see one another again. When I arrived at the house in Berkeley, I found some changes. My friends, together with their two children, now occupied the lower half of the house they lived in; the upper half was occupied by three maritally estranged feminists and their collective five children; together, all five adults and seven children were attempting some variant of cooperative living.

Richard was out when I got there at 8 P.M., but Eva welcomed me heartily and pulled me inside to the kitchen for coffee and kisses and laughter and words that tumbled one after another in some vague semblance of sentences meant to communicate meaning. After a while, one of the feminists from the top floor came down and joined us at the table. She was the estranged wife of a prominent New Left radical, life with whom she acidly described: "He was the intellectual and I was the earth mother." It became quickly clear that she was now, heart and soul, given over to the women's movement. Within minutes we were all embroiled in serious, fast-moving movement talk—and within the hour I was being told I was a revisionist. It seemed I had too loose an idea of what constituted properly revolutionary behavior.

When Richard came home, he walked into the kitchen; I was very glad to see him and leaped out of my chair to hug him hello. He responded, was friendly for a few minutes, and then left the room. I expected him to return and so I simply sat down again and resumed the conversation, and it was 1 A.M. before I realized Richard had gone to his room with no intention of returning to the kitchen.

We, the three women, continued to talk movement talk until 3 A.M. Movement talk, of necessity, is composed of a constant intertwining of personal experience, tactical speculations (regarding activity in and out of the movement), and theoretical projections, all being fed continually through the mill of observation and analysis. Naturally, the men in our lives are part of the material we supply for model cases and situations. Naturally.

I wasn't able to speak to Richard, who seemed abnormally preoccupied, until late the next day, and then I asked him why he hadn't come back into the kitchen the night before. He looked at me for a long minute, and then he burst out, "I've gotten to hate women. I can't stand them gathering in cliques, the way they do now. I just can't *stand* the constant cliquishness.

It reminds me of my mother, for God's sake. When I was a kid, my mother and her friends would gather in the kitchen like that, pushing the men—me and my brother and my father— out with their eyes and their sudden silences. Jesus. Now it's the same thing all over again. When I walk into my own kitchen I feel the invisible curtain suddenly coming down between me and the women. Suddenly, *I* am the enemy incarnate, *I* am the fucking oppressor, *I'm* the one to be watched and to be shut out." He gestured in disgust. "It's useless now. I really don't know what to make of the movement any more, and certainly I don't feel part of it at all."

I was stunned by his outburst. A great blot of sympathy began to be outlined in anger, and the outline thickened until it covered half the blot . . . and then I realized that both my sympathy and my anger were for Richard and for the women. For him and for me, for the cause and for the movement, for the depth of meaning sealed into this incident and for the insight it holds into the nature of the struggle that lies still so far ahead of all of us.

What is happening to Richard is happening to men (from liberals to revolutionaries) all over this country who have considered themselves spiritual partisans of the women's movement and feel, bewilderedly and angrily, that the movement itself is now beating them over the head daily with an indiscriminately wielded club marked "male chauvinist pig." (A really unhappy example of this: John Leonard's recent, startling battle in the *Times* with some of my sisters.) The entire action is amazingly reminiscent of the time only ten years ago when thousands of white middle-class liberals who had fought with patience and sincerity in the black civil rights movement were suddenly being called "ofay motherfuckers" by LeRoi Jones and Stokely Carmichael and told to get the hell out of *their* movement. It was as difficult then to sort out the right and the wrong of the matter as it is now, because the right and the wrong were then, and are now, all mixed up with the ugliness of emotional need so swollen and so distorted as a result of having been told so long it *does not exist* that blacks then, and women now, could not take in all at once both the full impact of their previous condition and their roaring need to see it change—and still retain their full capacity for humanist behavior. It is almost as though the very act of declaring oneself ready to do battle for one's humanity transforms one into something *other:* like the good and innocent men who go to war to fight for the sweetness of civilization and return killers.

But of course that is the whole sickening trickery in life— the idea that one cannot fight for one's humanity without, ironically, losing it—and it is a piece of trickery that the blacks sometimes seem helpless against and the women now sometimes seem helpless against, and, in the final analysis, that trickery is the real enemy and the very essence of the thing we must continually be on our guard against. For what shall it profit a woman if she gain an end to slavery in marriage and in the process lose her soul?

However, a liberal who was outraged ten years ago at the sheer "unreasonableness" of the blacks and is outraged now at the sheer "unfairness" of the women is a fool, and possessed of the kind of impatience that calls all of his early allegiance into question. For how is it possible that a man in one breath should proclaim his genuine understanding of women's deeply subordinated position in our society, and in the very next exclaim savagely against the forceful and sometimes "unreasonable" expression of rage now rising in women, an expression which inevitably accompanies the uprising of those who suddenly realize they have been cheated of their birthright, and which dies down only slowly and with the healing passage of time that brings real change and increased understanding? Does a woman suddenly understand the need to reverse the behavior of over 2000 years, and—*presto!*—that understanding makes her saintly? Or is it exactly the opposite? "Ye shall show the truth and it shall turn you into a monster. And only after a long siege of fever shall you become human again." After all, why did it take Moses forty years to cross the desert? Because God instructed him that he was not to return *slaves* to Canaan.

Many women are acting ugly now because they *feel* ugly. For a long, long time these women acted sweet when they didn't necessarily feel sweet. They did so because deep in their being, in a place beyond conscious thought, they believed their lives depended upon their being sweet. Now, when they think of that time, of all that life spent on their knees, they feel green bile spreading through them, and they feel that their lives *now* depend upon calling men "male chauvinist pig." That sweetness, then, was infantile, and this virulent aggression, now, is infantile. But a people are not kept for generations as children and suddenly, simply upon coming to realize that they have lived as children, become fully humanist adults, capable of measured proportion. That measured proportion is the kind of behavior that is *learned,* and it is learned only in a specific way: through the reinforcement of a repeated personal experience which perceives humanism, finally, as the only true and necessary and *satisfying* expression of the self. A people who have only just begun to emerge from a state of subjugation are in no position to be even-handed in this manner, and it takes much patience and understanding and good will on the part of the strong ones both in the subjugated group and in the group holding the power to provide an atmosphere of stability in which the frightened bravado on both sides of the fence can dissipate itself without increasing the chaos that is already intrinsic in the situation.

John Leonard was appalled by the out-of-focus fury of the sisterhood over his review of a number of feminist books, a fury that declared, finally, a man shouldn't be reviewing feminist books. Leonard, a long-time supporter of women's liberation, flew into a rage and in reply said that in that case *Moby Dick* should be reviewed by whales, and ended, in his turn, with an attack on the stupidities of the women's movement. It was so *obvious* to him that the feminists' response was an outrageous attack upon every civilized notion that allows a reviewer of intelligence and decency to call the shots as he sees them.

Leonard was right and he was wrong: the women were right and they were wrong. If I were in Leonard's place, I would have done precisely what he did—and regretted it five years later. On the other hand, I *am* in the feminists' place; I would not have done what they did, but I can see exactly why they did what they did.

Women's liberation is being called by many names today. It is called "the movement," it is called "the cause," it is called "the revolution." Often, the language—as language does—begins to take on a life of its own, and then the *idea* of women's liberation and the terms of description by which it is known begin to grow dangerously distant from each other. Even more important, those terms of description sometimes harden into dogma, and dogma in time becomes a kind of shorthand—first for explanation and then for response. When that happens, experience is on its way to becoming institutionalized, and the life at the center of that experience is slowly sucked away.

The liberation of women is, in my view, at one and the same time all the things it is called, and none of those things. For me, feminism is, more than any other single thing, not a movement, not a cause, not a revolution, but rather a profoundly new way of interpreting human experience. It is a vital piece of information at the center of a new point of reference from which one both reinterprets the past and predicts the future. In that sense, it is parallel to the great cultural movements that have so altered the shape of the twentieth century—Freudianism and existentialism. Feminism is a piece of emotional and intellectual insight that allows us to see that women's lives represent the effects of a piece of culture that has come to be known as "sexism": a determination—based on fear and the existential struggle for power—that women shall be declared natural inferiors, and taught that they are natural inferiors. The consequences of this insight, if it is perceived *instantly,* are as far-reaching as Freud's discovery of sexual repression and the existentialists' discovery of nothingness. For each woman and each man contains within herself and within himself a microcosm of the universe in feminist terms—just as each person also contains within himself and within herself a microcosm of sexual neurosis and existential angst—and thus feminism also is nothing less than a new form into which one pours old knowledge, thereby revitalizing and setting into motion anew the sources of psychic energy responsible for growth and change and altered behavior.

The conversion to feminism is also very much like the conversion to Freudianism and existentialism: for a long time one sees nothing, and suddenly one sees it all—whereupon absolute hell breaks loose. A woman suddenly *sees* herself in feminist terms (just as a prospect for psychoanalysis suddenly *sees* that his behavior is the response to repression); she grasps the fundamental *idea* in a flash (and that, by the way, is the last thing she is *going* to grasp in a flash); immediately she is surrounded by the "panic and emptiness" of a world in shambles, on the one hand, and the drunken exhilaration of a world overflowing with new possibility on the other. Utterly dislocated, a newly converted feminist is then like the man in Plato's parable who, coming out of the cave of ignorance, is blinded by the light and must grope slowly and painfully toward some coherent reassembly of the world—a groping, I might add, that is further retarded by the fact that the man is eager to accept each new object he stumbles on as the ultimate object, the one that really defines this giddy and fearful new atmosphere he now finds himself in.

But more significantly and more directly, the newly converted feminist bears a striking resemblance to the novitiate into psychoanalysis who, for an amazingly long time, is overwhelmed by the fact that his father never made him feel loved and that his desire for his mother deeply affected his ability to love other women, as well as by this amazing discovery of a world within himself of emotional scars, complicated repressions, unbelievable defenses—all busily going into operation every time a stranger says hello, all explained by an erudite world theory, all passionately seen as part of an enormous puzzle, there simply to be worked out—and *shazam!* on the very day the last piece of the puzzle is in place, those compulsions formed by that unanalyzed self begin to wither and die, one sheds the worn-out skin of defensive behavior, and a whole, new creature is born inside the familiar but now psychoanalyzed body.

All that is romantic fancy, as the unhappy analysand is quick to learn; should he actually piece the entire puzzle together, he has just begun his trip, and it is one of the cruelest journeys in the world—that journey that must be taken from the stunning point of initial conversion, quick understanding, and unquestioned belief in the miraculous powers of the language of faith, to the disenchanting point of realization that insight must be reinforced by and ultimately (through the formerly impotent tools of intelligence and will) replaced by an act of hard, drudging *work* in which the emotional habits of a lifetime are slowly and continually chipped away—inch by inch, moment by moment, day by painful day—in order that the analysand's life may perhaps begin to resemble that glorious possibility of existence glimpsed in the rarefied atmosphere of the analyst's office, hour after cathartic hour.

For the feminist, it is exactly the same. The woman who suddenly sees that she has been forced by cultural decision to remain a half-formed creature, never to have known actual autonomy or direct power, is as overcome by her revelation as is the new analysand by his. So violent is the nature of her insight that she is able in a shot to gather into her previously resistant understanding a new explanation for almost every identifiable piece of behavior that characterizes her life. She is able quickly to see her life—down to its smallest detail—as a microcosmic example of the larger and more theoretical idea: sexism. She sees the cultural and political system under which she has grown, suddenly, not as the familiar capitalist West but as a patriarchy in which men have direct power and women do not; in which women have been kept, essentially, as children, and men have assumed the responsibilities and the rewards of adulthood. When the feminist comes to see her life in this light, it is inevitable that she should see men—all men, the men in remote places of power as well as the men in her immediate life—as agents of her victimization. It is also inevitable that she be overwhelmed by an uncontrollable and very unhappy fury—just as the analysand is overtaken by a furious anger against his parents when he first realizes "what they did to him." It is only with enormous difficulty that the feminist—like the analysand—can get past the point of initial understanding and primary response. For indeed, if she does not, she, like the psychiatric patient who cannot stop explaining his behavior in terms of how his mother or father affected him in early childhood, is lost to genuine change. Man-hating, for the feminist, then becomes a waste of energy and a force for retardation rather than progress. It is exactly like taking a trip down an unknown country road in the middle of the night. One goes a short distance and falls into a ditch. One steps on the gas pedal, again and again, but to no avail. The force of acceleration makes it feel as though the car is moving, but in fact the wheels are only spinning. One must get out of the car, lift it from the ditch, and proceed down the road—to the end of the trip.

For in the final analysis, feminism, for me, is the journey deep into the self *at the same time* that it is an ever-increasing understanding of cultural sexism . . . and, more than anything, the slow, painful reconstruction of that self in the light of the feminist's enormously multiplied understanding.

Let me explain what I mean. Recently I was walking through midtown Manhattan with another woman. We had just had lunch and we were speaking warmly with one another. This woman is over fifty. She is very beautiful, she has two broken marriages behind her, a grown son, an amazingly gentle nature, and a terrifying history of alcoholism. She does not call herself a feminist, and yet she is certainly deeply affected by the women's movement; she is, in my view, a perfect candidate for feminist conversion. As we were walking, she said to me, "You know, I've been reading Ti-Grace Atkinson, and I'm beginning to think perhaps she's right, perhaps separatism is the answer for us. I realized, as I was reading her, that love, being in love, had always been to me exactly what alcohol had been. I mean, when I was in love, it was just like being high; I would experience exhilaration, a sense of strength, and a marvelous conviction of freedom . . . do you know what I mean? And then, after a while, love—like alcohol—would begin to wear off, and the high would end in depression. Perhaps, then, I should abstain from love as I have abstained from alcohol."

I felt a terrible rush of confusion and unhappiness as she spoke. "No," I said hotly, "no." It seemed to me that the lesson to be learned from that experience is not that we must stop loving men, but that we have *all* been taught a corrupting version of romantic love and we must learn *better* how to love. That high of love is like something on the cover of the *Saturday Evening Post*. It is falling in love with the *ritual* of love, not with a human

being, and experiencing the emptiness that follows when ritual
is perceived to be without substance; and women do it a thousand
times more often and more easily than men because "falling
in love" is what women wait to do.

Imagine a bride as she is prepared for the ordinary American
marriage: there she is draped in masses of queenly white, surrounded by adoring subjects (family, friends, neighbors) ready
to worship at her prize-winning feet, intent on absorbing every
detail of this high-mass ceremony: the gathering of gifts, silver,
wedding rings, honeymoon plans, dressmaker details, wedding-
hall plans . . . the actual man who is actually being married
slowly recedes into the unreal background . . . delicious! Suddenly it's over. They are married, and it is all over. Nothing
remains but to prepare for the next high: having a baby. In
one sense or another—given higher or lower degrees of spiritual
and intellectual pretension— thousands of people marry in precisely this manner, mistaking circumstance for personality. Although we alone are not the victims, we, the women, are the
ultimate victims of these marriages—because marriage is so damnably central to a woman's life. And precisely because we *are*
the more genuine victims, it is incumbent on us to understand
that we participate in these marriages because we have no strong
sense of *self* with which to demand and to give substantial love,
it is incumbent on us to make marriages that will not curtail
the free, full functioning of that self. If giving up "romantic"
love, then, is the price that must be paid for a new kind of
marriage, let it be a price we pay gladly, and once and for all
have done with the hellish lies attached to the whole damned
business so that we can look forward with pleasure to a new,
free, full-hearted, eminently proportionate way of loving. That,
for me, is the feminist lesson to be learned from the realization
that love is an institution of oppression, as Ti-Grace so accurately
puts it.

It breaks my heart to hear a woman speak of "ripping off" a
man, of another calling a man she lives with—and has every
intention of continuing to live with—a "male chauvinist pig"
twenty-nine times a day, or another reveling in the open hostility

she displays toward every man she sleeps with. It breaks my heart because I know equally well the confusion and the despair and the frustration behind such a woman's words. I know that her emotional wheels are spinning, and that she can't see her way past her present position. And I know also that somewhere inside her, perhaps well below the conscious level, she apprehensively feels that displaying the same emotional viciousness toward men that they have displayed toward her may be suspicious proof of the female's crippled ability to assume responsibility for the making of her own life.

And I want to say: have faith, my sister. The place in which we now find ourselves is unavoidable, but soon it will prove insupportable. Soon it will prove emotionally unsatisfying, and with that emotional dissatisfaction comes another leap toward understanding, and with that, the automatic courage to press further and be off down that road once again. It is insufficient to the cause to concentrate on man-hating; it exhausts your energy and makes you lose sight of the real aim of the struggle. It is not the action that will return your life to you; it is not the way to the end of that road, and the end of that road is all that counts.

None of which is to say that the fight against sexism is not very real, or that it must not be fought daily by the women's movement—in the courts, in the streets, in the offices, in the bedrooms—or that those in power are anywhere *near* ready to relinquish that power. It is only to say that I believe that the thrust of feminism should not be the reforming of old institutions so much as the creation of new ones:

—I do not wish to batter down the doors of male institutions, crying "Let me in!," so much as I simply wish to walk away from those institutions, thereby causing them to fall, as women make of themselves human beings who simply will not participate in the male scheme of civilization.

—I wish to see every feminist take a solemn vow: "Let there never be another generation of women for whom marriage is the pivotal experience of psychic development."

—I wish to see every feminist say to herself, "Yes, the patriarchy has taken my life from me, but also I have given it. I am not going to waste the rest of it in an avalanche of reproach. I am going to fight the patriarchy, but my real energy goes to the hard, drudging work of making myself human—as well as humane. Men may have taken my life from me, but they cannot give it back to me. Only I can do that, fighting inch by inch to reverse the emotional habits of a lifetime."

All much, much easier said than done—especially for us, the women between thirty and forty, the truly brave and sacrificial, transitional generation. But it is, I believe, the only true direction that we—as women, as human beings, as intimate possessors of the final understanding of "liberation"—can travel. Yes, men are also in chains. Yes, "powerful oppressor" is, for most men, a painful farce. Yes, it is the sexual liberation of everyone that is required. But history has now passed the ball to us, the women, and it is *our* liberation that is demanded, *our* liberation that must be of paramount concern, *our* liberation that will, by default, insure the liberation of all. And it will come, all of it, not so much through the development of a political dogma or a revolutionary apparatus or a sweeping commitment to feminist ideology, as through the slow, irreversible conversion to a new psychology of the self on the part of thousands of women today, and millions more tomorrow. Against that force, the operating principles of the old male civilization will be utterly helpless. Against that force, the denial of female autonomy will be as a leaf in the wind.

It is for these reasons that I believe that the heart and soul of the feminist movement is the small, anonymous consciousness-raising group. It is here that the real work is being done, here that feminism struggles to life, here that it takes hold with rooted strength, transforming the soul of a woman, biting deeply and slowly—like acid on metal—into the ready heart beneath the encrusted surface, so that it becomes forever impossible for that woman to turn back on what she now knows or to make whole again that old, false self.

The existence of the women's movement as a source of support and strength for thousands of women who will come slowly to feminism is invaluable. On the other hand, the movement is also a source of apprehension in that it nurtures the irresistible tendency toward doctrinaire indictments, the easy out of man-hating, the often false solidarity of ideological "sisterhood." In the short time since it first came into existence, the movement has already spawned hundreds of party hacks, women who are now "movement women," women whose line of defense grows more rigid with each passing day, women who have often exchanged one crudely held ideology for another.

To travel down that ideological road is not fatal—nothing can be fatal to the feminist movement, for it is alive in all parts and its desire for more life is omnivorous, feeding itself on anything and everything—and often it seems the only real road to be on. But in the end ideology is regressive and dangerous to a movement that prides itself on having as its ultimate goal the humane treatment of all human beings.

For myself, I can only say: I fight the polemicist in me daily. I fight not to destroy it, but merely to hold it in balance. To hold it in balance. And I must *fight*, because it is such a temptation for me simply to surrender to it. The excitement, the energy, the sheer voluptuous sweep of feminist ideology is almost erotic in its power to sway me. The mind grows sharp, the responses come quickly, the illuminations and connections are irresistible, as one piece of the puzzle after another begins to fall swiftly into place no sooner do I allow a single sentence to dominate my being: "Everything in man's experience makes him an oppressor, everything in women's experience makes her a victim." That's all. Just a single sentence. No more than that. And yet . . .

Something in me holds back, some part of me struggles up in painful confusion to say softly, No, that's not entirely true. That is certainly not entirely true. I cannot say to a man who has loved me, "You goddamn sexist" (as I have said) without feeling a terrible numbing pain as I look upon his dismayed face and the whole of our deeply woven experience together flashes before me. No, I cannot say I am a total victim as I feel the energy of life rushing through me and I exult in my growing independence. I cannot say these things—and I think it is the best part of my feminism that will not allow me to say them.

Feminism has within it the seeds of a genuine world view.

Like every real system of thought, it is able to refer itself to everything in our lives, thereby rescuing the old, forgotten knowledge that is locked deep inside each of us. But if, in the end, in our ideological lunge toward retribution, we use it as a means of abdicating our responsibility *to be true to every part of our experience*—we are lost.

(December 1970)

Consciousness

In a lower Manhattan office a legal secretary returns from her lunch hour, sinks into her seat, and says miserably to a secretary at the next desk, "I don't know what's happening to me. A perfectly nice construction worker whistled and said, 'My, isn't *that* nice,' as I passed him, and suddenly I felt this terrific anger pushing up in me. . . . I swear I wanted to *hit* him!"

At the same time, a thoughtful forty-year-old mother in a Maryland suburb is saying to a visiting relative over early-afternoon coffee, "You know, I've been thinking lately, I'm every bit as smart as Harry, and yet he got the Ph.D. and I raised the girls. Mind you, I *wanted* to stay home. And yet, the thought of my two girls growing up and doing the same thing doesn't sit well with me at all. Not at all."

And in Toledo, Ohio, a factory worker turns to the next woman on the inspection belt and confides, "Last night I told Jim, 'I been working in the same factory as you ten years now. We go in at the same time, come out at the same time. But I do all the shopping, get the dinner, wash the dishes, and on Sunday break my back down on the kitchen floor. I'm real tired of doin' all that. I want some help from you.' Well, he just laughed at me, see? Like he done every time I mentioned this before. But last night I wouldn't let up. I mean, I really *meant* it this time. And you know? I thought he was gonna let me have it. Looked mighty like he was gettin' ready to belt me one. But you know? I just didn't care! I wasn't gonna back down, come hell or high water. You'll just never believe it, he'd kill me if he knew I was tellin' you, he washed the dishes. First time in his entire life."

None of these women are feminists. None of them are members of the women's liberation movement. None of them ever heard of consciousness raising. And yet, each of them exhibits the symptomatic influences of this, the movement's most esoteric practice. Each of them, without specific awareness, is beginning to feel the effects of the consideration of woman's personal experience in a new light—a political light. Each of them is undergoing the mysterious behavioral twitches that indicate psychological alteration. Each of them is drawing on a linking network of feminist analysis and emotional upchucking that is beginning to suffuse the political-social air of American life today. Each of them, without ever having attended a consciousness-raising session, has had her consciousness raised.

Consciousness raising is the name given to the feminist practice of examining one's personal experience in the light of sexism—that theory which explains woman's subordinate position in society as a result of a cultural decision to confer direct power on men and only indirect power on women. The term of description and the practice to which it refers are derived from a number of sources—psychoanalysis, Marxist theory, and American revivalism, mainly—and was born out of the earliest stages of feminist formulation begun about three years ago in such predictable liberationist nesting places as Cambridge, New York, Chicago, and Berkeley. (The organization most prominently associated with the growth of consciousness raising is the New York Redstockings.)

Perceiving, first, that woman's position in our society does indeed constitute that of a political class, and, second, that woman's "natural" domain in her feelings, and, third, that testifying in a friendly and supportive atmosphere enables people to see that their experiences are often duplicated (thereby reducing their sense of isolation and increasing the desire to theorize as well as to confess), the radical feminists sensed quickly that a group of women sitting in a circle discussing their emotional experiences as though they were material for cultural analysis was political dynamite. Hence, through personal testimony and emotional analysis could the class consciousness of *women* be raised. And thus the idea of the small "women's group"—or consciousness-raising group—was delivered into a cruel but exciting world.

Consciousness raising is, at one and the same time, both the most celebrated and the most accessible introduction to the women's movement and the most powerful technique for feminist conversion known to the liberationists. Women are *drawn*, out of a variety of discontents, by the idea of talking about themselves, but under the spell of a wholly new interpretation of their experience, they *remain*.

Coming together, as they do, week after week for many months, the women who are "in a group" begin to exchange an extraordinary sense of multiple identification that is encouraged by the technique's instruction to look for explanations for each part of one's history in terms of the social or cultural dynamic created by sexism—rather than in terms of the personal dynamic, as one would do in a psychotherapist's group session. (Although there are many differences between consciousness raising and group therapy—for example, the former involves no professional leader, no exchange of money—the fundamental difference lies in this fact: in consciousness raising one looks not to one's personal emotional history for an explanation of behavioral problems but rather to the cultural fact of the patriarchy.)

Thus, looking at one's history and experience in consciousness-raising sessions is rather like shaking a kaleidoscope and watching all the same pieces rearrange themselves into an altogether *other* picture, one that suddenly makes the color and shape of each piece appear startlingly new and alive, and full of unexpected meaning. (This is mainly why feminists often say that women are the most interesting people around these days, because they are experiencing a psychic invigoration of rediscovery.)

What *does* take place in a consciousness-raising group? How *do* the women see themselves? What *is* the thrust of the conversation at a typical session? Is it simply the man-hating spleen-venting that is caricatured by the unsympathetic press? Or the unfocused and wrongheaded abstracting insisted upon by the insulated intellectuals? Or yet again, the self-indulgent contemplation of the navel that many tight-lipped radical activists see it as?

"In this room," says Roberta H., a Long Island housewife speaking euphemistically of her group's meetings, "we do not generalize. We do not speak of any experience except that of the women here. We follow the rules for consciousness raising as set out by the New York Radical Feminists and we do not apply them to 'woman's experience'—whatever on earth that is—we apply them to ourselves. But, oh God! The samenesses we have found, and the way in which these meetings have changed our lives!"

The rules that Roberta H. is referring to are to be found in a mimeographed pamphlet, an introduction to the New York Radical Feminists organization, which explains the purpose and procedures of consciousness raising. The sessions consist mainly of women gathering once a week, sitting in a circle and speaking in turn, addressing themselves—almost entirely out of personal experience—to a topic that has been preselected. The pamphlet sets forth the natural limitations of a group (ten to fifteen women), advises women to start a group from among their friends and on a word-of-mouth basis, and suggests a list of useful topics for discussion. These topics include Love, Marriage, Sex, Work, Femininity, How I Came to Women's Liberation, Motherhood, Aging, and Competiton with Other Women. Additional subjects are developed as a particular group's specific interests and circumstances begin to surface.

When a group's discussions start to revolve more and more about apparently very individual circumstances, they often lead to startling similarities. For instance, a Westchester County group composed solely of housewives, who felt that each marriage represented a unique meaning in each of their lives, used the question, "Why did you marry the man you married?" as the subject for discussion one night. "We went around the room," says Joan S., one of the women present, "and while some of us seemed unable to answer that question without going back practically to the cradle, do you know?, the word love was never mentioned *once.*"

On the Upper West Side of Manhattan, in the vicinity of Columbia University, a group of women between the ages of thirty-five and forty-five have been meeting regularly for six months. Emily R., an attractive forty-year-old divorcée in this group, says: "When I walked into the first meeting, and saw the *types* there, I said to myself: 'None of these broads have been through what I've been through. They couldn't possibly feel the way I feel.' Well, I'll tell you. None of them *have* been through what I've been through if you look at our experience superficially. But when you look a little *deeper*—the way we've been doing at these meetings—you see they've *all* been through what I've been through, and they all feel pretty much the way I feel. God, when I saw *that!* When I saw that what I always felt was my own personal hangup was as true for every other woman in that room as it was for me! Well, that's when *my* consciousness was raised."

What Emily R. speaks of is the phenomenon most often referred to in the movement, the flash of insight most directly responsible for the feminist leap in faith being made by hundreds of women everywhere—the intensely felt realization that what had always been taken for symptoms of personal unhappiness or dissatisfaction or frustration was so powerfully and so consistently duplicated among women that perhaps these symptoms could just as well be ascribed to *cultural* causes as to psychological ones.

In the feminist movement this kind of "breakthrough" can occur nowhere else but in a consciousness-raising group. It is only here, during many months of meetings, that a woman is able finally—if ever—to bring to the surface those tangled feelings of anger, bafflement, and frustrated justice that have drawn her to the movement in the first place. It is only here that the dynamic of sexism will finally strike home, finally make itself felt in the living detail of her own life.

Claire K., a feminist activist in Cambridge, says of women's groups: "I've been working with women's groups for over two years now. The average life of a group is a year to eighteen months, and believe me, I've watched a lot of them fold before they ever got off the ground. But, when they *work!* There is a rhythm to some of them that's like life itself. You watch a group expand and contract, and each time it does one or the other it never comes back together quite the same as when the action started. Something happens to each woman, and to the group itself. . . . But each time, if they survive, they have *grown*. You can see it, almost smell it and taste it."

I am one of those feminists who are always mourning after the coherent and highminded leadership of the nineteenth century. Often, when I observe the fragmented, intellectually uneven, politically separated components of the women's movement, I experience dismay, and I find myself enviously imagining Elizabeth Cady Stanton and Lucretia Mott and Susan B. Anthony sitting and holding hands for forty years, performing an act of mutual sustenance that gave interwoven shape to their lives and their cause. And I think in a panic, Where would we be without them? They thought it all out for us, and we've got not one inch beyond them. Lately, however, I have changed my mind about that. . . .

I was on my way to a meeting one night not too long ago, a meeting meant to fashion a coalition group out of the movement's many organizations. I knew exactly what was ahead of me. I knew that a woman from NOW would rise and speak about our "image"; that a Third Worlder would announce loudly she didn't give a good goddamn about anybody's orgasms, her women were starving, for chrissake; that a Radicalesbian would insist that the women's movement must face the problem of sexism from within *right now;* and ten women from the Workers' Socialist party would walk out to protest against middle-class "elitist" control in the movement. I knew there would be a great deal of emotional opinions delivered, a comparatively small amount of valuable observation made, and some action taken. Suddenly, as the bus I was on swung westward through Central Park, I realized that it didn't matter, that none of it mattered. I realized it was stupid and self-pitying to be wishing that the meeting was going to be chaired by Elizabeth Cady Stanton; what she had done and said had been done and said profoundly in the idiom of her time, and in the idiom of *my* time no woman in the movement was her equal, but something else was: the consciousness-raising group.

I saw then that the small anonymous consciousness-raising

group was the heart and soul of the women's movement, that it is not what happens at movement meetings in New York or Boston or Berkeley that counts but the fact that hundreds of these groups are springing up daily—at universities in Kansas, in small towns in Oregon, in the suburbs of Detroit—out of a responsive need that has indeed been urged to the surface by modern radical feminism. It is here that the soul of a woman is genuinely searched and a new psychology of the self is forged. I saw then that the consciousness-raising group of today is the true second front of feminism; and as I thought all this I felt the ghost of Susan B. Anthony hovering over me, nodding vigorously, patting me on the shoulder and saying, "Well done, my dear, well done."

That ghost has accompanied me to every movement meeting I have attended since that night, but when I am at a consciousness-raising session that ghost disappears and I am on my own. Then, for better or worse, I am the full occupant of my feminist skin, engaged in the true business of modern feminism, reaching hard for self-possession.

And now let's go to a consciousness-raising session.

Early in the evening, on a crisp autumn night, a young woman in an apartment in the Gramercy Park section of Manhattan signs a letter, puts it in an envelope, turns out the light over her desk, gets her coat out of the hall closet, runs down two flights of stairs, hails a taxi, and heads west directly across the city. At the same time, on the Upper West Side, another woman, slightly older than the first, bends over a sleeping child, kisses his forehead, says goodnight to the babysitter, rides down twelve flights in an elevator, walks up to Broadway, and disappears into the downtown subway. Across town, on the Upper East Side, another woman tosses back a head of stylishly fixed hair, pulls on a beautiful pair of suede boots, and leaves her tiny apartment, also heading down and across town. On the Lower East Side, in a fourth-floor tenement apartment, a woman five or six years younger than all the others combs out a tangled mop of black hair, clomps down the stairs in her Swedish clogs, and starts trudging west on St. Marks Place. In a number of other places all over Manhattan other women are also leaving their houses. When the last one finally walks into the Greenwich Village living room they are all headed for, there are ten women in the room.

These women range in age from the late twenties to the middle thirties; in appearance, from attractive to very beautiful; in education, from bachelor's degrees to master's degrees; in marital status, from single to married to divorced to imminently separated; two are mothers. Their names are Veronica, Lucie, Diana, Marie, Laura, Jen, Sheila, Dolores, Marilyn, and Claire. Their occupations, respectively, are assistant television producer, graduate student, housewife, copywriter, journalist, unemployed actress, legal secretary, unemployed college graduate, schoolteacher, and computer programmer.

They are not movement women; neither are they committed feminists; nor are they marked by a special sense of social development or by personal neurosis. They are simply a rather ordinary group of women who are drawn out of some unresolved, barely articulated need to form a "women's group." They are in their third month of meetings; they are now at Marie's house (next week they will meet at Laura's, and after that at Jen's, and so on down the line); the subject for discussion tonight is "Work."

The room is large, softly lit, comfortably furnished. After ten or fifteen minutes of laughing, chatting, note and book exchanging, the women arrange themselves in a circle, some on chairs, some on the couch, others on the floor. In the center of the circle is a low coffee table covered with a coffeepot, cups, sugar, milk, plates of cheese and bread, cookies and fruit. Marie suggests they begin, and turning to the woman on her right, who happens to be Dolores, asks if she would be the first.

DOLORES *(the unemployed college graduate):* I guess that's okay. . . . I'd just as soon be the first . . . mainly because I hate to be the last. When I'm last, all I think about is, soon it will be my turn. *(She looks up nervously.)* You've no idea how I *hate* talking in public. *(There is a long pause; silence in the circle.)* . . . Work! God, what can I say? The whole question has always been absolute hell for me. . . . A lot of you have said your fathers ignored you when you were growing up and paid attention only to your brothers. Well, in my house it was just the opposite. I have two sisters, and my father always told me I was the smartest of all, that I was smarter than he was, and that I could do anything I wanted to do . . . but somehow, I don't really know *why,* everything I turned to came to nothing. After six years in analysis I still don't know why. *(She looks off into space for a moment and her eyes seem to lose the train of her thought. Then she shakes herself and goes on.)* I've always drifted . . . just drifted. My parents never forced me to work. I needn't work even now. I had every opportunity to find out what I really wanted to do. But . . . nothing I did satisfied me, and I would just stop. . . . Or turn away. . . . Or go on a trip. I worked for a big company for a while. . . . Then my parents went to Paris and I just went with them. . . . I came back . . . went to school . . . was a researcher at Time-Life . . . drifted . . . got married . . . divorced . . . drifted. *(Her voice grows more halting.)* I feel my life is such *waste.* I'd like to write, I really would; I feel I'd be a good writer, but I don't know. I just can't get going. . . . My father is so disappointed in me. He keeps hoping I'll really do something. Soon. *(She shrugs her shoulders but her face is very quiet and pale, and her pain expressive. She happens to be one of the most beautiful women in the room.)*

DIANA *(the housewife):* What do you think you will do?

DOLORES *(in a defiant burst):* Try to get married!

JEN *(the unemployed actress)* and Marie *(the copywriter):* Oh no!

CLAIRE *(the computer programmer):* After all that! Haven't you learned yet? What on earth is marriage going to do for you? Who on earth could you marry? Feeling about yourself as you do? Who could save you from yourself? Because that's what you want.

MARILYN *(the schoolteacher):* That's right. It sounds like "It's just all too much to think out so I might as well get married."

LUCIE *(the graduate student):* Getting married like that is *bound* to be a disaster.

JEN: And when you get married like that it's always to some creep you've convinced yourself is wonderful. So understanding. *(Dolores grows very red and very quiet through all this.)*

SHEILA *(the legal secretary):* Stop jumping on her like that! I
know *just* how she feels. . . . I was *really* raised to be a wife
and a mother, and yet my father wanted me to do something
with my education after he sent me to one of the best girls'
schools in the East. Well, I didn't get married when I got out
of school like half the girls I graduated with, and now seven
years later I'm *still* not married. *(She stops talking abruptly and
looks off into the space in the center of the circle, her attention wandering
as though she's suddenly lost her way.)* I don't know how to describe
it exactly, but I know just how Dolores feels about drifting. I've
always worked, and yet something was always sort of confused
inside me. I never really knew which way I wanted to go on a
job: up, down, sideways. . . . I always thought it would be the
most marvelous thing in the world to work for a really brilliant
and important man. I never have. But I've worked for some
good men and I've learned a lot from them. But *(her dark head
comes up two or three inches and she looks hesitantly around)* I don't
know about the rest of you, but I've always wound up being
propositioned by my bosses. It's a funny thing. As soon as I'd
be doing really well, learning fast and taking on some genuine
responsibility, like it would begin to excite them, and they'd
make their move. When I refused, almost invariably they'd begin
to *browbeat* me. I mean, they'd make my life miserable! And,
of course, I'd retreat. . . . I'd get small and scared and take
everything they were dishing out . . . and then I'd move on. I
don't know, maybe something in my behavior was really asking
for it, I honestly don't know any more.

MARIE: There's a good chance you *were* asking for it. I work
with a lot of men and I don't get propositioned every other
day. I am so absolutely straight no one *dares*. . . . They all think
I am a dyke.

SHEILA *(plaintively):* Why is it like that, though? Why are men
like that? Is it something they have more of, this sexual need
for ego gratification? Are they made differently from us?

JEN *(placing her coffee cup on the floor beside her):* No! You've just
never learned to stand up for yourself! And goddammit, they
know it, and they play on it. Look, you all know I've been an

actress for years. Well, once, when I was pretty new in the business, I was playing opposite this guy. He used to feel me up on the stage. All the *time*. I was scared. I didn't know what to do. I'd say to the stage manager: That guy is feeling me up. The stage manager would look at me like I was crazy, and shrug his shoulders. Like: What can *I* do? Well, once I finally thought: I can't stand this. And I bit him. Yes, I bit the bastard, I bit his tongue while he was kissing me.

A CHORUS OF VOICES: You bit him????

JEN *(with great dignity):* Yes, dammit, I bit him. And afterward he said to me, "Why the hell did you do that?" And I said, "You know goddamn well why I did that." And do you know? He respected me after that. *(She laughs.)* Didn't like me very much. But he respected me. *(She looks distracted for a moment.)* . . . I guess that *is* pretty funny. I mean, biting someone's tongue during a love scene.

VERONICA *(the assistant TV producer):* Yeah. Very funny.

LAURA *(the journalist):* Listen, I've been thinking about something Sheila said. That as soon as she began to get really good at her job her boss would make a pass—and that would pretty much signal the end, right? She'd refuse, he'd become an S.O.B., and she'd eventually leave. It's almost as if sex were being used to cut her down, or back, or in some way stop her from rising. An *instinct* he, the boss, has—to sleep with her when he feels her becoming really independent.

LUCIE *(excitedly):* I'll buy that! Look, it's like Samson and Delilah in reverse. *She* knew that sex would give her the opportunity to destroy his strength. Women are famous for wanting to sleep with men in order to enslave them, right? That's the great myth, right? He's all spirit and mind, she's all emotion and biological instinct. She uses this instinct with *cunning* to even out the score, to get some power, to bring him down—through sex. But look at it another way. What are these guys always saying to us? What are they always saying about women's liberation?—"All she needs is a good ----." They say that *hopefully. Prayerfully.* They know. We all know what all that "All she needs is a good ----" stuff is all about.

CLAIRE: This is ridiculous. Use your heads. Isn't a guy kind of super if he wants to sleep with a woman who's becoming independent?

MARIE: Yes, but not in business. There's something wrong every time, whenever sex is operating in business. It's always like a secret weapon, something you hit your opponent below the belt with.

DIANA: God, you're all crazy! Sex is *fun*. Wherever it exists. It's warm and nice and it makes people feel good.

DOLORES: That's a favorite pipe dream of yours, isn't it?

SHEILA: It certainly doesn't seem like very much fun to me when I watch some secretary coming on to one of the lawyers when she wants a raise, then I see the expression on her face as she turns away.

MARIE: God, that sounds like my mother when she wants something from my father!

VERONICA *(feebly)*: You people are beginning to make me feel awful! *(Everyone's head snaps in her direction.)*

MARIE: Why?

VERONICA: The way you're talking about using sex at work. As if it were so horrible. Well, I've *always* used a kind of sexy funniness to get what I want at work. What's wrong with that?

LUCIE: What do you do?

VERONICA: Well, if someone is being very stuffy and serious about business, I'll say something funny—I guess in a sexy way—to break up the atmosphere, which sometimes gets so heavy. You know what I mean? Men can be so pretentious in business! And then, usually, I get what I want—while I'm being funny and cute, and they're laughing.

DIANA *(heatedly)*: Look, don't you see what you're doing?

VERONICA *(testily)*: No, I don't. What am I doing?

DIANA *(her hands moving agitatedly through the air before her)*: If there's some serious business going on you come in and say: Nothing to be afraid of, folks. Just frivolous, feminine little me. I'll tell a joke, wink my eye, do a little dance, and we'll all pretend nothing's really happening here.

VERONICA: My God, I never thought of it like that.

LAURA: It's like those apes. They did a study of apes in which they discovered that apes chatter and laugh and smile a lot to ward off aggression.

MARILYN: Just like women! Christ, aren't they always saying to us: *Smile!* Who tells a man to smile? And how often do you smile for no damned reason, right? It's so *natural* to start smiling as soon as you start talking to a man, isn't it?

LUCIE: That's right! You're right! You know—God, it's amazing!—I began to think about this just the other day. I was walking down Fifth Avenue and a man in the doorway of a store said to me, "Whatsamatta, honey? Things can't be *that* bad." And I was startled because I wasn't feeling depressed or anything, and I couldn't figure out why he was saying that. So I looked, real fast, in the glass to see what my face looked like. And it didn't look like anything. It was just a face at rest. I had just an ordinary, sort of thoughtful expression on my face. And he thought I was *depressed.* And I couldn't help it, I said to myself, Would he have said that to you if you were a man? And I answered myself immediately: No!

DIANA: That's it. That's really what they want. To keep us barefoot, pregnant, and *smiling.* Always sort of begging, you know? Just a little supplicating—at all times. And they get anxious if you stop smiling. Not because you're depressed. Because you're *thinking!*

DOLORES: Oh, come on now. Surely, there are lots of men who have very similar kinds of manners? What about all the life-of-the-party types? All those clowns and regular guys?

CLAIRE: Yes, what about them? You never take those guys seriously. You never think of the men of real power, the guys with serious intentions and real strength, acting that way, do you? And those are the ones with real responsibility. The others are the ones women laugh about in private, the ones who become our confidants, not our lovers, the ones who are *just like ourselves.*

SHEILA *(quietly):* You're right.

LUCIE: And it's true, it really does undercut your seriousness, all that smiling.

SHEILA *(looking suddenly sad and very intent):* And underscore your weakness.

DOLORES: Yes, exactly. We smile because we feel at a loss,

because we feel vulnerable. We don't quite know how to accomplish what we want to accomplish or how to navigate through life, so we act *feminine*. That's really what this is all about, isn't it? To be masculine is to take action, to be feminine is to smile. Be coy and cute and sexy—and maybe you'll become the big man's assistant. God, it's all so sad. . . .

VERONICA *(looking a bit dazed):* I never thought of any of it like this. But it's true, I guess, all of it. You know *(and now her words come in a rush and her voice grows stronger).* I've always been afraid of my job. I've always felt I was there by *accident,* and that any minute they were gonna find me out. Any minute, they'd know I was a fraud. I had the chance to become a producer recently, and I fudged it. I didn't realize for two weeks afterward that I'd done it deliberately, that I don't *want* to move up, that I'm afraid of the responsibility, that I'd rather stay where I am, making my little jokes and not drawing attention to myself. . . . *(Veronica's voice fades away, but her face seems full of struggle, and for a long moment no one speaks.)*

MARILYN *(her legs pulled up under her on the couch, running her hand distractedly through her short blond hair):* Lord, does *that* sound familiar! Do I know that feeling of being there by accident, any minute here comes the ax. I've never felt that anything I got— any honor, any prize, any decent job—was really legitimately mine. I always felt it was luck, that I happened to be in the right place at the right time and that I was able to put up a good front and people just didn't know . . . but if I stuck around long enough they would. . . . So, I guess I've drifted a lot, too. Being married, I took advantage of it. I remember when my husband was urging me to work, telling me I was a talented girl and that I shouldn't just be sitting around the house taking care of the baby. I wanted so to be persuaded by him, but I just couldn't do it. Every night I'd say, "Tomorrow's the day," and every morning I'd get up feeling like my head was full of molasses, so sluggish I couldn't *move*. By the time I'd finally get out of that damn bed it was too late to get a babysitter or too late to get to a job interview or too late to do anything, really. *(She turns toward Diana).* You're a housewife, Diana. You must know what I mean. *(Diana nods ruefully.)* I began concentrating on my sex life with my husband, which had never been any too good, and was now getting really bad. It's hard to explain. We'd always been very affectionate with one another, and we still were. But I began to crave . . . passion. *(She smiles, almost apologetically.)* What else can I call it? There was no passion between us, practically no intercourse. I began to *demand* it. My husband reacted very badly, accused me of—oh God, the most awful things! Then I had an affair. The sex was great, the man was very tender with me for a long while. I felt *revived*. But then, a funny thing happened. I became almost hypnotized by the sex. I couldn't get enough, I couldn't stop thinking about it, it seemed to consume me; and yet, I became as sluggish now with sexual desire as I had been when I couldn't get up to look for a job. Sometimes, I felt so sluggish I could hardly prepare myself to go meet my lover. And then . . . *(She stops talking and looks down at the floor. Her forehead is creased, her brows draw together, she seems pierced suddenly by memory. Everyone remains quiet for a long moment.)*

DIANA *(very gently):* And then?

MARILYN *(almost shaking herself awake):* And then the man told my husband of our affair.

JEN: Oh Christ!

MARILYN: My husband went wild. . . . *(Her voice trails off and again, everyone remains silent, this time until she speaks again.)* He left me. We've been separated a year and a half now. So then I *had* to go to work. And I have, I have. But it remains a difficult, difficult thing. I do the most ordinary kind of work, afraid to strike out, afraid to try anything that involves real risk. It's almost as if there's some *training* necessary for taking risks, and I just don't have it . . . and my husband leaving me, and forcing me out to work, somehow didn't magically give me whatever it takes to get that training.

LAURA *(harshly):* Maybe it's too late.

DIANA: Well, that's a helluva thought. *(She crosses her legs and stares at the floor. Everyone looks toward her, but she says no more. Jen stretches, Claire bites into a cookie, Lucie pours coffee, and everyone rearranges themselves in their seats.)*

MARIE *(after a long pause):* It's your turn, Diana.

DIANA *(turning in her chair and running thin hands nervously through her curly red hair):* It's been hard for me to concentrate on the subject. I went to see my mother in the hospital this afternoon, and I haven't been able to stop thinking about her all day long.

JEN: Is she very sick?

DIANA: Well, yes, I think so. She underwent a serious operation yesterday—three hours on the operating table. For a while there it was touch and go. But today she seemed much better and I spoke to her. I stood by her bed and she took my hand and she said to me, "You need an enormous strength of will to live through this. Most people need only one reason to do it. I have three: you, your father, and your grandmother." And suddenly I felt furious. I felt *furious* with her. God, she's always been so strong, the strongest person I know, and I've loved her for it. All of a sudden I felt tricked, I felt like saying to her, "Why don't you live for yourself?" I felt like saying, "I can't take this burden on me! What are you doing to me?" And now suddenly I'm here, being asked to talk about work, and I have nothing to say. I haven't a goddamn thing to say! What do I do? After all, what do I do? Half my life is passed in a fantasy of desire that's focused on leaving my husband and finding some marvelous job. . . . At least, my mother worked hard all her life. She raised me when my real father walked out on her, she put me through school, she staked me to my first apartment, she never said no to me for anything. And when I got married she felt she'd accomplished everything. That was the end of the rainbow. . . .

DOLORES *(timidly):* What's so terrible, really, your mother saying she lived for all of you? God, that used to be considered a moral virtue. I'm sure lots of men feel the same way, that they live for their families. Most men hate their work . . . .

MARILYN: My husband used to say that all the time, that he lived only for me and the baby, that that was everything to him.

LUCIE: How did you feel about that? What did you think of him when he said it?

MARILYN *(flushing):* It used to make me feel peculiar. As though something wasn't quite right with him.

LUCIE *(to Diana):* Did you think something wasn't quite right, when your mother said what she said?

DIANA *(thinking back):* No. It wasn't that something wasn't quite right. It seemed "right," if you know what I mean, for her to be saying that, but terribly wrong suddenly.

LUCIE: That's odd, isn't it? When a man says he lives for his family it sounds positively unnatural to me. When a woman says it, it sounds so "right." So expected.

LAURA: Exactly. What's pathology in a man seems normal in a woman.

CLAIRE: It comes back, in a sense, to a woman always looking for her identity in her family and a man never, or rarely, really doing that.

MARIE: God, this business of identity! Of wanting it from my work, and not looking for it in what my husband does . . .

JEN: Tell me, do men ever look for their identities in their wives' work?

VERONICA: Yes, and then we call them Mr. Streisand. *(Everybody breaks up, and suddenly cookies and fruit are being devoured. Everyone stretches and one or two women walk around the room. After fifteen minutes . . .)*

MARIE *(peeling an orange, sitting yogi-fashion on the floor):* I first went to work for a small publicity firm. They taught me to be a copywriter, and I loved it from the start. I never had any trouble with the people in that firm. It was like one big happy family there. We all worked well with each other and everyone knew a bit about everybody else's work. When the place folded and they let me go I was so depressed, and so *lost.* For the longest time I couldn't even go out looking for a job. I had no sense of how to go about it. I had no real sense of myself as having a transferable skill, somehow. I didn't seem to know how to deal with Madison Avenue. I realized then that I'd somehow never taken that job as a period of preparation for independence in the world. It was like a continuation of my family. As long as I was being taken care of I functioned, but when I was really on my own I folded up. I just didn't know how to operate. . . . And I still don't really. It's never been the same. I've never had a job in which I felt I was really operating responsibly since that time.

SHEILA: Do you think maybe you're just waiting around to get married?

MARIE: No, I don't. I know I really want to work, no matter what. I know that I want some sense of myself that's not related to a husband, or to anyone but myself, for that matter. . . . But I feel so lost, I just don't know where it's all at, really. *(Five or six heads nod sympathetically.)*

CLAIRE: I don't feel like *any* of you. Not a single one.

DOLORES: What do you mean?

CLAIRE: Let me tell you something. I have two sisters and a brother. My father was a passionately competitive man. He loved sports and he taught us all how to play, and he treated us all exactly as though we were his equals at it. I mean, he competed with us exactly as though we were twenty-five when we were eight. Everything: sailing, checkers, baseball, there was nothing he wouldn't compete in. When I was a kid I saw him send a line drive ball right into my sister's stomach, for God's sake. Sounds terrible, right? We loved it. All of us. And we thrived on it. For me, work is like everything else. *Competitive.* I can get in there, do the best I can, compete ferociously against man, woman, or machine. And I use whatever I have in the way of equipment: sex, brains, endurance. You name it, I use it. And if I lose I lose, and if I win I win. It's just doing it as well as I can that counts. And if I come up against discrimination as a woman, I just reinforce my attack. But the name of the game is competition.

(Everyone stares at her, open-mouthed, and suddenly everyone is talking at once; over each other's voices; at each other; to themselves; laughing; interrupting; generally exploding.)

LAURA *(dryly):* The American dream. Right before our eyes.

DIANA *(tearfully):* Good God, Claire, that sounds awful!

LUCIE *(amazed):* That's the kind of thing that's killing our men. In a sense, it's really why we're here.

SHEILA *(mad):* Oh, that love of competition!

MARIE *(astonished):* The whole idea of just *being* is completely lost in all this.

JEN *(outraged):* And to act *sexy* in order to compete! You degrade every woman alive!

VERONICA *(interested):* In other words, Claire, you imply that if they give you what you want they get *you?*

DIANA *(wistfully):* That notion of competition is everything we hate most in men, isn't it? It's responsible for the most brutalizing version of masculinity. We're in here trying to be men, right? Do we want to be men at their worst?

LUCIE *(angrily):* For God's sake! We're in here trying to be *ourselves.* Whatever that turns out to be.

MARILYN *(with sudden authority):* I think you're wrong, all of you. You don't understand what Claire's really saying. *(Everyone stops talking and looks at Marilyn.)* What Claire is really telling you is that her father taught her not how to win but how to lose. He didn't teach her to ride roughshod over other people. He taught her how to get up and walk away intact when other people rode roughshod over *her.* And he so loved the idea of teaching that to his children that he ignored the fact that she and her sisters were girls, and he taught it to them, anyway. *(Everyone takes a moment to digest this.)*

LAURA: I think Marilyn has a very good point there. That's exactly what Claire has inside her. She's the strongest person in this room, and we've all known it for a long time. She has the most integrated and most *separate* sense of herself of anyone I know. And I can see now that that probably has developed from her competitiveness. It's almost as though it provided the proper relation to other people, rather than no relation.

SHEILA: Well, if that's true then her father performed a minor miracle.

JEN: You're not kidding. Knowing where *you* stand in relation to other people, what you're supposed to be doing, not because of what other people want of you but because of what you want for yourself . . . *knowing* what you want for yourself . . . that's everything, isn't it?

LAURA: *I* think so. When I think of work, that's really what I think of most. And when I think of *me* and work, I swear I feel like Ulysses after ten years at sea. I, unlike the rest of you, do not feel I am where I am because of luck or accident or through the natural striving caused by a healthy competitiveness. I feel I am like a half-maddened bull who keeps turning and turning and turning, trying to get the hell out of this maze he finds himself in. . . . I spent ten years not knowing what the hell I wanted to do with myself. So I kept getting married and having children. I've had three children and as many husbands. All nice men, all good to me, all meaningless to me. *(She stops short and seems to be groping for words.)* I wanted to do something. Something that was real, and serious, and would involve me in a struggle with myself. Every time I got married it was like applying Mercurochrome to a festering wound. I swear sometimes I think the thing I resent most is that women have always gotten married as a way out of the struggle. It's the thing we're encouraged to do, it's the thing we rush into with such *relief,* it's the thing we come absolutely to hate. Because marriage itself, for most women, is so full of self-hatred. A continual unconscious reminder of all our weakness, of the heavy price to be paid for taking the easy way out. Men talk about the power of a woman in the home. That power has come to seem such a lopsided and malevolent thing to me. What kind of nonsense is that, anyway, to divide up the *influences* on children's lives in that bizarre way? The mother takes care of the *emotional* life of a child? The vital requirement for nourishment? Out of what special resources does she do that? What the hell principle of growth is operating in her? What gives a woman who never tests herself against structured work the wisdom or the self-discipline to oversee a child's emotional development? The whole thing is crazy, just crazy. And it nearly drove me crazy. . . . What can I say? For ten years I felt as though I were continually vomiting up my life. . . . And now I work. I work hard and I work with great relish. I want to have a family, too. Love. Home. Husband. Father for the children. Of course, I do. God, the loneliness! The longing for connection! But work first. And family second. *(Her face splits wide open in a big grin).* Just like a man.

LUCIE: I guess I sort of feel like Laura. Only I'm not sure. I'm not sure of anything. I'm in school now. Or rather "again." Thirty years old and I'm a graduate student again, starting out almost from scratch. . . . The thing is I could never take what I was doing seriously. That is, not as seriously as my brother, or any of the boys I went to school with, did. Everything seemed too long, or too hard, or too something. Underneath it all, I felt sort of *embarrassed* to study seriously. It was as if I was really feeling: "That's something the *grownups* do. It's not something for *me* to do." I asked my brother about this feeling once, and he said most men felt the same way about themselves, only they fake it better than women do. I thought about that one a long time, and I kept trying to say to myself: What the hell, it's the same for them as it is for us. But . . . *(she looks swiftly around the circle)* it's not! Dammit, it's *not*. After all, style is content, right? And ours are worlds away . . . .

VERONICA: Literally.

LUCIE: I don't know. . . . I still don't know. It's a problem that nags and nags and nags at me. So often I wish some guy would just come along and I'd disappear into marriage. It's like this secret wish that I can just withdraw from it all, and then from my safe position look on and comment and laugh and say yes and no and encourage and generally play at being the judging mother, the "wise" lady of the household. But then I know within six months I'd be miserable! I'd be climbing the walls and feeling guilty. . . .

MARILYN: Guilty! Guilty, guilty. Will we *ever* have a session in which the word guilty is not mentioned once? *(Outside, the bells in a nearby church tower strike midnight.)*

DIANA: Let's wrap it up, okay?

VERONICA *(reaching for her bag):* Where shall we meet next week?

MARIE: Wait a minute! Aren't we going to sum up? *(Everyone stops in mid-leaving, and sinks wearily back into her seat.)*

LUCIE: Well, one thing became very clear to me. Every one of us in some way has struggled with the idea of getting married in order to be relieved of the battle of finding and staying with good work.

DIANA: And every one of us who's actually done it has made a mess of it!

JEN: And everyone who *hasn't* has made a mess of it!

VERONICA: But, look. The only one of us who's really worked well—with direction and purpose—is Claire. And we all jumped on her! *(Everyone is startled by this observation, and no one speaks for a long moment.)*

MARILYN *(bitterly):* We can't do it, we can't admire anyone who *does* do it, and we can't let it alone. . . .

JEN *(softly):* That's not quite true. After all, we *were* able to see finally that there was virtue in Claire's position. And we are here, aren't we?

MARIE: That's right. Don't be so down. We're not a hundred and two years old, are we? We're caught in a mess, damned if we do and damned if we don't. All right. That's exactly why we're here. To break the bind. *(On this note everyone takes heart, brightens up, and troops out into the darkened Manhattan streets. Proof enough of being ready to do battle.)*

(January 1971)

Lesbians and Women's Liberation: "In Any Terms She Shall Choose"

A month ago I spent a weekend in the company of a prominent feminist, a dedicated and intelligent woman who, in the course of the time we passed together, spoke out passionately against the open recognition of lesbianism in the movement, claiming— along with *Time* magazine—that the women's movement would destroy its credibility out there in "middle America" if it should publicly support lesbians as a legitimate element in feminism and in the movement. I found this position appalling, and I feel now that it raises an issue that must be argued more specifically than I had recently thought. For just as it seemed transparently certain to that feminist that open recognition of lesbianism in the women's movement would imperil the life of the movement, so it seems equally clear to me that denial of lesbianism in the women's movement will insure the death of the movement.

Hundreds of women in the feminist movement are lesbians. Many of them have worked in the women's movement from its earliest days of organized activity. They were in NOW three and four years ago, working steadily along with heterosexual women for the redress of grievances that affected them all; they are scattered today across the entire political board of women's organizations. They probably have more to gain from feminism

than any other single category of women, both in the most superficial sense and in the more profound one. Certainly, they have
more to *teach* feminists about feminism than has any other single
category of human being—man or woman. And yet, until only
this past year, lesbians have lived the same crypto-life in the
movement that they live outside it. Sitting next to a heterosexual
feminist who might rise in distress at a meeting to say, "Oh,
let's not do *that.* They'll think we're a bunch of lesbians," the
lesbian in the next seat could not rise and say, "But I *am* a
lesbian," because her admission would have forced to the surface
a wealth of fears only half understood, which would then quickly
have been converted into panic and denunciation. It was an
old, old story to the lesbians, one for which they could have
written the script, and one which feminists should feel eternal
shame for having played a part in.

It is the very essence of the lesbian's life that she leads an
underground existence; that she cannot openly state the nature
of her emotional-sexual attachments without thereafter enduring
the mark of Cain; that in innumerable places and under all varie-
ties of circumstance she experiences every manner of insult and
injury to the soul that can be inflicted by the insensitive and
the unperceiving; that in every real sense she is one of the invisible of the earth. It is this element almost alone, separated out
from the multiple elements of her defining experience, that determines the character of the lesbian's life and often the shape
of her soul. To live with the daily knowledge that what you
are is so awful to the society around you that it cannot be revealed
is to live with an extraordinary millstone slung from one's neck,
one that weighs down the body and strangles the voice.

Imagine, then, the feeling of those lesbians who joined the
feminist movement only to find themselves once more unable
to be themselves. Here they were, women doubly cast out of
society, both as women and as homosexuals, joined together
in the feminist struggle for selfhood, being victimized by other
women. For there's no mistaking it: the heterosexual feminist
who disconnected herself, politically and spiritually, from the
homosexual feminist sitting next to her (and did so most especially when she was saying, "Look, I don't care what *anybody*

does in her private life, but there's no public place in the movement for that sort of thing") was disavowing that homosexual feminist, and thus victimizing her. The irony of it all was that in actuality the heterosexual feminist was victimizing herself even more, for that disavowal strikes at the bottommost roots of feminism, attacking the movement in its most vital parts, threatening its ideological life at the source.

Feminism, classically, has grown out of woman's conviction that she is "invisible" upon the earth; that the life she leads, the defining characteristics that are attributed to her, the destiny that is declared her natural one are not so much the truth of her real being and existence as they are a reflection of culture's willful *need* that she be as she is described. The feminist movement is a rebellious *no* to all that; it is a declaration of independence against false description of the self; it is a protest dedicated to the renunciation of that falsity and the courageous pursuit of honest self-discovery. The whole *point* of the feminist movement is that each and every woman shall recognize that the burden and the glory of her feminism lie with defining herself honestly *in any terms she shall choose.*

Sexual self-definition is primary to the feminist movement. After all, the movement's entire life is predicated on the idea that woman's experience has been stunted by society's falsifying views of the nature of her sexuality. Feminists are now saying to male civilization, "Your definition of my sexuality is false, and living inside that falsehood has now become intolerable to me. I may not know what I *am,* but I surely know what I am *not,* and it is offensive to my soul to continue to act what I am not." Thus, in essence, the feminist's course is really charted on the path of discovery of the sexual self. What *is* the actual nature of a woman's sexuality? What *are* its requirements? To what genuine extent does it exert pressure on her to fulfill herself through sexual love? To what extent will that miracle of force and energy—if diverted elsewhere—blossom into an altogether other and transformed kind of human being? Who knows? No one has the answers. We are only just beginning to formulate the questions.

Seen in this perspective, homosexuality in women represents

only a variant of the fundamental search for the sexual self-understanding that is primary in the struggle to alter radically the position of women in this culture. In a word: some feminists are homosexual, and others are heterosexual; the point is not that it is wrong and frightening to be one or right and relieving to be the other; the point is that *whatever* a woman's sexual persuasion, it is compelling, and she must be allowed to follow her inclinations openly and honestly without fear of castigation in order to discover the genuine self at the center of her sexuality.

That, for me, is the true politics of the feminist movement. It is woman recognizing that she is a fully developed human being with the responsibility to discover and live with her own self, which means creating an emotional environment in which that self can not only act but be prepared to take the consequences for those acts as well. The determination of what the self is, or should be, is a matter of individual choice that must be honored by the movement, and acknowledged as a legitimate reference to the movement's ultimate aims.

What is most astonishing in all this is that the open flare-up last year between homosexual and heterosexual feminists is living proof of this deepest influence of the feminist movement on the need to be oneself. After enduring in silence for a number of years the movement's virtual denial of their existence, NOW's lesbians suddenly emerged a year ago as the Radicalesbians, demanding acknowledgment, and forming a consciousness-raising group of their own, thereby taking the movement at its word and using feminism's most valuable technique for support and definition as well. Most heterosexual feminists were initially startled by the lesbians' outburst, but many immediately grasped that the deepest principles of feminism were involved here and offered ready alliance. The lesbians were demonstrating for all those who had eyes to see that much of the movement's rhetoric had never been tested, that the issue of sexual liberation was an amazingly complex one, that at last the question of sexual fear was being turned on themselves. Many feminists did not see these things, however, and many, to this day, continue to see the open acknowledgment of lesbianism in the movement as irrelevant, or a threat to the movement's survival.

The claim that the question of lesbianism is irrelevant to the movement—that the struggle for recognition as a lesbian belongs properly to gay liberation and not the women's movement— seems to me openly fallacious. The point is not that lesbians in the movement are homosexual; the point is that they are *feminists:* self-proclaimed, fully participating feminists who are being told, in a movement predicated on the notion that women are the victims of sexism, that the dominating principle of their sexuality is to be kept under wraps because the women out there in "middle America" simply wouldn't understand. This is the kind of emotional response masquerading as political analysis that panders to all our emotional and sexual fears. It encourages us to remain afraid of ourselves and to inflict injustice on each other in the name of our fears. And is that not what sexism is all about? If our emotional and sexual fears are not at the bottom of the condition that has brought us to feminism, what on earth is? Would we then not all profit immeasurably from the emotional daring involved in facing down the fear of lesbianism in the movement, and recognizing *it* for the true irrelevancy in the feminist struggle to reclaim our lives?

What I find more distressing than the charge of irrelevancy, however, is the aggressive talk from feminists that admission of lesbianism in the women's movement is a threat to the growth of the movement. From *Time* magazine I can take it, but from feminists it goes unbearably against the grain. If anything is a threat to the movement, it is the fear of taking just action in the name of political expediency. If anything will destroy this movement, it is losing sight of the fact that what feminism is genuinely all about is calling the shots as we see them. To be possessed of a bit of emotional truth, and then to go publicly against that truth because it is politically "wiser" to do so, is to totally misperceive the *real* politics of feminism—which has not to do with altering legislation or building a political party or taking over the government or uselessly increasing ranks. The real politics of feminism has to do with filling the social atmosphere with increased feminist consciousness and letting acculturation do its job. Nothing—absolutely nothing—is "wiser" than that, *Time* magazine and Kansas City housewives notwithstanding.

Really, the whole thing is so bewildering. Three years ago

the women's movement was a renegade movement, willing to speak truths nobody wanted to hear. Suddenly, on this issue, it is being told it must speak *only* those truths middle-class America is willing to hear. And this is absurd, for in reality all the apprehension is groundless. When Ti-Grace first said, "Love is an institution of oppression," everybody panicked. Now, a year and a half later, the most respectable ladies in the movement don't bat an eyelash when the guilty phrase is invoked, and *Time* magazine nods knowingly. Clearly, then, if we stick to our guns, the rightness of our perceptions will obtain, and in two years' time lesbianism in the movement will be a fact of boring respectability in Omaha.

And that is all it should ever be. In radical circles in the movement there is now a rather alarming swing left toward the suddenly fashionable superiority of lesbianism, and the half-assed notion that the only "true" relationships for a feminist are with other women. One hears the silliness of the intellectual decision to become a lesbian because it's good for you, and worse, one hears a belligerent arrogance in some lesbians that amounts to angry revenge. One morning on Nanette Rainone's WBAI "Womankind" program I heard a lesbian assert that a woman couldn't really be considered a feminist unless she "related" to women in every way. Now that is power politics—nothing more, nothing less—and it is up to the straining honesty in both homosexual and heterosexual feminists to keep the central issue uncluttered and free of hysteria.

And the central issue is the question of self-definition for all women. What must be learned from the acceptance of lesbianism in the movement is that radically different truths inform different lives, and that as long as those truths are not antisocial they must—each and every one of them—be respected. If feminism is to have any historical significance, it certainly will be because it has taken an important place in this latest convulsion of the humanist movement to remind civilization that human lives become painful and useless when they cease to feel the truth of their own experience.

In the end, the feminist movement is of necessity the work of a radical feminist sensibility, and the fear of open recognition of lesbianism is the work of a liberal feminist sensibility. The falseness of the liberal's position is that while she apparently sorrows over the pain of the world, she offers only distant sympathy, when what is needed is partisan courage. By offering sympathy instead of courage, she increases rather than reduces the pain of this world.

(March 1971)

On Trial for Acting
Like a Man

The facts of the case are these: In 1967 Gabrielle Russier, a divorced woman of thirty, the mother of nine-year-old twins, and the possessor of a brilliant academic record from the University of Aix-en-Provence, became a teacher of French literature in a high school in Marseilles. She was, in authoritarian France, an unusual teacher in that she considered her students people, saw life from their point of view, and drew close to them both as a friend and as a teacher. They, in turn, adored her, called her "Gatito" (little cat in Spanish), and addressed her with the familiar *tu.* Among her students was a boy of sixteen named Christian Rossi. Christian, a tall, husky, bearded young man, was a passionate Maoist and the son of two professors at the University of Aix-en-Provence (which is almost a suburb of Marseilles). Both Mr. and Mrs. Rossi were Communists, and Mr. Rossi had been the teacher of Gabrielle Russier. The boy Christian and the woman Gabrielle became intimate friends, and in June 1968, after the May uprising, they fell in love and began an affair.

Toward the end of that summer Gabrielle went to Christian's father and told him of her love for his son and of her desire to live openly with Christian. Professor Rossi flew into a rage and became determined to part the lovers. When this began to seem impossible—there were terrible raging scenes between father and son and the son finally ran away from home—the Rossis filed a complaint in court and Gabrielle was arrested for corruption of a minor. (By this time Christian was seventeen and Gabrielle thirty-one.) Gabrielle was imprisoned in Marseilles for a number of months under the law of preventive detention. At last, in July 1969, she came to trial in a closed court and was given a suspended sentence, which amounted to amnesty. Half an hour later, as a result of a telephone call from the Public Ministry, the prosecuting attorney gave Gabrielle's lawyer the astonishing news that the state would appeal the decision in a higher court and seek a stiffer penalty for Gabrielle Russier. The point of this was to make sure she would have a police record, thereby making it impossible for her ever again to teach anywhere in France.

Gabrielle, destroyed by her months in prison and the nightmare that had become her waking life, broke down entirely and was sent to a convalescent home to await a new trial. She returned to Marseilles—all alone—at the end of the summer, and on September 1, 1969, unable to stop brooding about her ruined life, she committed suicide.

The issues the case of Gabrielle Russier raises are obvious and painful. How could such a thing have happened? Why was she imprisoned? What was her crime? Could this have happened to her had she been a man? Why were the French authorities obviously determined to ruin her? What is the relation among all these questions?

One reads and rereads the facts of the case, and one falls into the well-developed habit of accepting bizarre premises as an unquestioned starting point. It all becomes so *easy* to understand: then she did this, then he did that, then they were faced with this consequence, then his parents were faced with that consequence, then The Law took over . . . and so it all neatly unfolded, it all followed a weird kind of logic, it all, in retrospect, seems "inevitable." And suddenly one's mind jolts to a stop— she is actually *dead!* it all really *killed* her—and the terrible emotional confusion that then crowds in on the brain wipes out the seeming reasonableness with which one has been "understanding" these events. With bitter lucidity one sees that the death of Gabrielle Russier was a kind of ritual offering demanded by a pack of savages playing an elaborate game in which the stakes genuinely are the life of the "other."

When I first read of Gabrielle Russier I thought, Clearly this all happened because she was a woman. Then I thought, No, perhaps it was simply that the outraged French bourgeoisie were determined, regardless of sex, to punish the renegade in their midst as they would not have punished either a man or a woman of say, the lower classes or even of the upper classes. Ultimately, I returned to my original conviction: regardless of other factors, Gabrielle Russier would not have been meted out the particular and fatal brand of justice she *did* receive had she not been a woman.

To begin with, how, everyone immediately wonders, could a woman be put on trial and hounded to death for having slept with a boy in the country that produced out of the very marrow of its culture a literature of print and film—including *Chéri, The Red and the Black, Devil in the Flesh, The Rules of the Game*—that demonstrates repeatedly with that incomparable mixture of French cynicism and passion that women of forty sleep with boys of eighteen, that what is often begun for sensuous profit deepens into some mysterious and vital connection that can be called nothing else but love, that whatever happens it's good for everyone involved, that this kind of relationship is, in actuality, formed commonly and continually?

Also, one wonders, how could this happen in a country that respects the intelligence and achievement of its women as they are never respected here in the United States? In France, a woman who demonstrates a first-rate intelligence is taken seriously much more easily and much more often than she is in this country, and once she demonstrates her ability she rises to high position without the opposition she eternally faces here. How, then, Gabrielle Russier?

The answer, in the first instance, lies in one word: *secrecy.* The very point of all these famous liaisons is that they take place in dead secrecy; the power of the woman lies in her skillful and complex ability to manipulate her official and respectable position as teacher to the boy, as friend of the family, as disinterested neighbor, never—under any circumstances—losing the essential operating tool of respectability. It is a game of odds: if she plays the odds well she is released into mastery; if she plays badly she forfeits her life. Nowhere in French literature are we taught these lessons so well as in *Les Liaisons Dangereuses*. Gabrielle Russier chose not to play any odds. She chose to live openly with her offensively young lover. She lost her head.

As for the second instance, women of high accomplishment are rewarded because the overriding passion of the French *in power* is intellectual attainment. Any eccentricity or freakishness in human life will be regarded highly in France if it should draw from its intellectuals astonished admiration. I sometimes think an ape could become president of France if it had a Ph.D. in Sanskrit. The question, then, for us to ask is: if an intellectual ape became president would all other apes be accorded equal human status? The answer is obvious.

The truth, then, of the position of women in France is that it is far worse than it is in America, that those who glitter so brilliantly and those who manipulate so spectacularly are a direct measure not only of the deep powerlessness of those who do not, but also of the even deeper contempt in bourgeois authoritarian France in which women are in reality held. Gabrielle Russier went on trial for something no man in France would ever have gone on trial for. She went on trial, therefore, for acting like a man.

And yet, it is also true, as the prosecuting attorney said, that "if she had been a hairdresser, or if she had slept with a young apprentice, it would have been different." She would not have been dealt with so harshly. She would not have been dealt with at all. Because who the hell could *give* a damn what a hairdresser did? Which works both ways: one of the vital concerns that arose out of the Russier trial (once the unthinkable had happened— that is, that an educated middle-class woman had been incarcerated) was the question of the law of preventive detention, under which someone charged with a crime can remain in prison for incredible periods of time awaiting trial. Well, thousands of "hairdressers" languish in preventive detention all the time. Who on earth—either in France or in this country—has ever known or cared or taken action?

But Gabrielle was not a hairdresser. She was a keeper of the culture. She was an educated woman of the most unbending middle class in the Western world, a middle class of the most vicious self-importance, a middle class that operates with extraordinary skill and talent inside a rigid set of behavioral rules and plays the Queen of Hearts without mercy when those rules are challenged, especially if they be challenged by a woman. (When there was an uproar over the state's appeal for a stiffer sentence for Gabrielle, the Public Ministry said it was only routine, while a hundred Parisian lawyers said, "Never! This kind of appeal hasn't been made ten times in the last forty years, and never has it been made for a charge such as this one.")

But Gabrielle was being charged by public opinion—and indeed, then by the government itself—with every obscenity imaginable. She was charged not with an actual crime, not with a set of legally damaging facts, not with vice, fraud, arson, rape, or murder, but rather with being a fallen woman. She was charged with having slept with a man fifteen years younger than herself. She was charged with being a whore, a nymphomaniac, a threat to public morality, a bad mother, a divorced woman. (In Mavis Gallant's memorable phrase, *"Divorced woman* clanged away with the regularity of a clock striking.") She was charged, in the final analysis, with having an insufficient character in the view of Parisian shopkeepers as well as in the view of the Public Ministry. (A lawyer in Paris said, "It is not the machinery of the law that is crushing her. It is only a few men with opinions.") She was charged, really, with not having a proper "soul." And for all of this she died.

In *The Stranger* Meursault also is tried for not having the proper soul. Clearly, he is not being adjudged guilty for the actual crime of having murdered someone, but for his inability to love, for his sacrilegious attitude toward his mother, for his insupportable separateness in the human community.

Years ago, a movie called *La Vérité* demonstrated the same French penchant for judgment according to some fearful middle-class assessment of character rather than according to criminal code. There, a woman goes on trial not really for the actual facts of her crime but for the distastefulness of her "soul," for the immorality of her past, for the number of lovers she has had.

According to Mavis Gallant, in her essay about the trial of
Gabrielle Russier, it is not likely in an actual court of French
law that Meursault would have been tried for the contents of
his soul; on the other hand, it *is* likely that the woman in the
movie would have been so tried. She recounts a series of cases
in French law where women on trial hear judges say things like
"I have searched everywhere in the record for your soul, and
I am unable to find it"; where a man charged with murder received eight years and the woman who supposedly incited him
to commit the crime received twelve years, where a woman
charged with murder was sentenced not because the facts against
her were incontrovertible but because the judge was horrified
by the number of lovers she had had (saying her life would
tempt the pen of a Balzac) and he disapproved of the books
she had read. Gallant, a Canadian writer who has lived in France
for many years, states categorically that it would be unheard-
of in the trial of a man that moral judgment of this sort be
substituted for facts.

What happens to a woman under these circumstances is that
she becomes a stand-in for self-punishment: what men cannot
bear to inflict on themselves they will often inflict on women;
whereas they will not pontificate over each other they will pontificate over a woman. In the terrifying course of that locked struggle between enlightened behavior and primitive fears, men have
come, often, to "forgive" themselves for uncontrollable hungers,
indiscreet honesties, unpredictable responses. A civilization's
courts of judgment are just such places in which men feel obliged
to battle over "forgiving" these transgressions or punishing
themselves for them. The truly powerful impulse is to punish—
and more often than not that impulse is followed. However,
when it is an "other" creature—like a woman—who sits in the
dock, then that internal conflict, without hesitation, is *snapped*
to attention, and the alien terror and hatred of the self that
has confided itself in society into law comes swooping to the
surface with ferocious relief. Gabrielle Russier was caught in
that tangle, and perished in it.

The book that Knopf has now put together, telling the story
of the unfortunate schoolteacher, is composed of an introductory

essay by Mavis Gallant; a shorter preface by Raymond Jean, a teacher and friend of Gabrielle's; and the letters from prison written by Gabrielle. Gallant's essay is brilliant; not another word need be said on the trial and its meaning within the context of French society after her essay. She tells the story of the two lovers from every necessary point of view: hers, his, the parents, the magistrates, the law, national customs, the power of French patriarchy, the influence of literature, the academic life in which they moved, the influence of the May uprisings—it is all satisfyingly and abundantly there, sadly and justly viewed through the ironic eyes of a deeply intelligent foreigner.

Raymond Jean is less interesting. A French Communist and a former professor of Gabrielle's at the University of Aix-en-Provence, his personal memoir serves to sketch in the character of the protagonist in this deathly melodrama, but he grows tiresome in his predictable railing against the "bourgeois courts."

It is the letters of Gabrielle herself, written from prison, that are finally the most penetrating part of the book. To read them is to be reminded of Chekhov's *Ward Six* and of the unspeakableness of truly changing places with one of the dispossessed of the earth. The letters, at first calm and literate, fall gradually into a depthless despair; it is the despair of a middle-class woman who in her wildest nightmares could never have dreamed that her life would finally become this stunning negation, this unprotected and abandoned *thing*, this absolute helplessness, this descent into corrupt madness.

"What have I done? Why am I here?" she writes, and I froze reading those lines. I felt that I stood behind her eyes, that I pushed that pen across the paper, that I, too, now suffered the dread and unthinkable reality that had, at last, overtaken her. There was no doubt in my mind, not for a fraction of a moment, that if it had happened to her it could happen to me too.

What nags at the heart, though, long after one has stopped reading, is the memory of Gabrielle among the other prisoners. Surrounded by a vast and hopeless corruption of the spirit, she sank into a kind of humiliated horror from which she never recovered and which surely was at the center of the suicidal depression that caused her to take her own life.

Again, Chekhov. It was the noble Russian doctor who said, "It is important that a human being never be humiliated. That is the main thing."

(October 1971)

Why Women Fear Success

Girls get dumber and dumber as they get older and older. We all know that. We have all *always* known that. The girl child matures early, levels off fast, and then slowly retrogresses. Thousands of females who are positively brilliant in grade school become merely bright in high school, simply very good in college, and, finally, almost mediocre in graduate school. It is a curious pattern of human development familiar to all of us, one that has come under formal observation very often in the past seventy-five years.

The explanation for this peculiar reversal has consisted of obscure references to something in the female that turns inward, something that is repelled by competition, some natural lack of aggression. Freud said it, Erikson said it, and the entirety of Western culture repeats it. All of our observations and predilections have traditionally supported the idea that women, in the long haul, simply do not have the constitution for normal competition; that, in women, the inner necessity to succeed that nourishes and sharpens the intelligence seems to be missing. In all the highly perceptive work done on the relation between motivation and achievement, none of the information contributed by women adds to our understanding of this powerful dynamic in human lives, because women seem unresponsive to the stimulus to achieve. In fact, they seem dominated by a profound wish to fail.

Seven years ago, Matina Horner, an experimental psychologist working on the relation between motivation and achievement at the University of Michigan, was as puzzled as the men in her department by the irregular and disturbing results that came exclusively from female subjects. All sorts of data based on information given by the men were successfully fed into the carefully worked-out test model, but when it came to the women, the model went crazy. Nothing meshed; no two tests of women came up with the same kinds of results—ever. In addition, the women tested out abnormally high on anxiety. Bewildered and dissatisfied, the psychologists reluctantly dismissed the women's data as indicating a hopeless "will to fail," impossible to cope with in achievement-motivation work. Dr. Horner, however, sensed that this was not an adequate explanation for what she felt was going on with the women; she stumbled, ultimately, on the idea that the women involved were not exhibiting a will to fail, but rather an active, anxious desire to *avoid success.*

Matina Horner, a dark-haired, dark-eyed woman in her early thirties, is now assistant professor of clinical psychology at Harvard. She teaches three courses in personality, one of them a graduate seminar in the personality development of women. Her office, in a new Harvard building, is a large bright room overlooking the city of Cambridge. Recently, I spent a morning in that room with Dr. Horner. We discussed her work, and inevitably— as we were not only a psychologist and a journalist, but two women as well—we discussed our own lives. (After all, were they not proper subjects for a study of the fear of success in women?)

Dr. Horner spoke slowly, in a soft voice; as she warmed to both her subject and her visitor she became more animated.

I asked Dr. Horner what had made her tumble to the idea that it was not the will to fail that was operating in the girl students she had tested but rather the desire to avoid success.

"Well," she said, smiling, "the desire to fail comes from some deep psychological conviction that the consequences of failure will be *satisfying.* These girls at Michigan were motivated by the opposite; they were positively anxiety-ridden over the prospect of success. They were not simply eager to fail and have done with it; they seemed to be in a state of anxious conflict over what would happen if they succeeded. It was almost as though this conflict was inhibiting their capacity for achievement."

Intrigued by the intellectual problem that these male-female sexual differences seemed to present, Dr. Horner had decided to work up another model for testing, one that would concentrate on discovering women's actual expectancies in relation to achievement. This approach made use of what is known in scientific jargon as an "expectancy-value theory of motivation." Here the experimenter aims to discover what a subject's expectations are regarding the consequences of an action he or she proposes to take. According to the theory, anxiety is aroused when one expects the consequences to be negative. Thus, anxiety acts as an inhibiting force and produces what scientists call an "avoidance motive." This motive doesn't tell us what someone *will* do, but it indicates clearly what he or she will *not* do.

Out of this approach came a theory Dr. Horner called "the Motive to Avoid Success." The compelling evidence for her theory came from a series of Thematic Apperception Tests she administered to 90 women and 88 men, all undergraduates at the University of Michigan. Known to psychologists as T.A.T.s, these tests require the interpretation of a picture or the completion of a story line. The results of those T.A.T.s were startling. As Dr. Horner explains in her first study:

> We asked Phil, a bright young college sophomore . . . to tell us a story based on one clue: *After first-term finals, John finds himself at the top of his medical school class.* Phil writes:
> *John is a conscientious young man who worked hard. He is pleased with himself. John has always wanted to go into medicine and is very dedicated. . . . John continues working hard and eventually graduates at the top of his class.*
> Now consider Monica, another honor student. She too has always done well and she too has visions of a flourishing career. We give her the same clue, but with "Anne" as the successful student. . . . Instead of identifying with Anne's triumph, Monica tells a bizarre tale:
> *Anne starts proclaiming her surprise and joy. Her fellow classmates are so disgusted with her behavior that they jump on her in a body and beat her. She is maimed for life.*
> Next we ask Monica and Phil to work on a series of achievement tests by themselves. Monica scores higher than Phil. Then we get them together, competing against each other on the same kinds of tests. Phil performs magnificently; Monica dissolves into a bundle of nerves.

The glaring contrast between the two stories and the dramatic changes in competitive situations illustrate important differences between men and women in reacting to achievement. . . .

In response to the successful-male cue *(After first-term finals, John finds himself . . .)* more than 90 percent of the men in the study showed strong positive feelings, indicated increased striving, confidence in the future and a belief that this success would be instrumental to fulfilling other goals such as providing a secure and happy home for some girl. . . . Fewer than 10 percent of the men responded at all negatively. . . .

On the other hand, in response to the successful-female cue, 65 percent of the girls were disconcerted, troubled or confused by the cue. Unusual excellence in women was clearly associated for them with the loss of femininity, social rejection, personal or societal destruction or some combination of the above. Their responses were filled with negative consequences and affect, righteous indignation, withdrawal rather than enchanced striving, concern, or even an inability to accept the information presented in the cue. For example:

Anne will deliberately lower her academic standing the next term, while she does all she subtly can to help Carl. . . . His grades come up and Anne soon drops out of med school. They marry and he goes on in school while she raises their family.

Anne is a code name for a nonexistent person created by a group of med students. They take turns taking exams and writing papers for Anne. . . .

Aggressive, unmarried, wearing Oxford shoes and hair pulled back in a bun, she wears glasses and is terribly bright.

In other words, women showed significantly more evidence of the motive to avoid success than did men, with 59 of the 90 women scoring high and 8 of the 88 men doing so.

"What was even more apparent," said Dr. Horner, swiveling her chair around to face me more directly, "was that the fear of success manifested itself mainly in women of demonstrably high intelligence, coming from homes where high achievement was much valued. Which makes great sense, when you think about it. After all, a girl who's not too bright and doesn't have much chance for success to begin with is hardly likely to be frightened by the prospect of success. Whereas a bright girl from a middle-class home, knowing she actually has it within her possible grasp. . . ."

What happens to most women of this type, continued Dr. Horner, is simple. In this age of lip service to equality and self-realization for all, parents encourage their daughters to fulfill their entire potential and allow them some of the advantages given to men. The encouragement, however, is essentially hollow. Somewhere around a girl's junior year in college, if not before, the parents' strong desire surfaces: that the girl be securely married, rather than take the unconventional and risky course of becoming a serious working person. The contradictory message that the girl gets, from society as well as from her parents, is that if she is too smart, too independent, and, above all, too serious about her work, she is unfeminine and will therefore never get married. (Speculation that the full brunt of anxiety over femininity and academic achievement begins to fall upon a woman student about halfway through college is supported by special studies. For instance, one study revealed that the fear of success in women ranged from a low 47 percent in a seventh-grade junior high school sample to a high 88 percent in a sample of high-ability undergraduate students at a prominent Eastern school.)

The woman student in her third year understands then—or primarily then—that she actually has been sent to college to find a husband and to fit herself out as an attractive and educated wife. The important aspect of this reversal of goals is the immediate capitulation in the girl's psyche, a capitulation that parallels the rapidity with which the fear of success then grows in the brightest women students. The implication, clearly, is that the girl is predisposed to accept this notion that femininity and academic achievement are incompatible; that some deep receptivity toward this idea has been developing in her personality almost from birth; some influence beyond the inauthentic encouragement of her parents to become an autonomously developed human being has caused her to internalize the traditional sexual stereotype of passive femininity. Once the thin crust of encouragement is broken, a deep well of social conditioning is discovered underneath. She goes into a tailspin of anxiety as she struggles to reverse her appetite for human fulfillment, an appetite she now learns is in direct contradiction to her *feminine* fulfillment.

As Dr. Horner succinctly puts it in her study:

Our data indicate that the emphasis on the new freedom for women
has thus far not been any more effective in doing away with this tendency
[to avoid success] than were the vote, trousers, cigarettes, and even
changing standards of sexual behavior. If anything, our most recent
data indicate something of a backlash phenomenon since the mid-sixties.
The negative attitudes we find expressed toward successful women have
increased to a disproportionately greater extent than have the positive
ones, and this is true of both male and female subjects.

Needless to say, such a contradictory state of being is unthinkable for a man, who is taught *from birth* that his human fulfillment
and his masculine fulfillment are one and the same. While it is
true that achievement-motivation work has uncovered the fear
of success in men, that fear is always coupled with philosophical
issues in the man's mind—that is, an apprehension regarding
the values of succeeding in a materialistic or socially amoral
culture. It is never coupled with a deep conflict over the crucial
and fundamental issue of his masculinity.

What happens inside the mind of a woman struggling with
such a conflict? Since it has never been properly acknowledged
until now, the question has remained unaddressed.

One day Dr. Horner separated out into two piles the results
of one of her T.A.T.s. She separated them according to the
data collected through other T.A.T.s, which had identified some
of these same subjects as low in fear of success, and others as
high in fear of success. The T.A.T. cue was *Anne is sitting in a
chair with a smile on her face.* Those low in fear of success had
responded to the cue with rather pleasant, neutral tales such
as:

*Anne is happy—she's happy with the world because it is so beautiful. It's
snowing, and nice outside—she's happy to be alive and this gives her a warm
feeling. . . .*

*Anne is alone in her room. It's a beautiful day. . . . Her two closest friends
have just met marvelous people and believe they are in love. . . . The beautiful
day and her nice friends' happiness create an aura of happiness about her. . . .*

The stories written by the girls high in fear of success were
startlingly different:

Anne is recollecting her conquest of the day. She has just stolen her ex-boyfriend away, right before the High School Senior Prom. . . . She wanted to hurt her friend, and succeeded by taking the boyfriend away underhandedly. . . .

Anne is at her father's funeral. There are over 200 people there. . . . Her mother, two brothers and several relations are there. Anne's father committed suicide. . . . She knows it is unseemly to smile but cannot help it. . . . Her brother Ralph pokes her in fury but she is uncontrollable. . . . Anne rises dramatically and leaves the room, stopping first to pluck a carnation from the blanket of flowers on the coffin.

(Anne), woman in her twenties, is sitting, smiling smugly, in a chair in a small restaurant in New York City. She has just successfully (so far) completed her first robbery (jewelry store). . . . Gun in hand, she is waiting for her stepmother to return home. A short time earlier, her father was murdered and she believes her stepmother did it. . . .

To think seriously on the meaning of these fantasies in the minds of women who long for and are morbidly afraid of autonomous fulfillment is to come away filled with fear and sadness. Our culture has made a deep split in the souls of its women, and the result is insupportable anxiety which can bear up only by transforming itself into the malevolence of what is known as passive-aggressive behavior. Behind the "passive" exterior of many women there lies a growing anger over lost energies and confused lives, an anger so sharp in its fury but so diffuse in its focus that one can only describe it as the price society must pay for creating a patriarchal system in the first place, and for now refusing to let it go.

And make no mistake, it is not letting go.

Last summer at Harvard University, Dr. Horner tested a group of undergraduate men in order to discover their genuine feelings about successful women. She gave them the T.A.T. cue that she had previously given to women at the University of Michigan: *After first-term finals, Anne finds herself at the top of her medical school class.* The answers, overwhelmingly, were along the following lines:

Anne is not a woman. She is really a computer, the best in a new line of machines. . . .

Anne rushes out of her smelly formaldehyde laboratory, and runs to the university bar where she knows she will find Bruno! The perfect man!

Anne is paralyzed from the waist down. She sits in a wheelchair and studies for medical school. . . .

This is the summer of 1970. This from Harvard University. This from the men who will marry the girls at Michigan.

"How has this happened to women?" I asked Dr. Horner. "And how can it *un*-happen?"

"Those are both extremely difficult issues even to *speculate* about," Dr. Horner smiled. "How does it all happen? When does it begin to happen? So fast, so early, that it is frightening. My daughter is five years old. One day she came into my room and said to me 'Mommy, Daddy must love you very much.' 'Why do you say that?' I asked her, pleased that she had made such an assumption. 'Because he doesn't want you to be tired,' she said. 'He does the dishes so that you won't be tired. . . .' Now, it was very nice that the conclusion she came to was that my husband cared for me because he washed the dishes, but the point is, it was a *problem* in her mind, one she had to find a solution for. At five—without any help from us, I can assure you—she knows something is funny if her daddy is doing the dishes!

"The sexual stereotypes are fixed in the minds of girls and of boys almost from birth, and God, do they ever *stay* fixed. I've observed it repeatedly in *myself*. Look, when I was up for my prelims, I went into a state of anxiety like nothing I'd ever known before. I carried on so I frightened my husband and finally, in desperation, he yelled at me, 'For God's sake, maybe women *shouldn't* be in graduate school!' Now, what was I afraid of? I had designed my own prelim. I knew everything I was responsible for. There wasn't the *remotest* possibility of failure; and yet, I was shaking, throwing up, screaming I was stupid and now they'd all know I was stupid.

"Interestingly enough, there was only one time that I remember facing an audience calmly. I rose to speak and was amazed at how quiet and good I felt inside. Then I looked down at myself, and I understood. There I was seven months pregnant. Nothing I was about to say could contradict *that*. It was my insurance—I was loved, I was about to have a baby, I was in there being a woman—nothing to be afraid of.

"To alter all this is the most complex problem we face now. And it's what we do here. We sit around and we think about these things. My students here at Harvard are marvelous: very bright, very quick, very much taken with these problems. We sit together in our seminars and we ask hard questions. It's exciting to see these ideas taking hold in their minds.

"What we have to do is to get to the bottom of what is genuinely natural in women. What we now call natural is only normative. It is what our culture has defined as normal for women and normal for men, but it sheds no light on what is *natural.* For instance the assertion that women have no natural aggression in them is absurd. Women can be very aggressive even while using 'passive' methods. Silence can be used aggressively. Two little girls getting together in a schoolyard and saying to each other, 'You be my friend and I'll be yours, and we won't be *her* friend'—that's aggressive! Aggression is a desire to exercise will. Passivity is not. Well, God knows, enough women are interested in exercising their wills. . . . So which is it? Is woman aggressive or not? What *is* her nature? This we know next to nothing about. It is this vast area of ignorance that we must explore.

"I think, as far as the future is concerned, that everything depends on where society goes. The counterculture offers some interesting possibilities, but even those, if you look closely enough, don't get to the heart of the matter as far as women are concerned. For instance, one of the ideas of the counterculture is that competitiveness is bad. You are a bad *person* if you compete. If this idea should begin to dominate the norm, and women seeking to develop themselves for the first time should then rise to high positions, well they're still in bad shape! Because men define the good. It is what *men* do that determines the values of the society, and this no less so in the counterculture than in the one they left behind.

"But perhaps all these issues—the counterculture, ecology, liberation from sexual stereotypes—can eventually feed into a new normative world in which women may finally be able to define themselves. I have great hopes."

I walked out into the Cambridge afternoon sun, feeling benign toward every unknown person whose path crossed mine. After all, this campus had given Matina Horner a place to work, a place to continue her search for new answers, and, perhaps more important, a place to examine and discard all those old questions. Here, her gift as a scientist had led her to ask *new* questions about women. And new questions are what women's liberation is all about.

(1972)

Why Radcliffe Women
Are Afraid of Success

Cambridge, Mass. On November 16 of this past year (1973), Matina Horner, a thirty-three-year-old associate professor of psychology at Harvard University, became the sixth president of Radcliffe College, the famed school for women founded in 1879 across the Cambridge Common from Harvard. For great numbers of people—both inside and outside the academic world—Matina Horner's inauguration was a moment of ritual rather than of ceremony, signifying the assumption of a post empty of genuine powers: a token title thrown to a woman academic under pressure from the government and the social atmosphere created by the feminist movement to end discrimination against women in the academy. It was not uncommon during the week of her inauguration to hear many generally well-informed people say of Matina Horner, "Well, I don't understand. . . . After all, Radcliffe is now part of Harvard isn't it? I mean, the school, for all intents and purposes, has been integrated for twenty years now, hasn't it? Radcliffe girls do sit in Harvard classrooms, don't they? And now they even live in Harvard houses. What is the meaning of yet another Radcliffe president?"

For great numbers of *other* people, however, Dr. Horner's assumption of the Radcliffe presidency has much meaning. For, in fact, Radcliffe has never formally merged with Harvard and is at this moment not merged with Harvard, and for those who see in this question of merger meanings of symbolic proportion, the personality and history of this newest Radcliffe president are of vital interest.

The issue of merger—prominent during the tenure of Radcliffe's last president, Dr. Mary Bunting—burst to the surface during the student uprisings that convulsed Harvard in 1969. Discussed by administrative councils and boards of trustees for two years, merger was sufficiently opposed by Radcliffe alumnae to force the ultimate decision into the kind of limbo much favored by academic and governmental bodies: "Let us form an investigative committee to study the question further." Thus, while over the past three years the lives of Radcliffe and Harvard students have been more radically integrated than ever before, and everyone in Cambridge speaks with gentle cynicism of the "nonmerger merger," Radcliffe's traditional separate-but-equal position in relation to the world-famous university that now grants its degrees remains one of uneasy ambiguity.

What is happening now with regard to the integration of women into Harvard University is a metaphor for what is happening throughout American society, and it is no accident that a woman like Matina Horner finds herself at the center of a metaphor. It is no accident that this scientist-turned-feminist will preside over the question of merger between Radcliffe and Harvard. It is no accident that during the second great wave of American feminism this experimental psychologist, who has spent the last seven years of her working life investigating the reasons for failure to achieve in intellectually gifted women, should now be in a position to affect the atmosphere that simultaneously both encourages and cripples intelligent women.

In the twenty-five years since the Second World War, Radcliffe has risen to the position of the top women's college in the country. When Mary McCarthy was asked after publication of *The Group* whether, if she had a daughter of college age, she would today send her to Vassar, she replied, "No, Radcliffe." It is a piece of conventional wisdom that the brightest, most talented, most serious young women in the country today make up the student body at Radcliffe. This was not always so. For the first seventy years of its existence, when the school—which has never actually had its own faculty—"rented a professor from across the Yard" (that is, paid Harvard professors to come to the Radcliffe buildings to teach), the school was good but not exceptional. After the war, however, when Radcliffe students crossed the Yard into Harvard classrooms, its reputation altered, its fame grew, and although in every other respect life at Radcliffe College remained essentially unchanged, the quality of its students became uniformly superior. Oddly enough, however, the women of Radcliffe failed in great numbers to fulfill their academic promise. These very brilliant women seemed suddenly, upon graduation, simply to disappear. And are still disappearing. Last summer at a convention of the American Council of Education, when a new and vigorous discussion about the advantages of single-sex institutions was under way, it was observed that jobs of responsibility are held far more often by the women of Bryn Mawr, Wellesley, Vassar, and Smith than by the women of Radcliffe. The women from Cambridge are simply not out there in significant numbers.

Why? Why should it be so that the most intellectually gifted women in the country, living and working in the most intellectually gifted community in the country, if not the world, should nevertheless fail to achieve? Should simply, upon graduation, fall away? (And what's more, while undergraduates, should test out a high 88 percent on Matina Horner's fear-of-success model?) Inevitably, some of the answers to these questions must lie in a closer look at the actual rather than the statistical features of the intermingled life of Harvard and Radcliffe.

Harvard is the oldest and without question the finest university in the nation. Its life is multitudinous, its intellectual innovation prodigious, its atmosphere graceful and deeply civilized. Raymond Lubitz, a Columbia economist who took his doctorate at Harvard, once said, "Columbia is the book and the classroom. You close those down and you close down Columbia. But not Harvard. Harvard has many lives outside of the book and the classroom." In a more passionate and less disinterested manner, C. Wright Mills was making much the same point when he said there were two Harvards: the Harvard of the scholarship intellectual and the Harvard of what Mills called the power elite. What both men were talking about is an atmosphere compounded of tradition, social connection, and aristocratic assumption that drenches the beautiful stone buildings, the tree-lined paths, the peace and civility of Harvard Yard, the nineteenth-century calm of the inner courts of the river houses. It is an atmosphere that somehow conveys an unmistakable message: from this place will come the men who will sit in the councils of power, the men who will occupy crucial positions in government and business, in scientific foundations and patronage of the arts, in social philosophy and interpretation of the law.

"It's hard to say exactly how it happens," puzzled Sven Holmes, currently a Harvard senior. "But after four years here you feel as though the world has been created to be led by Harvard men."

It is a series of accumulating images that contributes to Holmes's sense of things. To stand in the doorway of the Harvard Faculty Club dining room is to glimpse instantly one of these images. The ceiling is high, the floor carpeted, the windows are broad and graceful, the tables covered with white cloths and flowers in slim glass vases; and the people sitting at the tables are all middle-aged Anglo-Saxon men in gray suits and steel-rimmed glasses. One *knows* better. One knows that there are women in this room, and young people, and even beards. But one *feels* only the presence of men who look like Eastern bankers devoted to public service. One stands in the doorway thinking: Will the real T. S. Eliot please stand up?

The Faculty Room on the second floor of University hall in Harvard Yard is even more overpowering. The room is oak-paneled, high-ceilinged, filled with long arched windows, crystal chandeliers, Greek columns atop which sit plaster busts, and on the walls, innumerable very dark paintings of Harvard presidents of the past. The entire atmosphere is somber and again, somehow, bankerish. One does not here think, This is the university of Emerson. Rather one thinks, This is the university of tradition and good family. If one is not oneself of "good family," it is impossible to escape a sense of outsidedness, and if one should, into the bargain, be a woman, one is entirely dislocated. For no woman can stand in the doorway of the Faculty Room and help but think, What has all this to do with me? Surely, this room was not made to accommodate or include me in its doings. Here, I was never intended to belong.

But it is in the Harvard house system that the heart and soul of the making of a Harvard man resides. Modeled forty years ago on the life of the great English universities, the house system at Harvard was designed to replicate a kind of university within the university. Traditionally, Harvard men spent the freshman year in dormitories within Harvard Yard. After that, each student moved into one of the beautiful houses built around spacious inner courtyards that surround the Harvard campus, houses that bear such venerable American names as Winthrop, Lowell, and Eliot, and that are complete with elegant suites, dining halls, and common rooms. Each house is supervised by a master who lives in the house, and staffed by a group of tutors, both resident and nonresident, whose duties include responsibility for the academic, physical, and emotional welfare of the students in the house. Here, in the houses, each day at luncheon and again at dinner, professors, tutors, masters, and students meet to dine and talk together. Here—between faculty and students—friendships are offered, contacts are made, ideas take fire, work clarifies, and the traditions that bind the university into a unifying whole are carried forward.

When one turns from these features of Harvard life to the life that was actually lived until three years ago at Radcliffe, it is like stepping directly into the pages of Virginia Woolf's *A Room of One's Own*. Speaking in that minor masterpiece of the inequities beween the lives of men and women at "Oxbridge"— inequities that are often summed up in one famous image, "Partridge for the men, prunes and custard for the women"—Woolf produces an indelible portrait of the damage that is done to the souls of women in such circumstances. At one point, having sought entrance to one of the great libraries wherein lie a number of famous manuscripts she wishes to peruse, and having been denied entrance because she is not a Fellow (and, of course, as a woman could never *be* a Fellow), she turns from the library door with these words:

That a famous library has been cursed by a woman is a matter of complete indifference to a famous library. Venerable and calm, with all its treasures safe-locked within its breast, it sleeps complacently and will, so far as I am concerned, so sleep forever. Never will I wake those echoes, never will I ask for that hospitality again, I vowed as I descended the steps in anger. . . . I thought how unpleasant it is to be locked out; and I thought how it is worse perhaps to be locked in; I thought of the safety and prosperity of the one sex and the poverty and insecurity of the other and of the effect of tradition and the lack of tradition upon the mind of a writer.

Susan Cary Block, an experimental psychologist at M.I.T., and a resident tutor at Radcliffe's only genuine house—gleaming new Currier—was in the Radcliffe class of '64. Sitting in her house-apartment, her legs crossed upon a coffee table, her hair flung back from her face, she pushes her glasses back onto the bridge of her nose and says flatly, "There were no houses at Radcliffe. That's it. No houses at all. No suites, no common rooms, no tutors in residence, nothing. I lived in the dorms. I shared a room smaller than my [present] dining room with another girl. It was all as different from the spacious suites the boys occupied in those riverfront houses as could be. The inequities? All the way down the line. The libraries were closed to us, the common rooms, the houses, the fellowships, the prizes, the lot. . . . And how we fantasized about the life in the houses! It was a given that we sat around the table talking about dates and clothes and nervous complaints, while the boys at Harvard sat around and talked about 'things.' We were *brighter* than they were, but that's what it came to. Mrs. Bunting understood what all this meant. She tried desperately to create houses at Radcliffe. But without money—and of course there's never been any money at Radcliffe; the underendowment of women's colleges is notorious—her hands were tied. She slapped a few dorms together and insisted they were houses. But everyone knew better."

Carol Kay, a graduate student in English, also a former Cliffie and now a nonresident tutor at Winthrop House, says over lunch, "I was in the class of '67. Yes, we shared classes, but the institution always gave out the signals, and those signals said, 'You don't belong. You're not really a part of things.' Because we lived in dorms, we never ate lunch with the men and the faculty. As a result, you didn't make those contacts, those easy friendships, that led to being able to work with your favorite professor. When you graduated, your department was behind you as it was behind the men. But it didn't look forward to placing you. You hadn't made the friendships that counted.

"The doors were never closed, but you never felt free to walk through them. The feeling I was left with after four years here was, 'We train leaders, and women aren't leaders.'"

A student approaches our table, and Carol Kay breaks off to give him her full attention. They exchange a few words, and afterward she laughs, a bit primly, and says, "You know, until coresidential living, no woman was ever a tutor. If you weren't a tutor, you couldn't receive a key to the Senior Common Room. If you didn't have a key to the Senior Common Room, you couldn't make those contacts necessary to further your career. You simply didn't belong."

The words of these two women are echoed, and re-echoed, by Radcliffe graduates of the sixties who are now graduate students, research associates, and instructors—but almost never regular appointment faculty—across the Harvard campus. Their implications are corroborated in the massive statistics and commentary compiled in the April 1971 report presented by a Harvard faculty committee, cochaired by Carolyn Bynum and Michael Walzer, on the status of women in the Faculty of Arts and Sciences. In one striking paragraph about graduate students the committee observes:

The results of our questionnaire clearly indicate that . . . the difference between male and female expectations is significant. Even more significant is the fact that 26 percent of female respondents (as opposed to 11 percent of male respondents) answered that faculty members 'had told them or given them the impression that they were not serious students.' Moreover, 37 percent of the female respondents had been told, or had received the impression, that their sex was a drawback in their chosen careers. Graduate-student women we have consulted point out that such attitudes are particularly infuriating and depressing. We agree. Sex, like race and color, cannot be changed. It is discourteous and cruel to imply that it ought to be.

Dark-eyed, raven-haired, and with the gypsy-sallow complexion that is her Greek heritage, Matina Horner sits with me one October afternoon in the president's office in nineteenth-century

Fay House in the Radcliffe Yard. Her composure is enormous, her manner uniformly grave and quiet, her opinions offered with a moderation that some consider tentative, and others downright conservative. And, indeed, it is difficult to escape the impression that it is precisely for these observed characteristics that Dr. Horner was ultimately chosen by the Radcliffe president Search Committee. In a number of interviews, various members of that committee, all speaking a masked, genteel rhetoric filled with words like "forward-looking" and "challenging," seemed extremely taken with the amiableness of Dr. Horner and the promise of good working relations which her manner seemed to hold. As to her work, they were enthusiastic about it to the extent that it gave her the requisite stamp of scholar, but vague in their understanding of its significance. In fact, observed Prof. Zeph Stewart, one faculty member on the committee, Matina Horner's work was very nearly a drawback rather than an enticement to the committee, as there was some speculation about whether her extreme interest in women's problems might not be a hindrance to the even-handed performance of administrative work.

Across the campus, people (professors, students, administrators) of every political stripe have all spoken well of Matina Horner. For from this academic scholar who looks for all the world like a young suburban matron there issues an aura of hidden strength, intellectual integrity, and genuine attachment to the students. Although she is now president of Radcliffe, Harvard dean of Radcliffe College, and associate professor in the Harvard psychology department, Dr. Horner has refused to give up her teaching duties. She remains adviser and seminar instructor to some fifteen or twenty undergraduate honors students and graduate students whose work was being conducted in her field (motivation and personality theory) under her supervision before she was appointed president. "I remember how it would have felt to be dropped by *my* adviser." She laughs quietly.

The room in which we sit is oval-shaped and calm with its years, a study in whitewashed walls, green plants, wooden sills, modern furniture, and the sunlit trees that fill its windows. But the problems that come across its teak desk are rough and shapeless, and must all be dealt with by the woman who sits behind that desk.

"I took this job," Matina Horner says, "because I had studied the growth and education of women for many years—both as a researcher and as a psychologist—and I naturally was eager to take a job that would put me in the position of being able to put this information to use and influence future policy regarding women and their education. But I genuinely believe this is a time of study. A time to investigate the true position of Radcliffe, and re-evaluate our relation to Harvard. A time to re-evaluate the education of women and whether or not it can be best achieved through merger. I want to keep an open mind on merger. The advantages of a single-sex institution must be studied. At colleges like Bryn Mawr, Wellesley, Vassar, there is a far greater proportion of students in economics, government, physics, and mathematics than at Radcliffe, and one finds that Radcliffe women fill the jobs one would expect them to fill far less often than the women of these other schools. Inevitably, merger raises other questions. Radcliffe, of course, has many of its own traditions. For instance, there is no separate [residence for the] freshman year at Radcliffe. Freshmen have always lived with upperclassmen. If the schools merge, there is no question but that the Radcliffe traditions will give way to the Harvard ones. The kids know this, and they're against that.

"Right now Radcliffe still has the autonomy of separate admissions, a separate endowment, a governing board of trustees, and it is still a property-owning corporation. Many Radcliffe alumnae feel that the women stand to gain nothing and lose everything if they simply turn all that over to Harvard.

"For the present I have no answers. In fact, what I want are more hard *questions*. Harvard and Radcliffe have the resources to *ask* the right questions, and the potential for answering them if they would only try.

"I want very much right now to study our admissions records. I want to see exactly what our criteria really are, and why a particular class has been chosen. Do we select those who test well? Are we more inclined to admit the traditional versus the nontraditional student? And what does an applicant say during those interviews? What do we say? What happens there? Whom do *we* get accepted by, and whom rejected by? What happens to those who come here?

"I am asked if I will push for equal admissions.* I am not prepared to jump on that national bandwagon. If Harvard were to become 70 percent female tomorrow, it would still be a *male* university. An increase of female enrollment alone will not change things significantly for women here, and I am absolutely opposed to tokenism of any sort.

"On this question, as on many others of policy, my ideas have been interpreted by some as a stand against equal admissions, which is not the case. Unless we ask the more basic, not the token, questions, things will never change."

What *will* change things? Matina flashes her truly brilliant smile at me, rises from her seat, and says, "Come on, let's go pick up my kids. We'll talk in the car."

The Horners have three children: Tia, eight; John six; Christopher, three. Matina and her husband continue to live in their spacious brick house in suburban Belmont rather than in the president's house on campus because they feel uprooting the children would be bad. Thus, on a number of afternoons a week, Matina continues to pick up the two older children at the Cambridge Montessori School and to drive them home exactly as she used to do.

"I was asked if I thought my mother's duties would interfere with my work," she says as she swings her station wagon into Cambridge traffic. "Nonsense. Being a mother has been all to the good. The same pleasure I receive from watching the growth of my children is transferred to my students. . . . But to get back to what we are talking about. How can things change here with regard to women? So much of it lies with intangibles. Let

---

* Equal admissions is sex-blind admissions, one of the touchiest issues on the Harvard-Radcliffe campus. At one and the same time, the demand for equal admissions (1) is a response to social and political pressure to equalize men and women in the student body, (2) presupposes merger, and (3) worries those administrators who are keenly aware of the fact that Harvard's massive endowment depends upon alumni who hope to see their sons entered in the university.

me relate two incidents to you. Many meetings are now commonly called to deal with the H.E.W. directive to increase the number of women on the faculty of Harvard. At one such meeting recently, I was the only woman in the room. One of the men said, very seriously, very thoughtfully, 'How much will we have to lower our standards to fulfill these requirements?' I was so shocked by the question that I remained silent. Completely silent. Then, as one, every head in the room turned toward *me!* I was doubly shocked now, both by the question and the automatic head-turning, and again I couldn't find my voice. Soon, everyone looked extremely sheepish. Later, someone said to me, 'That was a brilliant tactic.'

"On another occasion, at another, similar meeting, the names of one of two women were tossed out for faculty-appointment consideration. Of one of these women, a professor I know well, said, 'Forget it. Her husband won't come here.' I exploded. 'For heaven's sake,' I said, 'you've got to stop doing that. You've got to stop making those assumptions. If you want a talented woman, you've got to go after her the way you would any talented man.' The man looked blankly at me for a moment. Then he nodded."

With that Matina reaches behind her to unlock the door that will admit a leggy little girl and a bemused little boy to the back seat of the station wagon. Her point is well taken. Matina Horner knows better than anyone else what sexism has to do with an attitude of expectations about women, often shared by both men and women, that has hardened into emotional habit, and that it is this attitude that must be altered, bit by bit, in the daily flow of life, in the slow, steady, repetitious calling of it, each and every time.

At the same time, what is implicit in Matina's little stories of how change will come about is the deeper recognition that merger is inevitable. For what she has described is the petition by women for full entrance to the community of men. What makes of Radcliffe and Harvard a microcosm of what is now happening throughout the worlds of business, government, and the arts as well as the academy is precisely that Radcliffe—unlike the rest of the Seven Sisters—has never been a separate institution. It has always had one foot in Harvard Yard, and it is as bitter and unrealistic to talk of withdrawing that foot as most radical feminist talk of separation is bitter and unrealistic. Yet, it is that one foot that has been the source of paralysis for so many of Radcliffe's women. For how crippling it is to experience apparent equality rather than actual equality. How crippling to attend a university entirely run and staffed by men, taught almost exclusively by men (there are only 23 women on a faculty of more than 700 members), surrounded by an atmosphere designed for men: where the ordinary man is demonstrably superior simply by virtue of his maleness, and the "brilliant exception" cannot struggle successfully to overcome the stigma of her femaleness; where a professor could observe to the committee reporting on the status of women at Harvard, "I feel an automatic barrier being raised when I talk to a department chairman about a woman for an open position. A not atypical response is, 'You're not serious, are you?' "; where an administrator could only last year be told by her male superior, in an offguard moment, "Any man who works for a woman has got to feel as though his balls have been cut off"; where a famous master could be widely quoted by two generations of students as having said, "When a woman enters the room, intelligent conversation leaves."

Of course, the atmosphere of change is—as it is everywhere in the nation—strong at Radcliffe and Harvard. Three years ago coresidential living was inaugurated, and now men and women live in both the Radcliffe and the Harvard houses. Many of the fellowships and prizes and, yes, even the libraries, are now open to women. The government has placed enormous pressure on Harvard to hire more women academics and administrators. The importance of these changes is registered most clearly in the altered perception that Harvard and Radcliffe students now have of each other. According to Prof. Bruce Chalmers, Master of Winthrop House: The Harvard man has always had a stereotyped portrait of the Radcliffe girl. She was, above all, intense. Uninteresting, unattractive, brighter than he, threatening, and altogether uncomfortable. Of course, since 80 percent of Radcliffe women marry Harvard men, when the Harvard man found his particular Cliffie she was always the exception. Now, with coliving, one sees that whole emotional involvement being defused. They sit at tables together, have a normal conversation, and then simply go their separate ways, like two ordinary human beings. . . . With all the fuss that was kicked up over this arrangement, you would have thought that Harvard was inventing coeducation."

Even more significant, the young women who are now entering Radcliffe have absorbed the atmosphere of change and seem to view themselves differently. Grete Bibring, a well-known psychoanalyst who has been connected with Harvard Medical School for more than twenty-five years and has conducted a seminar at Radcliffe for the last seven years, reports: "When I began this seminar the girls *hated* being here with me. They felt nothing important could be said because there were no boys in the room. That was 1965. The year before last when I asked them if they wanted boys in the seminar they all shouted, 'No! It's the only time we talk sense!' But last year I did have boys, and it soon became apparent that something strange was happening. The boys seemed extremely passive about their careers, whereas the girls were extremely *eager* for them. Almost, the boys were saying, 'Let *them* have it now.' " Dr. Bibring is not alone in her observations. Both Jerome Kagan of the psychology department and Michael Walzer of the government department have observed the same change in their students, the men of the last two years seeming weary and rather passive over "success," and the women newly involved in "ego gratification" and a hard-driving interest in their work.

But the genuine integration of women into the society that is Harvard must turn ultimately on the erosion of a centuries-long way of thinking about women and their place, and men and their rights. What meaning and effect, then, can the appointment of Matina Horner have with regard to these issues? Let those around her speak.

Bruce Chalmers, Master of Winthrop House: "I think Dr. Horner has less administrative responsibilities (read 'powers' if you wish) than Mrs. Bunting did. But this may be good. She will have access to President Bok and to the councils of power because she *is* president of Radcliffe and not just another dean, and thus she will have more influence."

Carol Kay, graduate student in English: "Horner can't do much politically. It's clear from the statements she's made already. She's constrained to be Harvard-politic. She's not for equal admissions. Well, how else are we going to break out of the circle? But it's all to the good that a feminist has been chosen. Someone whose work has been in women's studies and who understands."

Dennis Krebs, professor of psychology: "Bertrand Russell said power is the ability to move people. Well, there's the kind of power, here at Harvard, to hire and fire and to make decisions no one can overturn. That's political power. I don't think Matina has that power. On the other hand, there is the ability to move people through the force and influence of your personality, the persuasiveness of your ideas, your capacity to accumulate emotional and intellectual credits. This, I think, may well be Matina's power here. She was hired, I think, because she is full of feminine charm, nonthreatening, easy to take. But I don't think they know what they've gotten. I think she may surprise them with the strength and stubbornness that is hers, with her very genuine commitment to her ideas, with her ability to get what she wants."

Susan Cary Block, tutor in residence at Currier House: "Mrs. Bunting was a visionary. She was brought in to shape Radcliffe and she did. She pushed for this merger because she knew that it was full citizenship or nothing. Those who now hold on to the idea of the separateness of Radcliffe are romanticizing the past. Mrs. Bunting knew that even without equal admissions, once the women were admitted to Harvard there would be no going back, because Harvard protects its own. Three-quarters of the faculty and administration here look upon women as intruding on their lives. They would just love it if Radcliffe would disappear tomorrow, and the whole question of women's rights. Mind you, they don't object to the women being admitted so much as they object to being forced to deal with the question of their rights, and not be able to let them slip through, like moles in the dark or something.

"Horner is no visionary. But she symbolizes the issues."

(1973)

Toward a Definition of the Female Sensibility

IT IS USELESS TO GO TO THE GREAT MEN WRITERS for help, however much one may go to them for pleasure. Lamb, Browne, Thackeray, Newman, Sterne, Dickens . . . never helped a woman yet, though she may have learnt a few tricks of them and adapted them to her use. The weight, the pace, the stride of a man's mind are too unlike her own for her to lift anything substantial from him successfully. The ape is too distant to be sedulous. Perhaps the first thing she would find, setting pen to paper, was that there was no common sentence ready for her use. All the great novelists like Thackeray and Dickens and Balzac have written a natural prose, swift but not slovenly, expressive but not precious, taking their own tint without ceasing to be common property. They have based it on the sentence that was current at the time. (That sentence) is a man's sentence. . . . It was a sentence that was unsuited for a woman's use. Charlotte Brontë, with all her splendid gift for prose, stumbled and fell with that clumsy weapon in her hands. George Eliot committed atrocities with it that beggar description. Jane Austen looked at it and laughed at it and devised a perfectly natural, shapely sentence proper for her own use and never departed from it. Thus, with less genius for writing than Charlotte Brontë, she got infinitely more said.

—Virginia Woolf

Not so very many years ago educated and talented women were pleased to be told they wrote or thought like men, and often—

in mixed company—they argued hotly that there was no such thing as a "female" mind or a "female" sensibility: there were only writers or nonwriters, thinkers or nonthinkers. Today, there are, I believe, few women who would be pleased to be told they write like men, and there is much thoughtful discussion on the question of the "female sensibility." What is it? *Where* is it? Does it, in fact, exist? What—if it exists—are its components? How does it operate? A tide of novels, poems, and plays written by women about women is sweeping over us. Many of us examine these books with a mixture of excitement and criticism born out of restless, only half-formed perceptions that not so long ago would have been rejected out of hand but today are the basis for a kind of thought and a kind of insight that seems to be in the very air we breathe. For these works, and our approach to them, are in many ways a parallel to the growth of the women's movement in the past few years and they, like the movement, embody complex questions that, so far from being answered, are still being formed.

Another, more interesting parallel lies in another notion: there is, in a certain sense, a metaphorical shape to the growth of the women's movement that the novels and plays, both in their choice of subject matter and in the range of their accomplishments, reflect. For, if the movement represents anything larger than itself—and indeed it does—then it is the slow, difficult journey out of close-minded defensiveness into the open contemplation of change and experience: out of the fear that surrounds received ideas into the courage that accompanies primary insight. The cultural-political movement that is feminism today is symbolic of the renewing human effort to recover original life in the course of redressing political grievances: to dig out from beneath the stultifying layers of accumulated institutional response the human capacity for self-experience. The marvel of literature is that not only is it a detailed record of the progress of the effort, but it is *in its very self* a metaphor for the digging-out process. Virginia Woolf's recital of the difficulties of Charlotte Brontë and George Eliot in relation to "a man's sentence" is an accurate parallel to the difficulties of contemporary women writers trying in their work to come to their own experience—

even as all women, everywhere, struggle to come to their own experience.

The subjection of women, in my view, lies most deeply in the ingrained conviction—shared by both men and women—that for women marriage is the pivotal experience. It is this conviction, primarily, that reduces and ultimately destroys in women that flow of psychic energy that is fed in men from birth by the anxious knowledge given them that one is alone in this world; that one is never taken care of; that life is a naked battle between fear and desire, and that fear is kept in abeyance only through the recurrent surge of desire; that desire is whetted only if it is reinforced by the capacity to experience oneself; that the capacity to experience oneself is everything. The woman who knows *deeply* that she will marry and be "taken care of"—that this is the central event of her life—is in some vital sense being removed from the battlefield. She hands over her experiencing self to her husband: it becomes a surplus weapon for him in his own struggle. She stands aside and looks on. She grows drowsy and inert. She loses the sharp edge of desire. She cannot remember—can no longer *feel*—the shape of the action. She gains the philosophical distance. She becomes terrified of the battle and frozen into her fears. She loses her nerve and along with her nerve loses forever the point of it all: to experience oneself.

It is the re-creation in women of the experiencing self that is the business of contemporary feminism: the absence of that self is the slave that must be squeezed out drop by drop. Vast internal changes must occur in women in which old responses, old habits, old emotional convictions are examined under a new light: the light of consciousness. A new kind of journey into the interior must be taken, one in which the terms of internal conflict are redefined. It is a journey of unimaginable pain and loneliness, this journey, a battle all the way, one in which the same inch of emotional ground must be fought for over and over again, alone and without allies, the only soldier in the army, the struggling self. But on the other side lies freedom: self-possession.

In this sense feminism is akin to the process of psychoanalysis and to the process of artistic creation, both of which are also concerned with the re-creation of the self, and the promise of emancipation that re-creation brings with it. The artist creates out of the materials of his own life. He digs down into himself and dredges up, from the very bottom if he's any good, the elements of his own experience. These he holds up to a new light. Suddenly, he "sees" old experience as he has not seen it before. He rearranges what he sees: gives it new shape, new composition, and thus new content. It is this new content that is his art: experience transformed. In the act of recreating himself the artist is creating. Very nearly, his art is the *process* of re-creating. For it is not the moment of inspiration but rather the long, painstaking days and months and years it takes to write a book or finish a painting or compose a piece of music—the sheer *working* at it, the innumerable transformations that can take place only through the proper passage of time—that clarify the vision and bring internal coherence.

Thus it is with psychoanalysis. It is not the sudden insight or the moment of catharsis or the identification of trauma that is the analysis. Rather, it is the slow process of remembering, of recovering original experience, of holding it up repeatedly to the light of self-consciousness, that allows for the undoing of an old self and the creating of a new self. It is the process *itself*—the damnably hard work of living with an idea long enough so that it gradually becomes the basis for a new existence even as the old one is disappearing—that is actually the analysis.

Art and psychoanalysis are both reflections of the natural process of human growth: the adult body rises from the childish form, the mature mind flows directly out of the early personality. All is of a piece, all clearly related, logically concluded. The conscious relatedness of one's entire existence is what produces the integrated self; the recognition that what one is now one has always been—to hold live in one's hand the sense of what one has always been—is to have oneself. For the integrated human being there is no past: there is only the continual transformation of original experience.

Culturally speaking, women have a past, and the femaleness

of their experience lies buried in that past. To achieve wholeness they must become artists and analysands: they must break through to the center of their experience, and hold that experience up to the light of consciousness if their lives are to be transformed. They must struggle to "see" more clearly, to remember more accurately, to describe more fully who and what they have always been. . . . If only one could describe fully what one is! Then one would be free.

Our culture is a collective record of that hunger to "describe fully" in the hope that consciousness will end spiritual bondage. We write, we paint, we compose to express as wholly as we can who we are: what our own personal lives have been. In the course of so doing we transcend ourselves, and the record of our lives becomes a record of our common life. What we discover in the struggle to understand our own particular selves is what it is to be human. The very elements of our own identities become a metaphor for the condition of human life. It is an interlocking process out of which we create cultural civilizations by confessing who we are, and in turn being told who we are. . . . Inevitably, there comes a time when civilization must be told anew who we are.

For centuries the cultural record of our experience has been a record of male experience. It is the male sensibility that has apprehended and described our life. It is the maleness of experience that has been a metaphor for human existence. Literature, particularly, has been a vast reservoir in which has been cupped to overflowing the detailed description of human hungers and human fears as men have experienced them. The central image of a young man from the provinces going out into the world on a symbolic journey of self-discovery is the dominating image of our literature and it is, of necessity, a male image. In the twentieth century the nature of the journey has altered; the symbols have been reformed, the trip is now clearly an interior one rather than a deceptively physical one. No matter. It is still a journey that is characterized by a thrusting, piercing, aggressing motion: one in which man is pressing continually toward the center of his life, attempting to wrestle God, the elements, and his own demons to the ground as he goes. Naked, sweating, lost, terrified, he nevertheless pushes forward: defiance is the compelling force.

Now clearly this search, this voyage, this compulsive motion through a universe of darkness and pain, is one which speaks to the deepest impulses of all human beings. Thus, whether we are men or women, we recognize ourselves and make identification to one degree or another with what we find in the literature of our culture. Nevertheless, no woman could ever have written nine-tenths of the books that compose the body of our literature. What it took to write those books is a certain kind of arrogant self-confidence that has been utterly foreign to woman's life. This self-confidence reduces in men the universal human fear common to all human beings, and increases in them the arrogance necessary to aggress upon life. It shapes and controls fear in a very particular way, pushing it back, creating a space filled with light and air around the human spirit in which the illusion of omnipotence is permitted growth. It is a quality developed only by occupying a miniature universe in which one experiences oneself as a superior being. To a very large degree the superiority that men experience comes directly out of their relations to women. As Virginia Woolf remarked so dryly and so succinctly:

Women have served all these centuries as looking-glasses possessing the magic and delicious power of reflecting the figure of man at twice its natural size. Without that power probably the earth would still be swamp and jungle. . . . [For how else] is he to go on giving judgments, civilizing natives, making laws, writing books, dressing up, and speechifying at banquets, unless he can see himself at breakfast and dinner at least twice the size he really is?

The irony, then, is that the maleness of experience which has indeed contributed so very much to the growth of human consciousness is dependent for its very life on the spiritual purgatory of women.

What, then, is the *femaleness* of experience? Where are the compositional elements of a female sensibility to be found? Under what conditions does that experience and that sensibility become a metaphor for human existence, thereby adding, as the maleness of experience has added, to the small sum of human self-awareness? These are questions we are only just beginning to ask, ideas we are only barely beginning to articulate.

It is my belief that the growth of a genuine female sensibility, like the growth of a genuinely experiencing woman, is a generational task and will be a long time in the making. Rarely in the work now being written by women does one feel the presence of writers genuinely penetrating their own experience, risking emotional humiliation and the facing down of secret fears, unbearable wisdoms. Rarely is femaleness actually at the center of the universe, and what it is to be a woman used effectively to reflect life metaphorically. What is more common is the painful sight of writers still in the fearful grip of female anger and female defensiveness: even as Charlotte Brontë and George Eliot perhaps were.

There are works, however, it seems to me, in which one feels the heroic effort stirring: works in which the writer gropes magnificently for "her" sentence. One of the finest of these—chronologically not a contemporary—is Kate Chopin's *The Awakening*, published in 1899, and only recently "rediscovered." The story of this extraordinary novel is, briefly, as follows: Edna Pontellier, a twenty-eight-year-old American married to a Creole businessman and the mother of two children, is spending the summer at Grand Isle, an island off the coast of New Orleans where wealthy Creole families of the 1890s vacation. Between Edna and her husband—the rich, kindly, authoritarian Leonce—there exists an enormous gulf of spiritual and emotional sympathy of which he seems entirely unaware, and which she herself observes as though from across a great distance. But, then again, her entire life is observed as though at a great distance: blurred and without the sharpness of reality. Her marriage, her children, her memories of her family in Kentucky, her early fantasies— all have the quality of dream and accident: nothing moves, nothing speaks, nothing makes deep sense. There is, at the center of Edna's being, an awful stillness: a *female* stillness that is seen as a kind of swollen reflection of the emotional inertness of Anglo-American middle-class life.

In this, her twenty-eighth year, Edna is roused from her interior silence. A friendship that has formed with young Robert Lebrun, the son of the family running the hotel at which the Pontelliers are staying, flames into open sensuality. Her desire for Robert—which remains unacknowledged and unconsummated—mingles brilliantly with the sensuality of all about her that for the first time in her life penetrates: her skin, her flesh, her thought. She feels sun, wind, and sea as never before; always afraid of the water, she now learns to swim and experiences the sea in an act of narcotic daring; lying at midnight in a hammock she defies her husband's order that she come at once into the house, and realizes that for nearly the first time she is acting consciously, not automatically; from out of nowhere she finds herself saying to one of the Grand Isle wives, "I would give up the unessential; I would give my money, I would give my life for my children; but I wouldn't give myself. I can't make it more clear; it's only something which I am beginning to understand."

Abruptly, Robert Lebrun leaves for Mexico. The summer ends and the Pontelliers return to New Orleans. But Edna is a changed woman: bit by bit, the "awakening" she has undergone begins to dominate her life. She stops receiving guests, she ignores the house, forgets the children, spends hours painting, reading, thinking, walking, no longer hears her husband's voice. She is mesmerized by the growing discovery within herself of a separate, conscious spirit now making demands on her. When her husband goes off to New York on business, she moves out of his house and rents a tiny one of her own. Desire becomes an instrument of self-awareness: she responds to the advances of Arobin, a local Don Juan. Her hungers, now articulated, grow with inordinate speed. They become powerful, complex, demanding: and yet oddly sorrowful, tinged with a sense of foreboding. Robert Lebrun returns, and she forces a declaration of love out into the open between them. Lebrun, who is agonized by his desire for her, is nevertheless frightened by the extraordinary quality of Edna's new independence. He does not understand what she means when she tells him that now she belongs neither to her husband nor to him, but only to herself. As they are about to consummate their love, Edna is called away to attend the lying-in of a friend. When she returns to the house, Robert is gone. "Goodbye," he has scrawled on a scrap of paper. "Goodbye—because I love you." She sits up all night, thinking. In the morning she takes the ferry to Grand Isle. She takes off all her clothes on the beach where only last summer she first came to life. She stands for a moment naked in the wind and sun—and then she walks into the ocean.

It is only in the very last paragraphs of the book that the force of Kate Chopin's sensibility reveals itself. As Edna walks across the beach toward the ocean, which she now associates with freedom and self-discovery, she recalls her thoughts of the previous night:

She had said over and over to herself: "Today it is Arobin; tomorrow it will be someone else." . . . Despondency had come upon her there in the wakeful night, and had never lifted. There was no one thing in the world that she desired. There was no human being whom she wanted near her except Robert; and she even realized that the day would come when he, too, and the thought of him would melt out of her existence, leaving her alone. The children appeared before her like antagonists who had overcome her, who had overpowered and sought to drag her into the soul's slavery for the rest of her days. But she knew a way to elude them.

What Edna has seen in the night is the elusiveness of life, the power and insatiability of spiritual hunger, the meanness and smallness that is our socialized lives. She has looked into the future with a calm now drained of all conflict, and she has seen the men replacing one another, and the hunger of consciousness driving her on. For these men—Arobin and Robert—have helped arouse in her a wildness of longing that far surpasses them, a longing they can never satisfy, that nothing and no one can ever actually satisfy: for no ordinary human and no civilized circumstance is equal to the demands of that hunger once it is unleashed in a person of spiritual dimension. Edna has put her mouth to the primitive sense of spirit-freedom and spirit-fulfillment that haunts the human soul, and now that she has tasted of that exotic food, life without it would indeed be unendurable, a slavery of the soul. On the other hand, she cannot go back, cannot pretend to the old ignorant life; she has lost forever all hope of peace.

The swift visionary quality of Edna's insight—the sheer explosiveness of it—is directly proportionate to all the years of suppressed consciousness that have gone before it. If she had been a man, pursuing life at a normal rate of developing consciousness, Edna undoubtedly would have arrived at the age of sixty in possession of the same human despair: "For *this?* Is *this* what it was all for?" But as she was a woman—steeped in silence and unconsciousness nearly all her short life—the insight, when it came, came with pressure-cooker force: suicidal force. This perception is the power that irradiates *The Awakening.* This is experience transformed. This is femaleness used as a metaphor for life. This is the female sensibility in its most fully realized state.

In our time we have the novels of Paula Fox and the plays of Myrna Lamb as fine examples of the femaleness of life operating to illuminate human experience. Paula Fox creates out of Sophie in *Desperate Characters* and Annie in *The Western Coast* two protagonists whose significance lies in the womanness of their beings. Indeed, womanness is the compelling element in both novels. To deal with only one: *Desperate Characters* is a story of contemporary disintegration: a tale of human life sacrificed to the brutal disintegration of the city even as the souls of a man and a woman trapped in the equally brutal disintegration of an empty marriage are also being sacrificed. Jake and Sophie, a pair of well-to-do New Yorkers, live in comfort in a fine house in Brooklyn. Once an actively liberal lawyer, Jake is now financially settled and spiritually confused. Meaning has slowly ebbed from his work as well as from his marriage. Between him and Sophie there exists an uneasy truce. Their life together is marked by emotional silence, the death of passion, mutual suspicion. Inertia propels them forward. The city pushes in on them. Bit by bit, incident by incident, one feels Jake and Sophie surrounded by the filth, the menace, the hideous fear of civilization breaking down that is the dailiness of New York. Dread overtakes their lives: the city threatens and isolates them at every turn.

Seeking release, they drive out to their house in the country—
only to find the place horribly vandalized. In an anguish of helplessness Jake takes Sophie against her will. There is no escape
for these two: neither without or within. For, clearly, the paranoia
justifiably induced by the city is more than halfway met by the
emotional desolation of their interior lives. A tension is created
on which is balanced the two forms of deterioration. It is this
tension that makes Jake and Sophie desperate characters.

What is most remarkable in *Desperate Characters* is the way in
which the femaleness of Sophie's intelligence is made to operate.
It is, essentially, Sophie's story that is being told: it is through
her eyes, her thought, her experience that we see everything.
Sophie is the ultimate woman: she sees all, understands all, records all, and does nothing. Her intelligence is trapped, inert,
nonoperative. She observes with the dignified paralysis of a cate-
goric spectator. The choices of her life have rendered her incapable of action; she can only be acted upon. She experiences her
life as though at the center of a void with the antennae of her
observations surfacing only for a quick look around. Every now
and then, desire struggles toward motion, but soon enough it
dies down, overcome by the vast disconnectedness of her being.
Life is a series of single shots for Sophie; the camera of her
soul can register only the separate image.

The sense we have in contemporary life of being trapped in
our cities, trapped in our technology, trapped in emotional
death, unable to make the separate parts of ourselves cohere
becomes very powerful when seen against the trapped inertness
of Sophie's intelligence. For what Sophie communicates is a
sense of inescapable destiny: the natural fulfillment of the abdicating self that is femaleness incarnate. And what Paula Fox
communicates is that the femaleness is the best possible repre-
sentation of the spiritual abdication that is modern life.

The plays of Myrna Lamb come directly out of the American
feminist consciousness. Written in a stripped, metaphorical, sur-
real language, the plays, properly speaking, have a single subject:
the corrosive antagonism at the heart of all sexual relations between men and women. Lamb's plays—nearly all of which have
been produced in New York—appear in a collection called *The*

Mod Donna and Scyklon Z. The best of these are *But What Have You Done for Me Lately?* and *The Mod Donna.* The first—a remarkable piece of agitprop theater—is about a man who awakens to find himself in a silent, empty space. Something is wrong, terribly wrong; he can't quite tell what. A woman enters, dressed in doctor's white. She speaks, he speaks. Slowly, the man makes an incredible discovery: he has been impregnated. The woman is in a position to grant him an abortion. The man pleads desperately with her to do so. The woman becomes his interrogator. The empty space becomes a laboratory-courtroom. What follows is trial and indictment. (The effect of the reversed positions is extraordinary, similar to that of a white man turning black or a psychiatrist being confined in a mental hospital. He says, "I don't believe it. I can't believe this nightmare." She says, "Well, that is how many people feel upon learning these things." He says, "Do you know that I want to kill you? That is all I feel. The desire to kill you." She says, "A common reaction. The impregnated often feel the desire to visit violence upon the impregnator.") Gradually, it is revealed that the woman and the man were youthful lovers, that he impregnated and abandoned her, that he went on to become an important public figure (who is actively opposed to legal abortion), that she nearly died in childbirth, never let another man touch her again, and has clawed her way up, bitter and traumatized, to this moment. The speeches she delivers glitter with hatred and survival. The speeches he delivers cringe with fear and the consequence of emotional ignorance. The entire play is a spectacular exercise in the art of sexual vengeance, comparable to Duerrenmatt's *The Visit.*

The Mod Donna circles closer, approaching the genuine target of Lamb's central insight: the obsession with sexual desirability that characterizes women's lives—its meaning and its consequence. Two couples—Donna and Charlie, Jeff and Chris—play a weird game of sexual musical chairs. Chris, driven by dissatisfaction with her waning desirability, makes Jeff take Donna into their marriage. Donna, driven equally by the dissatisfaction of her "unused" desirability, consents to join the *ménage à trois.* The three live together, Donna and Jeff sleeping together, Chris watching and commenting. Donna's husband, Charlie, who works for Jeff and is humiliated by him, hates, loves, and is bewildered by Donna. He waits for her to come back, not knowing what else to do. Ultimately, Chris and Jeff betray Donna, going off to Europe by themselves, leaving her pregnant with the baby the "three" of them have begotten. In a final paroxysm of rage, jealousy, and frustration, Donna provokes Charlie into murdering her. The entire action of the play is a result of the maneuverings of the two women. As their speeches mount from self-deception to irony to rage, the obsessive psychic question that holds each of them in bondage—*Mirror, mirror, on the wall, who is the fairest of them all?*—stands surrounded by a fury of self-hatred: a fury that this, after all, only *this*, should be the question of her life, and thus the source of her inescapable destiny; for the questions one asks determine the destiny one receives. Each, then, moving with mad logic in an indisputably mad set of circumstances, thinks to cheat destiny at its own game, imagining that sexual manipulation will end sexual definition. The transparently murderous irony is, of course, the point of the play.

Myrna Lamb's work is, in three important respects, comparable to the work of Norman Mailer, and the comparison is here worth making. First of all, the power of her work—as with Mailer's—resides in neither her characterizations nor her dramatic plots, but rather in the force of her language. It is there, in the language, that the sensibility exists. It is there, in the shape and rhythm of the words and the sentences, that the story is being told. As the work moves closer to the bone, the language dives deeper and deeper, mounts higher and higher. We are caught in its anguish, impelled by its insistence, instructed finally by its pitch. What is actually happening to the characters is revealed to us by what is happening to the language.

Second, Lamb's language—again, as with Mailer—has a runaway quality to it: she does not always have her hands on the controls. Sometimes the language soars, sometimes it bucks and swerves, sometimes it sinks like a stone. But whatever it's doing—whether it's hitting the target or ricocheting off the walls—Lamb, like Mailer, is right in there with it, lurching, lunging, flying along, writer and language tied together, chasing down experience, bulling somehow toward the secret center of things.

Third, it is this compulsion to chase down experience, to penetrate the center, that powers the work of both writers. Mailer is driven by his vision of things. Not only must he be true to what he sees, but he must keep going until what he sees is *true*. He is thus forced to take emotional risks, to act with an emotional boldness that, win or lose, is exultant in its honesty. At her best, Lamb exhibits this same capacity for emotional risk taking, this same need to press forward until naked sight brings us to the only honesty possible.

The importance, of course, of thus comparing Norman Mailer and Myrna Lamb lies in the fact that Mailer's vision is entirely a product of the male sensibility, as is Lamb's of the female sensibility. What he digs and digs for, forever trying to root out, is the maleness of things. In the course of so doing he transforms his maleness, and it becomes an imaginative re-creation of the life we are living. Myrna Lamb, in reaching for her femaleness, is involved in the selfsame act of re-creation. What she is doing is precisely what Virginia Woolf said would have to be done if ever a first step was to be taken toward a generation of great women writers.

The novels of Joan Didion, Anne Roiphe, Lois Gould, and the Englishwoman Margaret Drabble seem to me works very much in the grip of the awful power of lingering defensiveness and conflict too dreadful to bear.

The most celebrated of these writers is Joan Didion, and the book that made her nationally famous is *Play It as It Lays*. Didion's great talent lies in her ability to evoke the stunning abstractness of southern California "dying in the golden light." Her images of people alone on freeways, beside mansion pools, in supermarkets at three in the morning, at despairing beach parties, on blistering streets with curlers in their hair and wedgies on their feet, are remarkable and compelling. And indeed, much of this sense of things pervades *Play It as It Lays*. The scene is moviepeople Los Angeles; the character is Maria Wyeth: model, actress, semi-estranged wife of a movie director, mother of a retarded child; the atmosphere is California drift. Maria drifts through the days of her life awash in a sea of empty friendships and corrupted emotions. Sex, drugs, abortion, and death roll themselves up on her tide, and then roll themselves back. Frightened of everything under the L.A. sun, suffering nameless dread and severe withdrawal, she feels safe only when she is driving the freeways. Nothing connects, nothing holds. People, scenes, events present themselves, one by one, before the camera's eye of Maria's attention; the camera strains to focus; misses; next, please. Disconnected is not the word for Maria. Chloroformed is more like it. People in the book keep asking Maria what she is thinking. "Nothing," she says. The people respond variously with cynicism, anger, awe. They think she's holding out on them. The reader, of course, knows better. The reader knows Maria speaks the truth, for that is what the book is all about: nothing, nothing, nothing. Maria knows what nobody else knows: that it is all nothing; that we go on "playing it" exactly as though we did not know it is all nothing.

The vision of nothingness haunts this century, and it is not uncommon that that vision finds expression through the portrayal of a woman breaking down in the face of the void. Nearly always, the breakdown is one of silence and withdrawal accompanied by irrational behavior that is never illuminated, never explained. Inevitably, this silence is imagined as having at its source some spiritual mystery, a deeper power, a secret heart of knowledge. Very quickly we are in the presence of a primitive myth: the belief in the magical properties of "strange" (that is, unreal) beings such as madmen, saints, idiots—and women. The important thing about this myth is that it is created and used almost solely by men in the ascendancy who are very far from mad and very far from silent. Knowing less than nothing about the silence or madness of women, they have used this conceit as a foil for their own often grandiose notions of existential angst, and its usage has degenerated into hack formulas for those who have a vested interest in the most cliché ideas of grief and madness in the modern world.

In our own time, the absolutely best place to find a superabundance of these significantly crazy ladies is in the movies, and in no movies more so than those of Michelangelo Antonioni. Put them all together and Antonioni's movies spell Monica Vitti: eyes rolling in her head, hand stuffed wildly in her mouth, mute as the tomb, tearing blindly at her Givenchy dress while any number of men implore, "What's *wrong?* Just tell me what's *wrong!*"—and the existential *meaning of it all* suffocates the moviegoers in their seats.

Maria Wyeth could have been written by Antonioni for Monica Vitti, so much a creation of that same usurped vision of contemporary torment does she seem to be. Which is not to say that thousands of women are not actually living out Maria's life; it is only to say that neither Maria Wyeth nor Monica Vitti tells me what it is like to be inside their heads. Coming from these two it's only hearsay. I am unable, through Maria and Monica, to hear these women speaking in their own voices or to feel them moving at the center of their own experience. What I hear and feel are the sounds and movements of puppets whose strings are manipulated by the fantasies of men.

I could not escape the sensation, as I read *Play It as It Lays,* that Maria's language was not her own: that her telescoped responses and significant silences had been placed in her mouth and behind her eyes by a generation of literary references created by an experience that was not the primary experience of the author. Thus, the story of Maria's life fails to become a convincing portrait of emotional removal; on the contrary, the story *itself* becomes an act of emotional removal. One feels onself in the presence of a writer who believed it good to be told she wrote like a man, and has—with the tools of talent and intelligence—knocked that belief into place: a shield between herself and her work.

Lois Gould's novels, which have been described as "bitchy," "tough," "honest," are an interesting variant product of the same kind of dishonesty that plagues *Play It as It Lays:* the dishonesty of defensiveness. Gould's novels do not actually tell stories; they fuse in my mind into one long monologue being spoken by an upper-middle-class New York Jewish woman who "knows the name of everything" and has a justifiable grudge against everyone. This poor little rich girl has met with coldness and malice everywhere, and has survived only through the use of irony. Her voice is brittle, hard-edged, vulnerable, and mean-spirited. She indulges in a stream of confessional detail about her (mainly sexual) life which is meant to be brutally honest. Very quickly, however, one perceives that the honesty is only a fashionable honesty: one whose limits have been set well in advance, and will in fact expose neither protagonist nor author to any unexpected emotions or insights. The honesty is a ploy: the more she reveals the more she conceals. Behind the toughness is a swamp of self-pity, an overpowering conviction of worthlessness. The writer-heroine is sealed defensively inside the toughness—and she'll be damned if we get in there, inside *that* fortress. From this kind of writing we can learn nothing: nothing about ourselves, or the world around us, or what it means to pass through life as a woman.

And then there is Anne Roiphe's *Up the Sandbox.* Written with grace and intelligence, this book has been hailed as a work that comes to realistic grips with the emotional-social bind of women's lives. It is nothing of the sort. What it is, though, is an important instance of the overwhelming *fear* with which a writer who also happens to be a woman begins to even sniff out the meaning of her own experience. The facing down of that fear is the point at which the female sensibility begins to grow, the point at which one *begins* to "come to grips" with one's subject. *Up the Sandbox* is a work in which fear is capitulated to rather than faced down; the lack of courage is fatal; it results in a dishonest book.

The story, very briefly, is as follows: Margaret is an intelligent, educated young mother and wife. Her husband is a graduate student at Columbia. They live a shabby-genteel life on New York's Upper West Side, waiting for the husband to finish his studies so life can improve. The husband, of course, is not really—certainly not solely—waiting. He is doing: it is his doing that delcares a period of suspension for both of them. But Margaret: she is *waiting.* She spends her days shopping, cleaning, taking her child to the park. She tries to convince herself that the raising of this child is the equivalent of her husband's work; that it is, in fact, life itself; that, therefore, the sensation of waiting for her life to begin is an illusion. But it doesn't work: the energy inside her remains muffled, trapped, alive, and insistent. This imprisoned energy is the subject of the book, and it is what

Anne Roiphe does with it that turns *Up the Sandbox* into a *Ladies'
Home Journal* story. Instead of gathering force and bursting
through to what*ever* is on the other side, the energy of her protagonist leaks out in safe little puddles, its pressure defused in a
series of park-bench fantasies. The fantasy life, to be sure, is
rich, funny, clever; but in the end cowardly and self-defeating,
shabby in its emotional use of self-deception. The chapter head-
ings clearly indicate whether this is a "fantasy" chapter or a
"real" chapter. The final chapter is headed "fantasy," and in
it Margaret discovers that she is pregnant again. In reality she
is, of course, pregnant. . . . The reader has been had. The book
stands revealed as one in which neither author nor protagonist
ever had any intention of moving into the eye of the conflict
that continues to hover like an anxious shadow at the side of
the head rather than directly face-front.

For a clearer view of the intelligent and talented avoidance
of conflict there is the work of Margaret Drabble, a remarkably
prolific Londoner whose novels are currently popular in this
country. Very well written and generously sprinkled with insight,
these books nevertheless remain, ultimately, women's magazine
fiction. *The Garrick Year* and *The Millstone* are two examples of
what I mean. In the former, a young woman named Emma is
married to a young man named David. She is beautiful and genteel, he is Welsh and an actor. They both speak the bright,
hip, suspicious language of sophisticated Londoners, and have
in fact married each other in an effort to "chain themselves to
wildness"; in other words, to keep alive their capacity for honest
emotion. Inevitably, she has babies and their life revolves about
his career. The story centers on a year in the provinces during
which David flourishes on the stage and Emma declines in boredom, jealousy, and a growing fear about the peripheral quality
of her own life. In a wonderfully perceptive passage Emma
watches David on the stage and understands what acting means
to him.

As I watched him I saw at last why we were here . . . why he had
been willing to submit me to unlimited boredom. . . . In the last scene
of the play he had some lines that came closer to him than anything
I had ever heard him say on the stage before. . . . All he wanted from

life was to be able to express, like this, to a mass of quiet people, what he felt himself to be. It was not merely pleasure that he had there on the stage: it was a sense of clarity, a feeling of being, by words and situations not of his own making, defined and confined, so that his power and his energy could meet together in one great explanatory moment. It was not enough for David that I should try to understand him or that his friends and employers should understand him, for we subjected him by the pressure of our needs and opinions to amorphous confusion: what he wanted was nothing less than total public clarity.

What is developing, of course, is Emma's realization that she needs the same thing. What *happens,* of course, is that after a lot of funny, English-ironic tumbling about, Emma has an abortive affair with the director and David is caught in humiliated confusion on a pile of packing boxes with the company sexpot. The supporting players disappear, David and Emma fall into each other's arms, she realizes she can never escape her marriage, he offers her a new life: a trip to the East Indies where he will make a film. The last passage is full of wisdom about snakes in the Garden of Eden, but the story could easily have appeared in *McCall's.*

It is, however, in *The Millstone* that the emotional cowardice which is the key to all these novels is to be found. Rosamund, a rising young academic, lives alone in London. She hangs out with writers and actors and is considered a swinger. Each of her boyfriends thinks she's making it with someone else. What no one knows is that she is a virgin. Determined to rid herself of her archaic condition, she sleeps one night with a man she barely knows, and becomes pregnant. She decides to have the baby: alone, unaided, without the knowledge of the father. The novel is the story of Rosamund's pregnancy and the first traumatic year of her baby's life. The writing is perceptive, detailed, and indeed a universe forms around Rosamund's clarifying emotions. But what is at the heart of it all is that Rosamund wants this baby because she feels only the baby can love her uncritically and, therefore, only with the baby can she risk revealing her own hungry need.

The need to love, the fear of risking that need, the dominating power that fear has over us—this, ultimately, is the crucial and determining element in all our behavioral constructions. The need is primary, the fear is infantile, the dominion is the crippling yoke from beneath which we must struggle our entire lives. We struggle, not against the need but against the fear, by attempting to own ourselves, and to bring to our lovers not our fears but our fulfillment. What has ever marked "women's fiction" is capitulation to the fear rather than a noble depiction of the struggle to conquer the fear. What makes of Colette a great writer is the courage and density with which she describes the struggle. What makes of Didion, Roiphe, and Drabble lesser writers is the meekness with which they elevate necessity to a virtue.

Ultimately, our art is a reflection of the progress of our desires chained to our fears. The meaning of a social movement is that it rises directly out of a gut need to defeat the ascendancy of fear. That need becomes an idea which takes hold slowly, and slowly forces emotional—hence cultural and political—change. The novels I have been describing are, as yet, for the most part dominated by fear. As the balance shifts for women—whose struggle toward selfhood is beyond question the newest incarnation of the primitive terms of conflict that is the politicalness of life—as they move closer and closer toward their own experience, impelled now by need rather than dominated by anxiety, so will the female sensibility grow, and the novels that will then be written out of that developing sensibility will, at one and the same time, become a reflection of and a guide to the true politicalness of contemporary feminism: the recapture of the lost, experiencing self.

(May 1973)

The Conflict Between
Love and Work

*Perhaps the greatest problem which any historian has to tackle
is neither the cataclysm of revolution nor the decay of empire,
but the process by which ideas become social attitudes.*

—J. H. PLUMB
New York Times Book Review

An idea whose time has come arrives with explosive immediacy,
creating the illusion of instant birth. But, of course, behind such
an idea lies a process of maturing that has been taking place,
subterraneanly, over a very great period of time—one that spans
decades if not centuries. What is remarkable about this process
is that up until the very moment of birth the maturing takes
place individually, in a great many separate people. Then—seem-
ingly overnight—the isolated perception of separate persons has
become the focused understanding of a people; the idea is no
longer simply an idea but has become a shared imperative.

Contemporary feminism, which seemed to burst suddenly
upon America ten years ago, embodies just such a process, and
for those of us who are living intimately with that amazing transformation of idea into imperative, the tracing of the process is
a source of endless—if not obsessive—interest. We reread history now—our own, America's, the century's, *anybody's*—with
new eyes, searching out the tracings, stumbling repeatedly upon
abundant proofs of the emotional accumulations in the culture

128

that have brought us to this moment. We read the novels we grew up on as though for the first time, we sit up late watching the movies of our childhood, we turn again to familiar memoirs and biographies of distinguished men and women. Everywhere, we are amazed at the isolated feminism that lies buried in the framed history. In the novels we see a metaphoric use of the femaleness of experience embedded in the social and political metaphors used to illuminate the human condition; at the movies—those marvelously literate movies of the thirties and forties—we laugh and cry over the ripeness of feminist perception masquerading as popular humor; in the biographies and memoirs we see men and women of large talents and large concerns struggling—as though armed with a flashlight in a vast dark tunnel—to place their male-female difficulties in the context of a serious life. We are embarked on a great voyage of rediscovery, one in which old experience is being recharted and old worlds lighted up with new insight.

It was in this spirit of rediscovery that I recently reread *Dorothy and Red,* Vincent Sheean's decade-old memoir of the marriage of Dorothy Thompson and Sinclair Lewis. I remembered the book as an intimate chronicle of a famous marriage lived at the center of a vital time: America between the world wars. I remembered it also as a compelling portrait of two enormously intelligent, talented people in continual conflict with a fiction of love and marriage that the two of them together created out of whole cloth: the cloth being a mutual emotional need to *not* face the fact that they had never really loved each other and were hopelessly mismated.

When I picked the book up again, what I found this time around was the record of a life—Dorothy Thompson's—which, *as a whole,* deserved to take its place in the collective history of the slowly maturing feminist consciousness; a life that was at once consciously defined—that is, defined itself—by the essential misogyny of its environment, and yet unconsciously, beneath the deceptively smooth surface of fame and accomplishment, was continually groping its troubled way toward those feminist questions that, if they had only been properly framed, would have suddenly thrown the whole of a severe emotional confusion into relieving focus. But how could these questions, in 1935, have been properly framed?

Dorothy Thompson was one of a generation of accomplished women who made no common cause with the general condition of women. She thought of her life as a self-willed one and, if she thought about it at all, would have said of other women's lives: Anyone with talent, energy, and drive can do what I have done, what's all the fuss about? Yet, she had in fact internalized the traumatic conflict of a human being living—by the dictates of her culture—an "unnatural" existence, and throughout her adult life the question of being a woman as well as a working human being dogged and confused her. It was a conflict that erupted again and again in her, flaring up, dying down, moving always toward the edge of full awareness, then falling back again into the half-truths that comprised intelligent thought on The Woman Question in the 1930s.

Thompson was one of the strongest, most independent, and most ambitious of women, capable of reaching to the furthest limit of political thought in her time, but—like all but the rarest of free spirits—*only* to the limit of her time. Thus, she absorbed the most highly intelligent confusions about what it is to be a woman, suffered grievously over the role of love in a woman's life, and in general confused and denied her own powers. Yet, so great was her vitality, so enormous her will to life, that the deepest dictates of her nature struggled successfully with the emotional dictates of her culture. She could not help but *be.* And in the very act of being she unconsciously helped push social time forward. Her life is a classic case of that two-steps-forward-one-step-backward, lurching, cumulative movement toward the moment when an idea becomes an attitude.

Dorothy Thompson was born, the daughter of a Methodist parson, in 1894 in upstate New York. She received a spare, American Protestant upbringing, attended Syracuse University (then a Methodist institute in her father's "conference"), and emerged from childhood a scrub-cheeked, large-boned, naïvely self-confident American girl possessed of a brash intelligence and a formidable eagerness for the world. She became a journalist, rose quickly in her profession, and by the early 1920s was a foreign correspondent in Central Europe. One day, having tea at the Ritz in Budapest, she looked up to see standing in the doorway the handsomest man she had every laid eyes on. She fell instantly, irrevocably in love with him—and she married him. His name was Josef Bard; he was a mediocre Hungarian-Jewish journalist, magnetically attractive to women, a man of lazy lust, emotional decadence, and one-raised-eyebrow morals (all qualities Thompson later came to identify with Budapest itself).

To the twenty-seven-year-old Dorothy, Bard was a poet: a man of depth and worldliness, the quintessential European who set in motion in her very young American self yearnings and longings she could neither identify nor resist. Needless to say, the marriage was a disaster. Bard unnerved her, humiliated her, and turned her into an anti-Semite ("You are so treacherous . . . they say it is a Jewish characteristic"). Nevertheless, it was many years before Dorothy could free herself of him. The man *was* complicated, he did teach her a great deal about herself, and he did introduce her to the artistic, intellectual, and political circles of Eastern Europe that made her worldly and developed her extraordinary gifts both for intelligent political analysis and courageous self-inspection.

Dorothy Thompson met Sinclair Lewis on her thirty-third birthday in July of 1927 in Berlin. She was at this time the chief Berlin correspondent for the Curtis newspapers. Lewis was forty-two and the most famous American writer alive. Each was on the verge of divorce from their first marriages. They met at a press conference, and he instantly determined to have her. She was taken aback, flattered, and flustered, and of course ultimately worn down. Within a matter of weeks they were both "desperately in love."

They really were two famous, lonely, emotionally suffering people, each drawn to a fantasy of the other, each fixed by a terrible *longing* to love the other. Lewis was in fact a dedicated alcoholic, a morbidly insecure and unaware man whose bottled-up sexuality was the cause of more hatred, cruelty, and anguish between them than anything else. Dorothy was an aggressively straightforward woman, eager as a college girl to "understand" everything, dedicated to the wistful notion that proper analysis brought instant correction. They never understood each other, or what each other's lives were all about. Above all, they never faced squarely their irremediable division—that the language of his expressive inner life was profoundly literary while the language of hers was profoundly political. Driven as they both were by emotional need, they were incapable of seeing what was so abundantly there to be seen. Thus, they lied to themselves, and the more they lied to themselves the more determinedly they lied to each other. They were married in 1928, lived thirteen hellishly unhappy years together, and separated with their emotional dreams of life broken.

Although the ostensible object of *Dorothy and Red* is the marriage, the dominant figure of the book is unquestionably Dorothy Thompson herself. Through her diaries and letters we find ourselves in the presence of that alone which makes a book come to life: a live human being struggling to make sense of herself and what she is living through. In this particular case, the human being struggling is positively impaled on the cross of femaleness.

The single most important thing about Dorothy Thompson is that she lived her life as "the brilliant exception." This made her both privileged—and freakish. The journalists, politicians, and intellectuals with whom she shared her work, her thought, and her concerns were all men; other women in her circle were wives. Her opinions were sought and respected, her work published and paid attention to—and at the same time a diplomat in Berlin addressed foreign press conferences with the salutation: "Mr. President, gentlemen, and Dorothy." Then, the marriages she made were both those of a political woman to literary men: a classic reversal that brought both admiration and snickering. The diaries she kept are exactly like those of most men of distinction leading public lives: magnificent mixtures of political analysis, social observation, and emotional angst, all thrown together; (for example, three paragraphs on the European crisis of the moment, followed by two on how Lewis is torturing her, and then one about the historical meaning of elitism; or, conversely, three paragraphs on Lewis ending with "Hindenburg made a damnfool speech last night"). They are the kind of diaries then accepted as stimulating in a man, uncanny in a woman.

She was surrounded at all times by a world of the most ordinary, respectable misogyny, one in which her authenticity as a woman was always suspect. Her own biographer, Vincent Sheean, a friend of thirty years, makes abundantly clear that while he loved Dorothy dearly he never quite considered her a natural woman. Early in *Dorothy and Red* Sheean writes: "She was beautiful, intelligent, and highly (perhaps too highly) informed, with a confident manner that was becoming to her fresh and original personality, although in other women it might not have been so." And Sheean writes of her first husband: "It is noteworthy indeed that Josef, when he wishes to praise the distinctive qualities of his remarkable wife, speaks of her energy, ambition, will power, her 'will-to-life,' and other elements in a character which sound more masculine than feminine."

Thompson would have denied—with a good deal of bravado—that any part of this pervasive atmosphere mattered a damn to her. "Any fool knows that distinguished women are as rare as distinguished men and cannot be judged by ordinary standards," she writes, thus avoiding the fundamental issues her peculiar position raised. But her private thoughts reveal the anxiety these issues caused her. In her diary for 1927 she records a conversation with a German writer:

Charles Recht . . . told me I was a biological monstrosity, that no man would stick to me because I'd give them all an inferiority complex, and a lot of other very hard, nasty, and I think, unjustified things. After all, he doesn't know me at all. . . . Recht made me sick too with the statement that all men experienced physical revulsion after intercourse with women. Said it was biological law! . . . I *know* what he says isn't true! . . . The damned man got under my skin, though.

Thus, although she was in essence a political creature with an intense, lifelong interest in the nature of government and the inner workings of society, she was always prey to the accusation that her exuberant pursuit of these interests was proof of her "unnaturalness." (Imagine her male counterparts having any part of their energies drained by a similar preoccupation!)

Absurdly, concomitantly, perhaps in reaction to her accusers, she was endlessly involved in her mind with the business of love, and she was haunted by the conviction that what she needed above all else to make herself whole was a "creative marriage." This conviction was her emotional downfall; it gave her the illusion of being deeply in touch with herself when in fact it sabotaged any genuine route to her real self; the illusion was fed by the wisdom of her day and experienced by her as natural desire.

In 1926, Dorothy wrote to her first husband: "I have in me the capacity to be deeply faithful to one man whom I love and who loves me; what I want is to find that person and build a life with him which shall have breadth, depth, creative quality, dignity, beauty and inner loyalty. If I do not find him I shall go it alone." The point of this important last sentence is that she *didn't really believe it.* (And neither until very recently did anybody else: it is painful to consider that it is exactly the kind of letter, with the same discrepancy between apparent and actual meaning, that thousands of women of my generation could have written as recently as ten years ago.) Secretly, although all her life she was an unstoppable workhorse, Dorothy Thompson was never actually convinced that for a woman love was not more important than work, and that if push came to shove she could *not* go it alone. Secretly—although life repeatedly forced upon her evidence of her own strength—she yearned for the one, the only, the magical man who would make it all come together for her. This man in her imagination—the one who would give her the "creative marriage" she needed to make herself "whole"—she mythicized, and to him she gave tremendous powers over herself. When she met Lewis she was a goner.

On September 27, 1927, Dorothy and Lewis were due to attend a fancy dinner party in Berlin. Dorothy had gotten a new dress and silver shoes for the occasion. An hour before the party Lewis was dead drunk and the evening was clearly lost. She went to his hotel room to attempt to revive him. Hopeless. The entry in her diary for that night reads:

Dead to the world. I was beside myself. I washed his face but he only came to enough to smile at me with fishy, dead eyes. (Those wide aufgerissene Augen). I cried terribly. Something in me collapsed. . . . All the time I was sobbing, I saw how everything is going. . . . I saw that everything has been a dream . . . like the dream of a child who says "When I grow up . . ." I saw all this and thought, "I will get up and go. Somehow I will reconstruct my life. There is still work. . . ." And I knew that there was not even that. I saw that being a woman has got to me, at last, too. I saw that if Hal [Lewis] goes now, I am finished. I cannot live by myself, for myself. All my heart cried out: this is my man, the one man, and he has come too late! Nothing left for me but to become brittle or to rot. All the time Hal was making love to me. Feebly, but tenderly. I kissed his breast and he yearned toward me. . . .

In the deepest part of herself she believed Lewis to be more important than she was. She believed her gifts were inferior to his gifts. She believed he was, ultimately, the stronger of the two, although, patently, she was the stronger of the two. Shy mythicized him, she never mythicized herself. In March 1928, in Italy waiting for Lewis's divorce to come through, she wrote to him:

I see you with your torn open eyes, your face scarred as though with flames, your long-legged body leaning against the wind, the pain in you, the sweetness in you, the mad anger in you which constantly rises to defend you against becoming one of the settled and contented of the earth; the urge in you to pain, to castigation, because in you is the world, in you is your own civilization, which you will castigate until it is pure and worthy to be loved. . . . But I do not castigate you; salvation is by passion and by understanding. You, beloved, furnish the passion. . . . I shall try to understand.

Above all, she mythicized her need for him. In November of 1927, in Russia on the greatest assignment of her life (the tenth anniversary of the Russian Revolution), an American woman traveling with the journalists dies suddenly of a brain tumor and Thompson writes to Lewis in Berlin:

And now all of a sudden, she's dead, from an abscess on the brain, or something. And I've wanted all day to run home to you, because

it scared me, and I don't feel quite safe anywhere except with you,
darling, darling.

A dozen letters follow this one, all bleating about how she can't
go on without him, how she can't pay attention to what's happening in Moscow, she can't she can't, she needs him she needs
him. What is hilarious and exasperating and deeply significant
about all this is: She *didn't* run home to Lewis, she stayed and
did her work, and produced an important series of articles on
Russia; but the effect on her emotional understanding (that she
was in fact work-independent first and love-dependent second)
was *nil.* She never got the message. And because she never got
the message, she never properly respected her relation to work;
she believed through much of her life that she plunged into
work in order to save herself from the emotional turmoil that
loving Lewis had inflicted on her—not that she plunged into
work because the expressiveness in her, the exuberant life force
in her, was so pre-eminently that of a working, thinking being.

Thus, she was a woman of power and potency who ignored
the lessons of that power and rejected the goodness of that
potency. Yet, she did no more and no less than millions of others
alive at that moment. Her confusions were at one with the confusions of her time. In that same fatal November of 1927 she
wrote in her diary:

The reason why modern women are so unhappy and why they unconsciously hate men, is because they have gotten better and men have
gotten worse. They will not let men swallow them up, because the
swallowers aren't good enough. I will give my body, soul and spirit
to a man who can use it up to make a Damascene blade, but not to
someone who will hammer out of it a lead paperweight. Women *know*
that making money . . . isn't worth the expenditure of whatever flame
of life is in them. . . . Leora [in *Arrowsmith*], protesting against any
cheapening of Martin's passionate dream, was only refusing to reduce
the price on her own complete gift.

This is pure Laurentian half-truth. ("It's because the men
aren't men anymore that the women have got to be.") It is both
an indictment of Western civilization between the wars and a
damnable usage in that indictment of the oldest, most wrong-

headed notion in the world of what Woman is, what Man is, and what the proper, ideal relation between the two is. Dorothy would give her "body, soul and spirit to a man who can use it up to make a Damascene blade." There she is—the strongest woman of her moment, at the top of her world—longing for the restoration of an ideal world in which she could give herself to a man who would do great deeds: instead of glorying in the great deeds that she herself would do, *was* in fact doing.

At the same time (there is no end to this mess), she knew. And in the knowing suffered bitterly. On February 13, 1929, six months after her marriage to Lewis, the following entry occurs in her diary:

I told him I didn't want to go to Florida because of my lecture date on the 21st. He then got angry and sneered at me: "You with your important little lectures. You, with your brilliant people. . . . *You* want to talk about foreign politics which *I* am too ignorant to understand!" When he talks so my heart freezes up. And then, in a minute he is very sweet again. Oh, my God, I really don't know whether I love or hate him—but tonight I was *bored* with him.

I say to myself "You are totally unimportant & you are married to a man of genius—if you give up your life to making him happy it is worth it."

But it isn't! It isn't! I can really do nothing for him. He is like a vampire—he absorbs all my vitality, all my energy, all my beauty—I get incredibly dull. If ever I begin to talk well he interrupts the conversation. He is not above calling me down in front of people because the dinner is bad—he did so when I had been too ill to bother about ordering the dinner, talking to me in a tone I would not use to a servant.

It's either give up my work or give up Hal. My work! I can't live and work in a world where I cannot plan from one day to the next. Yet if I give up work he will throw it up to me someday. . . . Indeed, he has already done so. . . .

And my very mind degenerates. . . . I know so well what I want of life:

I want to understand all manner of things better. I know I have taste and a good head. My creative gifts are negligible. But I should like to contribute to a clearer and deeper understanding of the things I understand. My gifts are preeminently social.

What I need: more knowledge.

What I prize: human relationships, of all kinds, passionate, tender, intellectual understanding.

What I want: a home which will be a center of life & illumination for people who can really contribute to the development of the humanities.

My gifts: interpretive: power to draw out and record others.

My interests: all humanites; politics; literature insofar as it is not precious but deals with living ideas; economics; all the attributes of civilized living—cooking—house-furnishing—manners.

My passion: creative men.

And this leads me to this relationship where what I prize, what I want, what interests me—my gifts—all are stultified and rendered sterile.

It is a heartbreaking document, this diary entry; heartbreaking and deeply important. *"My passion:* creative men." In a single sentence she has entirely undercut the noble manifesto that precedes it, demonstrating superbly the power of blind emotion over penetrating intellect. She has thrown into relief the net of socially determined awareness in which are caught even the most psychologically astute minds, the most feeling intelligences, the most energetic of spirits. Thompson "understood" everything, but her emotional sense of herself as a woman had been molded by the thought of her time, and in the end that psychological factor dominated her and made her more closely resemble the spirited, "rebellious" heroines of nineteenth-century novels than the women who would come two generations after her.

On August 25, 1934, Dorothy Thompson was expelled from Nazi Germany by decree of the secret police. She was the first American correspondent to be expelled from a foreign country. Overnight, she became internationally famous. Within months she was one of the most influential political journalists in the world. Throughout the war years, she was consulted by presidents and prime ministers, read daily by millions, and known to every household in America. Sheean writes:

When all is said, it is through and in politics, both national and international, that Dorothy takes her place in the history of the time. . . . She had a sense of mission about the real and present danger (the rise of fascism), as she saw it, both to the U.S. and to the Western world. This was the passion of her work and gave it an incredible intensity at times, more like a crusader's call to arms than like anything normally known in journalism.

Her fame, when it came, was hateful to Lewis. It finished their marriage. Although she "knew" better, she could not bear to see the marriage actually going. The early 1940s—even while she is running about the world trying to help save Europe from fascism—are filled with anguished letters to Lewis; letters in which she tries to explain their love, to give it significance, to rescue their life through what was always of paramount importance to both of them: words. She could not let go; not then, not for years afterward.

The liberation of women is the longest, most complicated revolution on record. Thompson was, in every real respect, a soldier in the army of the revolution. While she could not see the shape of the war, she nevertheless participated in a number of its battles. Today, thousands of women who are neither as intellectually or emotionally developed as Dorothy Thompson know, with clarifying power, about their lives that which she with all her sumptuous gifts could not know about her life. But if she had not lived her life—exactly as she lived it—we would not today know what we do.

(May 1975)

Outsidedness Personified

Many people are natural outsiders. There is the artist, whose outsidedness turns on temperament and unshared vision. There is the Jew, whose outsidedness turns on the political and social viciousness of national insecurities. And there is the woman, whose outsidedness turns on a birth defect: having been born into the wrong sex. Now, to be a Jew and a woman and to have the temperament of an artist: *there* is a combination of outsidedness worth examining.

Rahel Levin Varnhagen was born in Berlin in 1771. She was the offspring of a Jewish merchant who left all his money to his sons and none to his neurotic, hungering, unbeautiful, extraordinarily intelligent daughter. Thus, Rahel—endowed with neither looks, money, family, nor education—grew up equipped only with wit, appetite, intelligence, and a terrible desire for the world. As her biographer writes of her:

Excluded from society, deprived of any normal social intercourse, she had a tremendous hunger for people, was greedy for every smallest event, tensely awaited every utterance. The world was unknown and hostile to her; she had no education, tradition, or convention with which to make order out of it; and hence orientation was impossible for her. . . . No aristocratic elegance, no exclusiveness, no innate taste restrained her craving for the new and unknown; no knowledge of people, no social instinct, and no tact limited or prescribed for her any particular proper conduct toward acquaintances. . . . Rahel talked with everybody about everything.

The world that Rahel Levin was excluded from and spent her entire life attempting to penetrate was the world of Berlin society during the last quarter of the eighteenth century and the first quarter of the nineteenth. For Hannah Arendt, Rahel's famous biographer, the stigma of her Jewishness—and how she dealt with it—is not only the major factor in Rahel's despairing relation to that society but a reflection as well of the humanist convulsion of that time and that place which, symbolically, first swept up into its orbit the Jews of Germany and then contemptuously threw them down again.

In the 1790s (when Rahel came of age) European society was galvanized by the French Revolution, and for one brief moment in historical time life was open to all who could attract attention to themselves not by virtue of *who* they were in the rigid social structure that prevailed but rather by virtue of *what* they were. The Enlightenment produced the romantic movement, which in turn produced the powerfully seductive notion that one could—out of the materials of one's own particular mind and soul—literally create one's own life; that, in fact, the only genuine art *was* the creation of one's life. The implications of this idea were that history, politics, and social structure were immaterial forces to be ignored; only the force of the "cultivated personality" was to be heeded. In this atmosphere Rahel thrived.

Although the "right" people, under the Enlightenment, meant "nothing," Rahel had nevertheless managed to meet enough of them to become a salonkeeper, and now in a time of social recklessness and literary boldness, her Jewishness (that is, her political disfranchisement), her uneducated wit, her unmarried state, her crude intellectual brilliance (she was the first to bring Goethe to the attention of Berlin society)—previously unqualified negatives all—became alluring features, and drew many of the major literary and political figures of the time to her artistic "garret" on Berlin's Jagerstrasse. In a word: Europe was being reborn and Rahel Levin, Jewess, was being reborn with it. She, too, became convinced that she could "create" her life out of the raw materials of immediate experience, that she could successfully ignore her hated Jewishness, and that only the uniqueness of Rahel would prevail, thereby bringing her everything she had ever wanted. She would never again in her life be as gay, as self-confident, as stylishly aggressive as she was during these years.

But by 1806 the ideals of the Enlightenment were dead. The Napoleonic Wars were under way, nationalism flared up anew, burning more brightly than ever before, and the brief, curious "assimilation" of the German Jews was a thing of the hedonistic past. Rahel now sat alone in the Jagerstrasse: day after day, month after month, year after year. She could hardly understand what had happened. The aristocratic men who had fallen in love with her bold and striking manner in the Jagerstrasse now disavowed her in public, the women who had made a confidante of her crossed the street when they saw her coming.

Rahel, like many other Jews, had always known that she must somehow escape her Jewishness in order "to be" in the world; but, unlike many others who had "become German" by marrying or buying or converting into society, she had thought, especially in the Jagerstrasse, to remain free in her soul and *still* make it. Now, at the turn of the century, she saw this was impossible and she became obsessed with ridding herself of her "infamous birth." Somewhat toward this end, she fell violently in love with and became engaged to a weak, unintelligent count, Karl von Finckenstein. Their affair dragged on for years, and in the end von Finckenstein, frightened by the fierce and demanding quality of her emotions and the ultimately sobering fact of her Jewishness, gave her up. Rahel's grief knew no bounds. She raged, she wept, she flung herself to Paris and back, and knew at last that to the end of her days she would by punished for having been born Jewish. Her friendships narrowed and intensified.

In 1801 she met Friedrich Gentz, an aristocratic intellectual who loved beauty (a result of the romantic movement) and then power (he later became an adviser to Metternich). Gentz was deeply drawn to Rahel and she to him; but they both knew he would never have the courage of this liaison. Their friendship was platonically passionate and lasted a lifetime, surviving a thousand public betrayals on Gentz's part and raging accusations on Rahel's. This friendship was perhaps the most important and symbolic one in Rahel's life: through Gentz she "lived"—but she lived subversively.

She fell in love again. This time, the secretary of the Spanish Legation, Don Raphael d'Urquijo, and, once again, a man weak, shallow, and vain who felt violated and confused by the sweep of her emotions. Her associations grew steadily more inappropriate; the people who gathered about her were young, poor, unconnected, awed by this "great, bold, divinely diabolic creature." In 1814, at the age of forty, she married August Varnhagen, a penniless, uneducated, social-climbing twenty-six-year-old man who, with regard to human gifts, was by his own description "a beggar by the wayside." Varnhagen's sole virtue was his worshipful adoration of Rahel. This adoration lasted throughout their life together, and if it had not been for Varnhagen's collected letters, journals, and diaries Rahel would have disappeared into history without a trace.

In 1833, at the age of sixty-three, Rahel died. On her deathbed she said, "The thing which all my life seemed to me the greatest shame, which was the misery and misfortune of my life—having been born a Jewess—this I should on no account now wish to have missed."

Hannah Arendt wrote this book in 1933—one hundred years after Rahel's death—when she herself was a Jewish woman in flight from the ultimate Germanic revulsion of the Jews. In Rahel Varnhagen's life she saw a quintessential tale of Jewish destiny: a profound and metaphorical outsidedness, the existential meaning of the pariah, the overwhelming defeat of self-denial and, conversely, the curiously gathered victory of self-assertion. Given the narrower and wider circumstances of both Rahel's and Arendt's life, it was perfectly understandable that Arendt should have seen Rahel's life in this light only. What was not, perhaps, so easy for the distinguished historian to "see" (that is, to consciously attend to) was the fact that Rahel's destiny was so unalterably that of an outsider every bit as much because she was a woman as because she was a Jew.

The most striking element in this very interesting biography is the nature and character of Rahel Varnhagen's neurotic behavior. She was, for instance, obsessed with intelligence: other people's intelligence. Her need to surround herself with intelligent responsiveness was extraordinary: intense and desperate. Conversation for Rahel was not a genuine exchange; it was rather the ability to perform verbally, and to have that performance received intelligently. Arendt writes:

The true joy of conversation consisted in being understood. The more imaginary a life is, the more imaginary its sufferings, the greater is the craving for an audience, for confirmation. . . . A morsel of reality lay hidden in other people's intelligent replies. She needed the experience of others to supplement her own. . . . The more people there were who understood her, the more real she would become.

This conviction of the unreality of the self—of the hidden, cut-off being bereft of direct experience—is one that haunts the lives of countless women, and many have acted under its pressures exactly as Rahel did. The compulsive talker, the indiscriminate confessor, the person whose attachment to others is clearly based on responsiveness rather than objective interestingness is four times out of five a woman; and four times out of five she induces in the people around her the same response to naked deprivation that Rahel brought on. Her need is both fascinating and repellent: fascinating because wherever there is some native wit or intelligence the need produces inventive and energetic human entertainment, repellent because ultimately the need is so ever-present, so insatiable, that it threatens to suck dry the lives of everyone in the room. . . . Thus, it is difficult indeed to know whether the attraction-repulsion with which Rahel met almost all of her life was due to the distasteful intensity of her Jewish hunger or her intelligent woman's hunger. (Or are they, existentially speaking, one and the same?)

Now let us look at Rahel's love affairs. She knew some of the most intellectually and politically powerful men of her time (in fact, the chapters of this biography are arranged so that each man who "taught" Rahel is described and placed). Yet she loved only weak, shallow, unintelligent men; some of these men were vain and self-adoring and some were worshipful of Rahel, but *all* were her students, intellectually. A textbook piece of anxiety: she hungered all her life for people of intelligence, she dared not risk herself emotionally with men of intelligence. Inevitably, at the bottom of such fears was her femaleness, inextricably bound up with her deepest sense of worthlessness.

And then there is the shape of Rahel's letters. The letters, diaries, and journals of ambitious men—long before the eighteenth century, and certainly after it—reveal the ever-growing consciousness with which men of wit, appetite, and intelligence view their worldly progress as a process of education: an education which—for the *truly* ambitious—embodies not only their own lives but signifies as well the education of a class, a time, a nation, the race itself. By contrast, the letters, diaries, and journals of *women* of wit, appetite, and intelligence are strikingly void of the sense that their lives constitute the story of an education. Significantly, the letters of such women are, for the most part, tales of neurosis and outsidedness, detailing not a journey through life but rather a holding action. They are the works of creatures of developed consciousness looking on—sometimes weary and subdued, sometimes ferocious and flailing—while the main action passes them by, and they must turn their considerable abilities of observation and analysis to the weary business of maintaining themselves, to holding on and *getting in.*

Rahel's letters bear a striking resemblance—a dominating resemblance—to the letters of such women. They are, beyond question, far more the letters of an intelligent woman sighing for the world and obsessed with the business of marrying well in order to get into that world than they are those of the socially deprived Jew obsessed with "passing" (although they are that, too).

The dual outsidedness of Rahel Varnhagen's life is—to this reader—compelling. Unfortunately, the story of Rahel's life, as it is here presented, is not. Hannah Arendt, who must be commended merely for bringing Rahel to us, nevertheless does not do justice to her subject's uniquely interesting life. Arendt declares at the outset that she intends neither to judge nor to psychoanalyze; she intends only to present Rahel's life to us as Rahel herself would have seen it. So far from this being a simple way to construct a biography, it is a very difficult way, and a most ambitious one, too (a method rather more fitted for an artist, I should say, than a historian). Arendt fails at what she sets out to do.

To begin with, she *does* analyze, and certainly she judges (neither of which action do I take issue with, as I think it a perfectly respectable function in a biographer and I happen to agree with nearly every one of Arendt's judgments and analyses, finding them fine as far as they go). Second, the pages of this book are dense with a reconstruction of the very history that Arendt tells us Rahel failed accurately to perceive! (A very large part of Arendt's thesis in this biography is that Rahel's life embodies the strange and wrenching passage of the Diaspora Jew through European social history: a passage more often than not conducted in fatal ignorance by the Jews themselves, who, after all, were only human beings living their lives up against immediate need, without a Tolstoyan overview of the meaning and consequence of their actions.) Third, Rahel was above all a creature of feeling rather than abstract intelligence, and this book is often painfully abstract. . . . The result of these emotional and intellectual confusions is that Rahel herself emerges from the printed word all too rarely. The live woman is only occasionally felt and seen, more often described and placed. Our sense of her is historic, not immediate, and we know (because Arendt has told us so) that not until she was on her deathbed did Rahel have a historic sense of herself.

Having said all this, I must, however, also say that the speculative intelligence behind this biography is absorbing, the historic sense exciting, and the introduction to the *meaning* of Rahel Varnhagen's life altogether worthwhile.

(1975)

The Women's Movement
in Crisis

On Tuesday, November 4, the people of New York State will go to the polls to vote on whether or not the Equal Rights Amendment should be added to the constitution. The amendment requests that: "Equality of rights under the law shall not be denied or abridged by the State of New York or any subdivision thereof on account of sex."

This vote is important for a multitude of reasons, the most obvious of these being that if the people of New York vote yes to the ERA, the women of New York will become entirely equal with men under the law. Beyond this immediate good, New York's yes to the ERA will provide other states with the impetus to vote yes also, thereby helping to achieve the required ratification by three-fourths of the states for an amendment to become part of the Constitution of the United States—and thus making it possible, after more than a century of struggle, for the women of this country to be declared legal persons equal with men before the law of the land.

This vote is also important because its campaign has brought to the surface a significant contradiction in the world that surrounds feminist effort. On the other hand, there has been a ferocious amount of anti-ERA campaigning: alarming in 1975. To think! After nearly ten years of steadily growing feminist thought and action the opposition in this country is still so simple-minded and so ignorant that it can instruct its listeners that ERA means women will have to go to the bathroom with men, women will be forced to work, women will be forced to contribute

50 percent of all household expenses, and so on, *ad nauseam.* On the other hand, there has been a tremendous amount of support from people who did little or nothing about the ERA in previous years. Organizations of all sorts, politicians at every level, ordinary citizens, all have joined in a genuine coalition to help the ERA pass in New York. It is exciting and heartlifting to observe this true people's effort in the service of women's rights.

But this vote is, in my view, most important because it has given rise to a peculiar debate within the women's movement itself. That debate can be summarized as follows: "The women's movement seems to be falling apart. The organizations are dying, our ranks are split and fragmented, we are involved in the most dreadful internecine warfare, absolutely nothing seems to be happening, the only thing we are all able to rally around is the ERA. Only five years ago we were involved in large and profound issues, and now all we seem to have left is this old warhorse, the ERA. It is exactly like the great feminists of the nineteenth century being gradually reduced to the issue of suffrage. . . . Is *this* what we have been fighting for? Is this *all* that it has all been about?"

I would like here to enter *my* argument in the debate.

To begin with, it should be useful rather than disheartening to compare ourselves with the nineteenth-century feminists; if we look long and hard at this comparison, we will see that the differences between us are more compelling than the samenesses, and those differences, of necessity, lead our feminist lives to different conclusions. In the nineteenth century the feminists stood alone; they had no one but themselves and each other; the world was massively aligned against them; they could not make a dent in the ordinary culture.

This isolation produced two important results: on the one hand, it insured the unbroken solidarity that nurtures the coherent growth of revolutionary thought; on the other hand, it insured the cumulative weariness that comes from banging your head against a stone wall for forty years, and that disintegrates the most dedicated of human efforts. Thus, women like Lucretia Mott and Susan B. Anthony became truly great theoreticians and leaders—and in the end had nothing to lead but the fight for the vote.

We, on the other hand, born into a significantly different world, have everything to lead—but we have no leaders. We have not produced—and I prophesy will not produce—the intellectually coherent leadership that characterized nineteenth-century feminism. But paradoxically, we have, in less than a decade, made our voices heard throughout the land, persuaded thousands of people of the rightness of our vision and our cause, forced government to respond to our demands, and put into the world a piece of consciousness that will not—cannot—be gone back on.

In short: they of the nineteenth century were the children of the socially conscious segment of the Victorian upper classes. We are the children of the grass-roots, egalitarian twentieth century. We are profoundly different people living in profoundly different times. It is impossible that what we make and do and live through should ever simply amount to a repeat of their history. Each set of feminists has its own merits and limitations, and each set makes a vital and distinctive contribution to the struggle as a whole.

We are a genuinely broad-based movement that is dependent for its life not on the existence of a structured leadership but on the internalized awareness that each and every one of us— in her own person, her own work, her own life—is a force for feminist dissemination. We talk about reaching the people. We forget: we *are* the people. Every feminist, wittingly or unwittingly, is an organizer at large among the people. Every feminist every moment of her principled, deciding life is increasing, osmotically, the social atmosphere in which the gathering force for change takes root.

And it is happening, it is happening. All over this country, in small towns and cities, in places where they never heard of Betty Friedan, where they know nothing of Gloria Steinem, or the Redstockings, the women are changing, the tiny daily challenges increase, the bravery of independent thought begins. I have traveled this country many times in the last five years. I have listened to housewives, students, factory workers, and clerks—women who would hesitate to call themselves feminists who, nevertheless, speak about themselves and their lives in ways that would have been unthinkable ten years ago; ways that clearly indicate a growing sense of self that of necessity must produce a radically different generation of women-in-the-world.

A year ago a housewife in Iowa wrote to her cousin in New York:

> Although I think I am a typical suburban housewife, I don't think any of my friends would call me typical. I like to read, teach part-time, worked hard for McGovern, adopted a black child, and, yes, at dinner parties I challenge some of the "male chauvinist" attitudes. (Man: "Women doing the dishes is just a natural division of labor." Me: "Not natural, *learned.*") This sort of thing makes me somewhat different. I'm not quite a misfit, but I don't quite fit in.
>
> Our neighborhood has a homeowners' association that faces periodic crisis. One night I was arguing for a particular course of action, I looked around and realized I'm the only woman who ever says anything at the meetings. It honestly never dawned on me before, but I suddenly saw the truth: nobody expects the women to talk. It bothers them all—especially the men—when a woman talks.
>
> I met a new friend whose husband is a radiologist (smart, right?). Word reached me through the grapevine that this man was uncomfortable around me because I was too smart. I had *never even held* a conversation with him.

This woman, at the end of her letter, said—sweetly, superfluously—that she has not joined any organized groups but that she is definitely in sympathy with the women's movement.

Now, beyond question, it is true that if it had not been for the development of an organized women's movement this woman would never have written this letter. But it is also true that the organized women's movement is no longer guiding her political destiny. There is in this letter a power of growing self that has a life of its own. We, the organized movement, helped bring this power into the world, but it is now often beyond us, out there in political time and space. It is this consciousness that is the strength and meaning of feminism today; this consciousness that puts feminism on the map of social revolution, and makes it a thrilling part of the great egalitarian thrust of this century. It is this consciousness, also, that again marks the differences between us and the nineteenth-century feminists. For they stood isolated, their consciousness running upstream against the social currents of their century, and thus everything they said and did and thought stood out in important relief. We, on the other hand, stand smack in the middle of the deepest social currents of *our* century. Our consciousness is the open floodgate behind which stand ready to run the deepest desires of the time and will now, I believe, run almost regardless of what we in New York and Berkeley and Chicago say and do and think.

For these reasons, the internecine warfare among feminists strikes me as both sad and foolish. At one and the same time, the self-importance to which it speaks seems outrageously off the mark and the lack of generosity behind it indicates a serious waste of useful energy. What happens inside the movement now is important only because those happenings determine whether or not the movement will continue to be an effective instrument for the dissemination of the consciousness that it helped set in motion; on the other hand, that consciousness clearly has a life of its own now, one that pays relatively little attention to the quarrels of the New York "leadership," and will proceed on its course with or without us.

It is dismaying, almost tragic, that after a few years of near silence the invaluable group of radical feminists known as the Redstockings—the group that coined the terms "consciousness raising" and "the politics of housework"—should have re-emerged with its great revolutionary energy focused on denouncing Gloria Steinem and *Ms.* magazine as dangerous enemies of the women's movement. Dismaying because bringing charges against Steinem is so wrongheaded an action. (I looked at those tabloid-sized charges and I thought, So young, and already we have our first purge.) Tragic because it is so meaningless an exercise in terms of feminist activity.

This preoccupation with the "betrayal" by *Ms.* magazine that involves so many feminists is typical of the curious kind of help-lessness that the movement is inflicting upon itself with its inter-nal quarrels. For after all, what is the reality, finally, of the "trai-torousness" of *Ms.*?

A number of years ago, about fifty women gathered in Gloria

Steinem's living room to discuss the possibility of starting a feminist magazine. The women in that room occupied every space on the feminist political spectrum I'd ever heard of, and some I'd never heard of. Everyone had different ideas and different approaches to the question of a feminist magazine. I, for instance, wanted to start a newspaper that would resemble Susan B. Anthony's *Revolution* and would be given over to good, strong writing. Others wanted to start a glossy magazine that would appeal to all those women "out there." I wanted to finance my newspaper through feminist contributions; others wanted to "rip off the Establishment for $9 million." The exchange went on for hours. Meanwhile, at one end of the room sat a number of well-dressed women quietly jotting figures on paper: women who *clearly* knew how capitalist enterprise works. The upshot was, I (and everyone else like me) walked away from that meeting, went back to my working life, and forgot about the magazine. Gloria Steinem and her friends with the pieces of paper went seriously at it, and the result was *Ms.*

It was inevitable that *Ms.* would reflect the style, personality, taste, and politics of those who ran it. It could not reflect the style, personality, taste, and politics of those who walked out of that room. Steinem and *Ms.* could do nothing but become themselves. Their self, as it turned out, was not my self, or the self of many other feminists. The magazine proved to be slick, conservative, philistine (Ellen Willis hit it right on the head when she said *Ms.* was interested in editors, not in writers). Its intellectual level is very low, its sense of the women "out there" patronizing, its feminist politics arrested at the undergraduate level.

For many of us the magazine was a great disappointment. For others, disappointment escalated into anger. For still others, anger developed into flaming belligerence and the conviction that the magazine was distorting and betraying the movement. For myself, I could never figure out what all this fuss was about. After all, I thought, what the hell did *Ms.* owe me? Nothing. If I didn't like the magazine I was free to organize another one. And as far as the movement was concerned, did *Ms.* "own" the movement that it could distort and betray it? The movement had embraced as many different political positions as there were feminists; this kind of tolerance was a vital strength; why should it now be that if the politics of this magazine (which, after all, could only be the politics of those who ran it) was not agreeable to me it was dangerous to me? If *Ms.* existed did that mean I did not exist? If *Ms.* had a following did that mean that my friends and I did not have a following? If *Ms.*'s feminism was not my feminism did that mean it was "the enemy"? Surely, that way lay the oldest political madness in the world.

The women who run *Ms.* are not my political sisters or my working colleagues or my bosom pals. I cannot make natural community with them. Their view of the world is not my view of the world, their values are not my values. For all that, they are feminists—and as such we are allies in the larger cause that binds us all together.

Gloria Steinem and *Ms.* are not the enemy. The enemy is sexism. The enemy is the absence of feminist consciousness. The enemy is all those who actively hate and deny the growing autonomy of women.

That we should be calling each other the enemy instead of keeping our eyes on the real target is a cause for sorrow and alarm. The Old Left at least partially destroyed itself because the socialists and the communists were involved for so long and so bitter a time in savaging each other. If we in the feminist movement repeat this fatal pattern of political behavior we will turn ourselves over lock, stock, and consciousness to our deepest insecurities—and hence to that weakening from within that the real enemy only profits from.

And in the name of what is all this happening? And toward what end? We are only midwives; the baby is already born; it is true, it is only a weak, squalling infant, and possibly, without nourishment or care of any kind, it may die. But babies are sturdy creatures; once given a taste of life they cling to it, fight for it, pretty much make their own way in the world.

The fight for the ERA is important—but not that important. It can never—not in the next thousand years—mean what fighting for the vote at the end of the nineteenth century meant. That fight was the signal that the war was over, and the feminists had lost; the vote was the territorial bone thrown the vanquished by the victor. The ERA means exactly the opposite: the war is on its way to being won, and the recalcitrance over the ERA is a last-ditch stand made by a steadily losing side. If the ERA does not pass this year, it will pass next year. Of that there can no longer be any doubt.

Which does not mean that we sit back and not campaign, or worse yet, not go to the polls. We must call every shot every damned day of our lives; we must struggle over every law, protest over every daily discrimination, march endlessly to Albany and Washington, challenge every man at every dinner table, fight for jobs, credit, housing, and the equal care of children.

But: understand all the while what it is we are fighting for, what the nature of that struggle is, and what the real position of each and every one of us is in that struggle.

The campaign this year for the ERA gives us a chance to see that while we've come far, we still have a very long way to go. So we plunge back in and keep slogging along. The real question for me is: On that long trudge ahead who will give me more sustenance, the housewife from Iowa or my leaders in the movement? At the moment I'd say the housewife. The housewife, living in her small community "out there," daily risks becoming a pariah for the sake of her growing feminism. For my money, *she* is the brave soldier in the army of the revolution. My leaders in New York are in danger of being conned by their own press releases into forgetting that revolution, like art, is neither agony nor ecstasy but only sheer hard work; work done always in the service of the slowly growing consciousness which— like the gathering of a natural force—cannot tell the leaders from the followers.

No one of us has "the truth," or the word, or the correct view, or the only way. Each feminist is a microcosm of feminism, and as discrete as each one's feminism is, it *still* contains the whole of things. That is the glory of the movement at its best; that is what makes us so intensely a part of our time; that is the life within I think we should fight very hard to protect.

(November 1975)

Here's News: Fathers Matter as Much as Mothers

Jane Lazarre's thoughtful piece on mothering fathers in the September 22 issue of the *Village Voice* reminded me of an experience of my own related to this subject, which, in its entirety, was extremely revealing of (1) how deeply experience is tied to social attitudes and the conventional wisdom those attitudes serve, and (2) how resistant to change in those attitudes the entire society—from top to bottom—is.

Two years ago an editor from a well-known woman's magazine called me and asked if I would write an article for the magazine. What the editor had in mind was a piece on a men's consciousness-raising group in Cambridge. Nothing could have been of less interest to me than this subject but, in financial need-greed, I said okay, I'd look into it. With my first phone call I discovered that the group was falling apart and there wasn't much of a story there after all. Nevertheless, I asked the man on the other end of the line who he was and what he did in Cambridge. He was a psychologist and, it turned out, he was working on something that might be of interest to me. "What was that?" I asked. "The natural tie between the father and the child," he said. "You don't say," I perked up. "That *is* interesting." "Maybe you'd like to come up to Boston and take a look at what I'm doing?" he suggested. "Maybe I would. Why don't you send me something to read and we'll talk again."

Within a week I had part of Milton Kotelchuck's Harvard dissertation, and I knew that here was a genuine and important story. I marched up to the magazine's midtown offices, walked into the editor's room, and said, "Now here is something worth writing about." I talked for fifteen minutes about Kotelchuck's work, about the controlled experiment he'd been performing in Cambridge, the overwhelming data he seemed to have collected to indicate that chidren are as attached from infancy to their fathers as they are to their mothers, how important such work was at this time, of what a fine thing it would be for her to run the story of this work in her magazine.

The editor sat quietly in her chair, listening carefully to me. Then, when I stopped talking, she said to me, "You mean you want me to tell our readers that everything we've been telling them all these years isn't true."

I couldn't believe my ears. I was sure she was putting me on. Then I saw she wasn't. She really meant that incredible question. Suddenly, I wanted very badly to see this story run in this magazine—with its nearly 14 million readers.

"Look," I said softly, "that's an unnecessarily conservative response. Trust your readers a little more than you do. Motherhood is not an unmixed joy. This story will give them a little breathing space, that's all. It's not going to turn them into overnight revolutionaries or, worse yet, make them drop their subscriptions. Believe me, they'll welcome such information."

The editor thought it over and with much nervous hesitation agreed that I should write the story. I then went off to Boston to spend three days with Milton Kotelchuck and his videotape machines, his one-way glass walls, and his babies, mothers, fathers, and strangers.

The background of Kotelchuck's experiment and the experiment itself are substantially this: For generations people have believed that the relationship between the infant and its mother is a very special one: unique, irreplaceable, rooted in biological instinct. This belief in the almost inborn relationship between mothers and infants has certainly been upheld by the work of the social scientists, particularly those psychologists who have studied the mother-infant bond in humans as well as in primates.

To begin with, the psychologists believed that dependency was at the heart of the bond: the mother satisfies those needs the child cannot satisfy for himself; therefore, he is naturally devoted to her. Then, in the late 1950s, University of Minnesota psychologist Harry Harlow placed a baby monkey in a cage. In the same cage Harlow also put a wire monkey with a bottle of milk attached to it and a soft, terrycloth monkey with no food attached to it. The baby monkey clung all day long to the terrycloth monkey. When he grew hungry he swung over to the wire monkey, sucked at the bottle until he was satisfied, then swung back to the terrycloth monkey. "It is not dependency on food that we experience as infants," Harlow concluded, "it is dependency on love."

"Dependency," said English psychologist John Bowlby, "is the wrong word. Dependency is a passive state. The infant is *actively* engaged in making a connection with his mother. If you watch him you will see that many of his motions and expressions are an attempt to bind his mother to him emotionally. He clings, smiles, cries out. He is exhibiting an instinctual need for love, for human *attachment.*" Bowlby's views were supported by the American psychologist Mary Salter Ainsworth; together, these two have convincingly demonstrated that the child does seem to need and encourage human connection from early infancy on.

At no time, however, did any of the attachment psychologists—especially Bowlby and Ainsworth—question the idea that it is the mother who is the indispensable "connection" parent. For a mother to be separated from her infant at any time before the formative years are over, the psychologists contended, is to risk irreparable damage to the growing child.

These theories developed right after World War II, when everyone craved a return to "normalcy." Everybody wanted to believe the pronouncements of the psychologists, who said the mother was the most important person in a growing child's life, that she provided the one emotional relationship from which all others were learned and was the one necessary source of socialization and spiritual stability.

Even then, however, at least one strong voice was raised

against the conclusions of the attachment psychologists. As early as 1954, Margaret Mead wrote that the relationship of the child to its biological mother and its need to be cared for by human beings were becoming "hopelessly confused" in the growing insistence that child and biological mother "must never be separated, that all separation even for a few days is inevitably damaging," and that if it goes on long enough, "it does irreversible damage."

"This," Mead said, "is a new and subtle form of antifeminism in which men—under the guise of exalting the importance of maternity—are tying women more tightly to their children than has been thought necessary since the invention of bottle-feeding and baby carriages." There is no real anthropological evidence, Mead insisted, to establish such a tie between mother and child. In fact, studies of other cultures suggest that a child makes the easiest adjustment if he or she "is cared for by many warm, friendly people."

At the time, these words produced an uproar. Today, 20 years later, they seem neither dreadfully radical nor inflammatory. The feminists of the late 1960s altered the cultural atmosphere so severely that many people began to find it perfectly respectable to ask similar questions: Who says mothering is superior to fathering? What actually makes the mother the more necessary parent? Where is the hard evidence for the "natural" (rather than the culture-created) tie between mother and infant? How do we know that fathers can't be equally adept at child care? Have we ever given them a chance? And do we actually know that fathers do *not* influence their young and growing children? What exactly *do* we know about the relationship between fathers and infants as it presently exists?

Enter Milton Kotelchuck: Harvard graduate student in psychology in the late 1960s. Kotelchuck's interest in the relationship between infants and their fathers actually dated back to his undergraduate days at Johns Hopkins, where he studied with Mary Salter Ainsworth. He became fascinated with the subject of attachment, and much of what Ainsworth and Bowlby said struck him as eminently plausible. Yet, "I could not accept the idea," he said, "that the attachment between mothers and infants was unique or biologically built in. I had taken demography courses. I knew how many women died in childbirth. Where then did that leave the adoptive mother? Or the grandmother? or the nanny? You couldn't say that all children raised by women other than their biological mothers grew up neurotic or psychically damaged. That didn't make any sense. I started wondering about children raised by more than one mother—multiple mothering."

At Harvard he attempted to continue work on multiple mothering. However, in Cambridge he had trouble finding enough families whose living arrangements featured multiple mothering. Suddenly it occurred to him *fathers* were a component of multiple motherhood: "They're always there: they help out in time of need; they share educative tasks."

The more he thought about it, the more Kotelchuck realized that "no one really *knows* how children feel about fathers. There have been almost no studies directly observing fathers interacting with their young children. The work done on attachment between children and mothers always ranges mothers against strangers. Then, of course, the attachment between child and parent is clearly unique. But what about *other* familiar persons? What about fathers? How would a child respond if you had him in a room with his mother, his father, and a stranger?"

Kotelchuck had the basis for his experiment. He would examine a child's behavior in the presence or absence of the child's mother, his father, and a stranger. For his sample, he selected 144 infants, 12 boys and 12 girls at the ages of 6, 9, 12, 15, 18, and 21 months. Twelve women served as the strangers, and each saw 12 children, one boy and one girl at each age. The setting of the experiment was a playroom stocked with enough toys to attract the children, but not so many that they would be utterly absorbed and oblivious to the comings and goings of the adults.

The experiment began with the infant located in the center of the playroom, surrounded by toys and facing his or her parents, who were seated at one end of the room. The parents were instructed not to initiate contact with the child. If the child approached them or seemed upset, they were to respond naturally but briefly. The strangers were given the same instructions. Every three minutes, one of the adults was signaled either to enter or leave the room. Each schedule lasted 39 minutes, and was composed of 13 arrivals and departures which either left the child alone with one of the adults, or in the company of two of them, in all possible combinations.

Kotelchuck gave me a videotape demonstration of his experiment. The TV screen showed a playroom. In the middle of the floor sat a fifteen-month-old girl surrounded by toys. Annie, Kotelchuck explained, had never been in the room before. A man and a woman, whom he identified as her parents, were sitting reading in chairs pushed against the far wall. After looking at them to satisfy herself that they were there, Annie started to inspect the toys. Three minutes later her mother got up and left the room. Annie barely seemed to notice her departure. But then her eyes followed the stranger as she sat down in the chair previously occupied by her mother. Annie stared for a few seconds, then she got up and wandered over to her father, who continued to read. Annie became interested in the toys in the corner near her father's chair and remained playing there. Three minutes later her father got up and started to leave. Annie padded after him. When it became clear that he was really gone, she burst into tears. The stranger now attempted to make friends with Annie and managed to lure her back to the center of the room and to make her stop crying. But Annie still looked anxious and distracted. Three minutes later, her mother came back. Annie burst into tears and held out her arms to her mother, after which she quieted down and remained playing close to her mother's chair, her eyes never far from the stranger who was now sitting in the chair her father had previously occupied. Three minutes later the stranger left the room. Only then did Annie return to playing in the center of the room, exactly as she had done when left alone with her father.

"What you saw on that screen," Kotelchuck pointed out, "showed an important finding in our experiment; namely, that infants respond similarly to fathers and mothers. They will protest the departure of either parent but not the departure of the stranger. Moreover, it was clear that being left alone with a stranger in an unfamiliar room was what really disturbed the child, rather than the departure of her parents in itself. The child's comfort with *either* parent and the similarity of her responses to their departures and arrivals was significant. This is not to say that there were no differences in the response, only that the child's response to the father was more like the child's response to her mother than her response to the stranger."

The study in its entirety revealed that over 70 percent of the children observed were responsive to their father's presence, while a significant few showed a preference for their fathers over their mothers.

"It becomes clearer and clearer," said Kotelchuck, "that when another familiar person, like the father, is introduced into a setting, the presumed uniqueness of the mother-child relationship seems to disappear. Speaking more positively, when the father's presence rather than his absence is examined, it becomes evident that fathers are indeed important to their infants; the infants play with their fathers, give them toys, are comfortable in their presence. Children clearly *do* form specific relationships with their fathers; their behavior is often directly related to the father's presence or absence; fathers are missed when gone; the older the infant gets the more he interacts with his father."

Then Kotelchuck said that his experiments only gave further insight into what many psychologists *had known for a long time.* He cited the researches of two Edinburgh psychologists, Schaffer and Emerson, who in 1963 had followed the development of sixty Scottish infants for eighteen months. They discovered at the beginning that 65 percent of the infants were attached only to the mother, while only 27 percent formed multiple attachments from the outset. By the time they were eighteen months old, however, only 17 percent still were attached only to their mothers; 79 percent of them were attached to their fathers, sometimes jointly with their mothers, sometimes alone. Into the bargain, the Edinburgh study, as well as the findings of another Harvard study, indicate strongly that children who form attachments from the beginning to their fathers as well as to their mothers find it easier to form other attachments later.

These findings, Kotelchuck added, have never been made much of. In fact, they have never really been treated as findings; rather, they have been incorporated as casual observations.

So. What have we got here? Obviously, observations made before their time are rarely treated as discoveries; instead, they are treated as curiosities, perhaps aberrations, footnotes to a text that remains obdurately welded to the presumptions of the culture. The culture commands that the mother is more important to the chid than the father; and the social scientists will be damned if they'll discover otherwise.

I wrote up this experiment substantially as I have given it here. I returned with it to the magazine. The results were these:

1. I was asked twice to rewrite the piece; each time I did so my language became, somehow, mysteriously more subdued; above all, my *tone* seemed to melt into a peculiar neutrality.

2. The title of the piece as I handed it in was "The Natural Tie Between the Father and the Child." The title under which the piece was printed was "How Important Is a Father to His Child?"

3. I wrote: "This belief in the almost inborn relationship between mothers and infants is one that has certainly been upheld by the work of social scientists. . . ." This phrase appeared in the text, but it was *headlined* as "Up to now, the almost inborn relationship between mother and infants has been emphasized. . . ."

4. When the piece finally appeared it had been further cut, reorganized, and toned down without my knowledge or consent. When I called the editor to take issue with her over this unforgivable publishing practice, she retorted, "I had to do *something* to make it readable."

What she meant was: I'll give my readers the information but I'll do it in such a way that it won't make any impact on them. They'll never know what it all really means, and what it is actually telling them about their lives.

Are the women's magazines and the social scientists conspiring against the new knowledge of human relations and its far-reaching consequences for the structure of our society? Consciously: no. Unconsciously: yes.

Jane Lazarre's piece on paternity in the *Voice* counters mine on paternity in that magazine. Milton Kotelchuck's dissertation on paternity counters nine others on the uniqueness of motherhood. That's not quite enough. The only thing for it, then, is to increase our numbers. We must become more insistent about *our* "findings."

(1975)

Feminist Writers: Hanging Ourselves on a Party Line

It often seems to me that doctrine and doctrinaire opinion in the women's movement have developed as fast or even faster than has feminist thought itself. Almost from the beginning—even as women began to narrow their eyes with insight and men to stir with guilty defensiveness—there has been a growing tendency within feminist ranks to practice the curious self-censorship that accompanies the creation of a dogma. It has been considered a matter of urgency by many to "define" the feminist position; to ferret out "elitism"; to separate the "radicals" from the "liberals"; to suppress whatever is momentarily considered "politically inexpedient"; to insist on the "correctness" of certain opinions while vigorously denouncing the corresponding incorrectness of other opinions; to imply all relations with men amount to "collaboration"; and above all to use the word "sisterhood" like a club over the heads of all women whose thought and action follow the dictates of individual conscience rather than those of what has quickly become a closed system of response. As though what began so very recently as emotional conviction has already hardened for many into a tyranny of the mind: a state of being in which thoughtful response becomes a rigid polemic; a sudden realization is transformed into an insistent position; a single insight now constitutes a world view.

In short: within a very few years we have had the rapid development of what can only be called "party opinion" in the women's movement; the result of which has been astonishing and heartbreaking. Fierce and somewhat mad squabbling has often broken out among feminists. Outrageous accusations of "revisionism" have been leveled; an unthinking insistence on lesbian supremacy has blossomed; as well as bitter character assassinations in the name of "elitism" and harsh pressure toward conformist opinion in the name of "sisterhood."

Nowhere does the pressure of party opinion in the movement seem more appalling to me than within the sphere of literary and artistic criticism. While a great deal of opinion regarding works by or about women is genuinely thoughtful and seems to spring from an ever-widening frame of reference, all too often critical observation seems to flow from a political rather than an intellectual position. This political position, roughly speaking, incorporates the following principles: (1) if a work is "woman-identified," it is, *a priori*, good; if not, it is bad; (2) if a review is written by a man about work by or about a woman it is, *a priori*, evil or of no consequence; and (3) if a review is written by a woman about a work by or about a woman and the review is less than congratulatory, it is to be condemned as traitorous. As a consequence of this political mind set, many feminists reviewing work done by women seem to suspend the rigorous intellectual judgment they are clearly capable of and instead opt for lavish and embarrassingly *un*critical praise of their "sisters'" artistic efforts. Conversely, wherever some effort at objective intellectual judgment results in qualified praise or even critical rejection of a work by a woman, it is immediately denounced as sabotage.

Two striking instances of such political denunciation come immediately to mind: the one involving John Leonard, then editor of the *New York Times Book Review,* and the other involving Marge Piercy's novel *Small Changes.* The first instance invoked principle two of the political position; the second, principle three.

With regard to John Leonard: a few years ago Leonard wrote an omnibus review of a group of books written by women; most of the writers were avowed feminists, one—the actress Shirley

MacLaine—was not. In his review Leonard observed that while the feminists' books had a number of merits they were riddled with the language of political propaganda and to that extent they were, in his opinion, severely flawed; on the other hand, he found MacLaine's book altogether delightful and went on to say that the actress had, in all political innocence, made the case for feminism better than the feminists themselves had. The *Times* was then deluged with angry letters from feminists, all of whom, in one way or another, declared that Leonard was disqualified from reviewing these books simply because he was a man. Leonard—an open supporter of the women's movement almost from its inception—in his turn grew angry, and replied that if such was to be the case then "only whales could review *Moby Dick.*"

With regard to the Piercy novel: *Small Changes,* an openly feminist novel published two years ago this past spring, received highly mixed reviews. Among these reviews was one written by a woman and published in the pages of *Ms.* magazine. This review was also a mixed review; that is, it was a review that acknowledged the novel's accomplishments while criticizing its failings. Upon the appearance in print of this review, there arose from a large segment of the feminist community vigorous cries of: "Betrayal! Where, then, is sisterhood if this novel of all novels cannot receive a good review in a leading feminist journal?"

What are we to make of all this? What, in essence, is involved here in these instances of coercive opinion? The answer, apparently, lies in the oldest—the most totalitarian—confusion between art and politics in the history of the human struggle: the entirely mistaken notion that art is a *tool* rather than a *consequence* of political struggle; that art must embody the primitive idea of solidarity rather than represent the growth of individuation; and that art must merge with political doctrine rather than emerge from political insight.

It seems to me this growth of doctrinaire opinion in the women's movement can do nothing but retard the progress of modern feminism. For not only does dogma fail to nourish genuine solidarity among women—a true weapon in the struggle to come to a cultural maturity—but it undermines what are, for me at least, the extraordinary and exciting underpinnings of the second wave of feminism: namely, the desire and growing ability to see things as they are; to examine experience entirely in its own terms; to truly explore the country of self-determination. After all, did we not become feminists in order to think for ourselves? Was it not finally a gathered need in us—all of us—to press beneath the surfaces of automatic description that has bound us generation after generation into lives that have deprived us of the ability to experience ourselves? Did we not suddenly take a hard, thoughtful look inside ourselves at what was *actually there to be seen?* Does our politics not spring from the force of that initial insight? What earthly good could it do us now to *stop* looking at what is actually there to be seen; to exchange one set of automatic terms for another (for when you speak the rhetoric of dogma that is exactly what you are doing); to imagine that we are involved in anything but a process of growth; to forget that growth takes place as long as experience is live— not automatic.

What I mean by "live" as opposed to "automatic" is best implied simply by observing the altered effect of the term *consciousness raising.* Five or six years ago, when comparatively small numbers of women began slowly to stumble their way toward the dynamic process of group "testifying," the phrase had electric meaning. Women felt in their gut—with the amazing power of original discovery—the political meaning of personal history as they sat each week in a circle and discovered themselves through the process of describing themselves. Many women did not in the blessed anonymity of those very early days necessarily *know* what was happening to them, but they felt *compelled* by what was happening to them; and in that compelling quality lay the basis for all future feminist theory. That was consciousness raising when it was live experience, and when the term was used it conveyed the power and meaning of the experience.

Today, the term has passed into the lexicon of household usage. It is referred to with tiresome regularity by people who haven't the foggiest emotional sense of what it actually means; it is a piece of automatic rhetoric, good only for cocktail party reference and the mindless curriculum of bureaucratic lives; rarely, I believe, do women nowadays undergo the cathartic, transforming process that was once consciousness raising—and, indeed, it is impossible that it should be otherwise. After five years of regular exposure to the term in the pages of *Time* and *Newsweek,* is there a woman in the country who could come to the experience with the freshness and emotional "ignorance" required for original discovery?

It is easy to see how it happens—this quick drop from original insight into dogma and sloganism. Especially here: in this place at this time. America has always had the ability to subvert the power of radical and intellectual movements through the single expedient of mass absorption; this ability is at once the source of its stability and the cause for despair of change. We, too, are suffering now from this selfsame "absorption," the potency of our ideas drowning in a welter of words that once held living meaning and have now become automatic slogans that begin to deprive us—rather than support us—in our struggle to change our lives. Today, terms like *MCP* and *sexual object* are jargon, and they carry with them all the dangers of jargon. For jargon, after all, is shorthand; and the danger of shorthand is that it short-circuits thought; to substitute rhetoric for genuine thought, to use it as a kind of name calling or labeling, or as a nod of admission or a jerk of rejection, is to narrow experience once more: to deprive life of its complexity, its richness, and its infinite capacity for increased perception.

As I see it, this use of rhetoric is a luxury the women's movement cannot afford; for the women's movement is not in any conventional sense a political movement whose needs might best be served through the deliberate narrowness of classical revolutionary language and thought. It is, rather, a movement of social change whose ultimate aim is the re-creation of psychological reality; shimmering in the feminist distance is a world in which women are as real to men as men are to themselves. This is the heart of the matter; from this "reality of the self" flows all behavior, and from behavior flows all politics.

The movement is primarily a battle to alter behavior. In this battle a prime weapon is the continual revival of original insight.

Slogans deaden us. They reduce our ability to see clearly, to experience ourselves anew, to replenish the continually flagging urgency that must be kept alive at all times in this war of nerves and emotions that threatens at every turn to undo us. What is necessary is the ability to call the shots exactly as they are being played; to see our life in all its complexity; to recognize that sometimes we are the victims and sometimes men are the victims, but neither of us is always the victim. To fail to see that is to fail to see the truth of our lives, and without the truth we will never come close to possessing ourselves, for self-possession is the ability to face without fear life in all its contradictions. What has made men our oppressors is their inability to face the contradictions, but what will allow us to become strong is our increased ability to face the contradictions. That, to me, is feminism carried to its magnificent conclusion.

Self-possession. There's the magic word. That's the pot of gold at the end of the rainbow. That, finally, is what all the talk about changed realities and altered behavior and life experience comes down to. To possess oneself is, of course, everything. Artists and philosophers have always known that, and for centuries so, also, have psychologists and social thinkers known that. "The point of life," said Rousseau, "is to experience oneself." Why? Why to *experience* oneself? Because beyond the experience of the self lies the possession of the self. And there, finally, in the possession of the self, lies freedom.

At the visionary end of the road that feminism is now traveling is precisely that realization: to have power over the self through the means of self-possession is to be free of much that now defines our enslavement. If I own my mind, my spirit, and my behavior, who then can own my body, my soul, or my labor? This notion—of power as possession of the self rather than as manipulation of others—is what the entire twentieth-century civil rights movement is all about; and the spearhead of this movement is feminism. This is a social movement of have-nots whose have-not status has everything to do with the psychological exploitation that prevents possession of the self. It has to do with the fact that in a society that grants white adult males a host of unearned powers and unchallenged rights *at birth,* the rest of us must grapple all our lives to become only that which these men are at birth: human beings endowed with a certain psychological sense of their own reality that at least puts them on the map of struggling self-assertion.

To end, then, at the beginning: it seems to me that when a female reviewer writes a review in which she asks, "What, exactly, is being done here? How well, in its own terms, is it being done? And, finally, what is its value in relation to a context larger than itself?" she is struggling to possess her own soul—straining to think, to see things as they are, to grow herself an independent spirit. She is, by my lights, fulfilling and exulting in the promise of feminism. By the same token, when a female reviewer writes a review in which she says, "This book is not woman-identified enough," she reveals that she has a political agenda in her mind and she is ticking off the book against the items on that agenda. To have an agenda of this sort in the mind is, again by my lights, to have missed entirely the point of the feminist struggle; which, God help us, is surely not to turn us into card-carrying ideologues but rather to help us develop in ourselves the ability to think and feel clearly in order that each of us may better control this, our one and only life.

(July 1975)

Alice Paul

A woman sits in the gound-floor room in a large old house in Connecticut that has been turned into a nursing home. She is small and painfully frail, her body withered with great age. All around her, in the hall beyond this room and in the room itself, is the smell and feel of age and death. I stare at the woman. I have seen photographs taken of her when she was young: the body slim and strong, the eyes luminous, the hair rich, massive, piled high on her beautiful head. Now she sits before me in a wheelchair: the lovely dark eyes dim and colorless, the massive hair thin and white, the arms ropy, the mouth clumsy, as though filled with wooden teeth. I ask a vague, general question: how does she feel? The woman remains silent for a long while, as though she either hasn't heard or hasn't understood my question. Then she answers: abrupt, irritated, lapsing immediately back into silence, shrinking even further into her chair. Another question of the same sort . . . another answer of the same sort.

Then I ask her a specific question. The question is not about her health or any general sense of "life" she might have. The question is about the political movement she has given her entire life to. Her head straightens slowly on her neck, like a bird's feeling its way into safety, again an extraordinary silence lasts a very long while, and then she begins to speak. This time there is an amazing difference in her speech. Her voice grows full and strong, her words quicken with thought and memory, her sentences begin to shine with lucidity. An atmosphere accumulates arround her: calm, grave, steady. The atmosphere is transforming. The woman has become a presence, a force, a being alive with meaning beyond her tiny, withered self.

Alice Paul is ninety-one years old. The movement she has given her life to is the women's rights movement. The party that has been her instrument of political work is the National Women's Party. The issues of her life have been women's suffrage and the Equal Rights Amendment. She, the movement, the party, the issues are one. Inside her an entire history lives. It is not only the history of the women's movement in this country, but the history, as well, of the narrow, concentrated power of the human will in lifelong conflict with social injustice.

Alice Paul was born in January of 1885 in Moorestown, New Jersey. Her parents were well-to-do, middle-class Quakers whose lives were actively informed by the moral and humane principles of the religious sect to which they belonged. In later years when Alice Paul was asked what brought her to feminism, she said that it had always been there—in her home, in her young life. That is, she grew up with the assumption that men and women were equal, and only when she went out into the larger world did she discover this was not so. The discovery came as a visceral shock, the kind of shock that gives sudden form to that which has been inchoate. She realized that she was political to the bone, that her deepest being was aroused by the political. She saw the disfranchised condition of women in the light of political struggle, and she would never again see it otherwise.

She was very bright and full of intellectual curiosity; there was never any question of her not going to school. She began collecting degrees when she was twenty years old and didn't stop until she was forty-three (B.A., Swarthmore, 1905; M.A., University of Pennsylvania, 1907; Ph.D., University of Pennsylvania, 1912; LL.B., Washington College of Law, 1922; LL.M., D.C.L., American University, 1927–28).

She emerged from Swarthmore in 1905 as a social worker and became in that year a resident worker in the New York College Settlement. Her instinctive energy for the poor, the disorganized, those without voice or power, was as yet diffused. But that vital sense of disfranchisement that she carried with her into the sweatshops of New York and later into the slums of London was steadily narrowing. Its clarification required only

ALICE PAUL173

an igniting experience. And that experience, when it came in England, showed her who and what she was: a single-minded, single-hearted revolutionary who would travel one road only for the rest of her life.

Alice Paul went to England in 1907 at the age of twenty-two to study at the Woodbrooke Settlement for Social Work in Birmingham. In his incomparable history of feminism in America, *Everyone Was Brave,* William L. O'Neill writes:

> She came to England at a time when the fantastic Pankhursts were in full cry. Under the leadership of Emmeline Pankhurst and her daughter Christabel, the suffragist movement had been divided . . . and a spectacular minority, called suffragettes, who employed a kind of guerrilla warfare [had emerged]. Beginning in a small way with verbal protests, public demonstrations and the like, the suffragettes ultimately practiced arson and sabotage, mutilated artworks and physically assaulted cabinet ministers. When jailed they went on hunger strikes which compelled the government either to force-feed or release them. If let go they promptly began committing outrages again.

For Alice Paul the Pankhursts were electrifying. She instantly felt at one with them. They were the clarifying experience. They made her not only a lifelong suffragist, but a very particular kind of suffragist. In one swift visionary moment they showed her that women must adopt revolutionary methods, that no one was ever going to give them the vote; they must *take* the vote.

Alice Paul worked with the Pankhursts in England for three years; they proved to be the most formative years of her political life. Here in England she learned everything she, in fact, was going to learn about how to wage organized and vivid warfare for suffrage. She also learned how much punishment she could, and needed to, withstand: she demonstrated, she went to jail, she was force-fed. She returned to America in 1910 a dedicated, militant suffragist, ready to lay her talents and her experience before her own suffrage movement. But the American movement was so demoralized it was unable to make use of her.

In 1910, four years after Susan B. Anthony's death, active struggle for a federal constitutional amendment on woman's suffrage had all but come to an end. The suffrage amendment had never been brought to a vote in the House of Representatives, and in the Senate it had been voted on only once, in 1887. Nationally, not one politician was interested in or supportive of suffrage. Each president, in turn, had been oblivious to its merits if not downright antagonistic. Thus the National American Woman Suffrage Association (NAWSA) had in effect turned its entire attention to the states, hoping to make each state in turn enfranchise its women. The result was that between 1890 and 1911 the franchise had been granted to six Western states—Wyoming, Colorado, Utah, Idaho, Washington, California—and then: nothing. For years, nothing. The suffragists themselves were still vital, but the organization was all but moribund.

Alice Paul had become convinced in England that the only way to gain suffrage in America was through federal amendment; a continuation of state campaigns, she felt, was a crucial waste of time and energy. What's more, the traditional genteel methods NAWSA employed were not sufficient; something *more* was required. She went before NAWSA to persuade the organization to send her to Washington to work for a federal amendment. It took her two years to do so, and then it was only with the influential support of Jane Addams that she was able to make the national organization capitulate to her scheme—on the condition that she never ask them for money or support of any kind.

She arrived in Washington in December of 1912 with a list of names in one pocket, about $3 in the other pocket, and two coworkers: Lucy Burns and Crystal Eastman. These three together became the Congressional Committee of NAWSA. Within the next four years, as Alice Paul and her followers continued to come into conflict with the parent organization, the committee became the Congressional Union and then, finally, the independent National Woman's Party. Throughout each of its incarnations the committee, the union, the party—indisputably—was Alice Paul.

She proved to be an extraordinary organizer, fund raiser, and politician. She permitted nothing into her life or her consciousness that did not have a direct bearing on suffrage. She lived in a cold room so she wouldn't be tempted to read novels late at night. She worked for months at a time without removing her hat. Her manner was so intent, so direct, that it was often experienced as abominable rudeness. This manner induced in those around her either awe and loyalty or amazement and distaste. Once, when a volunteer who had worked very hard suddenly disappeared from headquarters, Alice Paul inquired after the woman. She was told that the volunteer was offended by Alice Paul's failure to thank her for her work. Alice Paul replied in wonder, "But she did not do it for me. She did it for Suffrage. I thought she would be delighted to do it for Suffrage."

Suffrage. That was the holy word. And precisely because it *was* a holy word for her she was able to swell the ranks of the Woman's Party to 50,000 in a few short years and induce an extraordinary solidarity in those who followed her. She brought to the flagging suffrage movement two things: the boldness of outrageous tactics and the idea—brought from England—that the suffragists must hold the party in power responsible for not passing the federal amendment. She organized massive demonstrations, the most famous of which took place on Pennsylvania Avenue in March of 1913, the day before Wilson's inauguration. Five thousand women marched. They were attacked by hoodlums, were not defended by the police, and the next day hit the front page of every newspaper in America, thereby immediately putting women's suffrage back on the American political map.

Alice Paul continuously organized disruptions at meetings, rallies, functions of all kinds. She threw a picket line around the White House—hers were the first suffragists ever to picket the White House—that consisted of women carrying signs that asked: "Mr. President, how long must women wait for liberty?" She and her followers got arrested, went to jail, hunger-struck, were force-fed, again made front pages across the country—and gained consistently growing attention and sympathy. For eight solid years Alice Paul and the Woman's Party kept up this kind of battering political activism—plus endless meetings, conferences, conventions, local and state demonstrations—never stopping, never relenting, creating an insistent atmosphere of social turmoil that demanded and gained national attention.

To Carrie Chapman Catt, the head of NAWSA, Alice Paul

and the Woman's Party were anathema. Mrs. Catt, the most powerful political leader the women's rights movement ever had, saw herself as comparable to presidents and heads of state, with the same responsibility to use traditional methods of political bargaining and compromise. To her, Alice Paul was an irresponsible radical whose idea of holding the party in power responsible was utterly wrongheaded and whose actions were detrimental to the cause of suffrage. In short, the Woman's Party was to NAWSA as—in our own time—the Radical Feminists are to NOW. The tragedy—than as now—was that neither the radicals nor the traditionalists saw that they were each necessary to the other. Carrie Chapman Catt could not see that Alice Paul's activism revitalized NAWSA and brought to an entire nation the urgency of woman's suffrage as probably no other kind of action could have. Alice Paul, for her part, never understood the need for conservative political behavior that determined Mrs. Catt's NAWSA policies. But beyond question, it was the two kinds of leaders, organizations, and policies that together pushed the cause of suffrage through to its victorious conclusion.

In one vital sense, however, Alice Paul's vision had an edge over Mrs. Catt's. Mrs. Catt was, at all times, prepared to use political expediency to gain suffrage. This required that she never challenge the myriad "protective" laws that governed American women's lives with regard to work, property, marriage, place of domicile, and obligations of citizenship. From the very first, Alice Paul saw suffrage and these protective laws as all of a piece, as all together speaking to the question of full citizenship for women. She said in 1913—and she kept on saying it—"Equality not protection." Mrs. Catt and NAWSA saw this statement as revolutionary and divisive nonsense. She told herself and her followers that once they gained suffrage all else would follow. Alice Paul said no, we'll have to fight for it just as we're fighting for suffrage.

In 1923, three years after suffrage was granted, Alice Paul and the Woman's Party drafted the Equal Rights Amendment, which stipulates that no right be abridged by either the federal government or the states on account of sex. That amendment was meant to be—and, indeed, certainly is—the proper accompaniment to the suffrage amendment; it is the other side of the coin of enfranchisement. Yet the struggle for suffrage had exhausted both the nation and the suffragists; most people simply did not have the emotional energy for the ERA. Only Alice Paul had the energy. For nearly twenty years she was able to keep the issue of the ERA alive before the Congress and before many state legislatures, but with the onset of the Second World War the entire question was submerged. The new wave of feminism in the late 1960s brought the ERA surging back into American life. It was there, ready and waiting to be rediscovered, only because of all those long years of steady, plodding work on the part of Alice Paul and her party.

The steadiness. Alice Paul said once in answer to a question about her unwavering steadiness in the cause of women's rights: "Well, I always thought once you put your hand on the plough you don't remove it until you get to the end of the row." The ninety-one-year-old woman sitting in the ground-floor room in the nursing home in Ridgefield, Connecticut, still has her hand on the plough. For her, there is no past; there is only an ever-accumulating present. Every day of her life she lives with the ongoing need to see the Equal Rights Amendment become federal law. This overriding "reality" is what made her a leader sixty years ago; it is what will make her a leader until the last breath passes from her body. A number of years ago, from the nursing home telephone, she directed the struggle for the passage of the ERA in the Maine Legislature. When I visited her she organized *me*. Halfway through one of our conversations she suddenly leaned across the little table on which her frail arms rested and said to me, "My dear, do you think you could get yourself elected to the New York State Legislature? We *need* someone there." And then again, when I was leaving her and promising to return in a week, her last words to me were: "Could you bring me news of what's happening in Indiana? It's a very important state, you know."

Her life has in no way been either ordinary or proportionate. She has been neither mother, wife, nor lover. Neither is she socially adept or culturally sophisticated. Her sense of historical balance is limited. She has no particular affection or understanding for the current generation of feminists; she does not see that the young radicals among them are exactly what she herself was sixty years ago. The gift of perspective is not hers.

What she has been, though, and what she is at this moment, is the embodiment of the revolutionary's narrow intensity and burning energy for "the cause." Her life has been a vessel into which the necessity of women's rights has been poured. She *is* the cause itself. And if Alice Paul had not lived, and been exactly what she is, we, the women of America, would not be today exactly what we are.

(June 1976)

The Price of Paying Your Own Way

For many years I feared the loss of poverty. I—like any good Marxist or capitalist—believed that to a large extent we are our circumstances, and I was not sure that I would ever have the strength of character to live outside mine. I looked around at everyone I knew who had entered the moneymaking middle class, and I grew very depressed. One and all, they seemed to become their possessions. Their will toward accumulation came to hold sway over social empathy and emotional adventurousness. Fuck it, I said to myself, I'll stay poor. In time, however, that semiwilled poverty became insupportable. I could no longer live in tenement apartments, unable to stay out late because I couldn't afford the taxi home, unable to eat out or buy books, unable to afford the simplest amenities of life. I decided I needed more money, I knew I could make more money, and I did make it.

Now, essentially, we're still talking about peanuts. Considering the sums of money made annually in this country I'd say, on a scale of one to ten, to begin with I made one and now I make four. But for me the Pandora's box was opened. I saw that I had the *option* to make money, and the existence of that option threw me (still throws me) terribly. I had something my parents had never had. Their lives had been fixed by the lack of options that is working-class life; and the social morality their poverty had imposed on them had been equally fixed. My life was now opened up by the presence of recognized options, and the social morality that had always been fixed for me was now something I would have to attend to myself.

My response to this new presence in my life was: I got crazy.
I took on certain obligations that posited the existence of money
in my life, and then fell into total disorder over the getting of
the money that was necessary to fulfill these obligations. For a
couple of years it was absolute madness Not only did I live
from hand to mouth, but there were times when three days
before the rent was due I had $75 in the bank and I couldn't
figure out how in hell that had happened. Money became a constant source of anxiety—as it had not been when I'd been poor
and lived a rigorously meager existence. I veered continuously
between wishing I were back in my tenement apartment and
wishing I had millions. One day I wanted puritanical socialism,
the next day I wanted to get to the top of the capitalist heap.

In the midst of all this, I became aware of an object in the
window of a certain shop that I passed daily in Greenwich Village.
The shop specialized in art deco, and this object was a lovely
painted-glass lamp of the thirties. The price tag on the lamp
was $300. Suddenly: I wanted that lamp. I began stopping every
day in front of the shop window, spending ten or fifteen minutes
staring at the lamp. After a while I began to scheme in my head
about how I could raise the money to get the lamp. One day I
said to myself: What the fuck are you doing? Even if you could
afford it, why the hell would you want to buy a $300 lamp?
You have never before in your life wanted such things. Why
now? What is going on here?

The craziness about money began to clear up a little bit after
that. Mainly, because I began to think about—instead of react
to—money, probably for the first time in my life. What did I
really want money for? What was I willing to do to get it? What
did I think it right to want and have, materially? What part of
my working life should be performed in order to get things?
Did I think it legitimate to have *anything* that caught my fancy
that I had the cash to put out for?

These were questions I'd never needed to ask myself; with
the ability to make money came a responsibility to discover and
face squarely who and what I really was in relation to money.
Only if I did that could I then begin to control the business
of money in my life.

I discovered that I really had no desire for luxurious living; I did not even want an abundance of "good" living. I didn't want cars, boats, houses, paintings, antiques, jewelry, furs, or vacations in first-class hotels on Caribbean islands. I didn't really want things. All I wanted was a good apartment in a decent building and money to eat out once or twice a week, to take taxis, to buy some books and a few clothes during the year, and to be able to spend a month in the country in summer. In short: I wished to live a decent, modest life free of poverty and economic anxiety.

Many women seem to agonize these days in an extraordinary way over whether or not they should make money, how much they should make, whether or not they should spend it, how and by whom the money should be managed, and so on. Women who have gained more than a degree of professional competence seem to fall into almost childish dishevelment over the question of their own money, their relation to their moneymaking capacity having become significantly complicated. Many of these women are of liberal and feminist persuasion, many of them have moved from working-class to middle-class status, many have been long married, and quite a few have been identified with the radical movement. Now, in the last five years or so, they have become moneymaking professionals, and the getting and spending of money seems to have thrown them terribly.

My friend Joyce is an example of what I'm talking about. Joyce and I have known each other for twenty years. We are the same age, we come out of the same working-class background, we were both educated at city colleges, and we have both struggled for years to attain professional status in our chosen work. The outlines of our lives, similar as they are, diverge, however, at one crucial point: Whereas I got twice married and divorced and am now childless and husbandless, Joyce got married and stayed married, and is now a wife of some fifteen years and the mother of three children.

Joyce, as it happens, is one of the most intelligent women I know. Her husband, David, a perfectly decent, competent man, is not nearly as intellectually gifted as Joyce. For many years, while David worked steadily and was a bulwark of emotional stability, Joyce stayed home, gave birth to and raised the children, and was a very nervous lady—strained, restless, sometimes verging on hysteria. So great in fact was Joyce's nervousness that her superior intelligence was forgotten: by both Joyce and David, as well as most of their friends and relatives. It was commonly assumed that Joyce was emotionally frail and that what made the marriage so beautiful, so tender, was the combination of Joyce's frailty and David's protectiveness.

Seven years ago Joyce entered law school. She went through the three-year course like lightning, graduated high in her class, and passed the bar exam first time out. Who could figure out what had happened? "All of a sudden": the cobwebs cleared out of her mind, the nervousness disappeared; she worked, she studied, she did brilliantly. And her marriage very nearly fell apart.

When Joyce entered law school, David was amazed and wonderfully encouraging—rather like a doctor with a patient: "You can do it, I know you can do it, do it for me." Then it became apparent that he did not really believe she could do it, that their entire marriage was predicated on the fantasy—shared by both and exploited by both—that she could not do it, that smart as she was she didn't have the strength of character or emotions required to *be* in the world. Now, when she was proving she did have it, David revealed—helplessly, inadvertently—that he had always believed her hopelessly weak. And Joyce—although she had secretly known of and exploited this belief all these years she was being "taken care of"—now smoldered with resentment at David. The tension in their house became unbearable, exploding four nights out of the week into bitter quarrels. Only a funny thing happened when they quarreled now: David sat staring at the kitchen table while Joyce slammed out of the house.

They survived this. They both loved their children very much, and their home, and they wanted to stay married. So they "worked" at it, and they survived. In certain ways they even flourished. Joyce got a fine job in a good law firm, within a short time was doing very well, both loving her work and bringing home a great deal of money. In fact, very quickly she was bringing more money in than David, whose job teaching history at a community college had always gained him only a modest income. They moved to a spacious apartment in a better section of the city, bought beautiful furniture, and sent their children to private schools and expensive camps.

In other ways Joyce seemed to flourish also. Her politics had always been very liberal, on occasion radical. The work she was doing allowed her to take many civil rights cases as well as perform many legal services for the neighborhood-community in whch she and David were now living. Her parents, who had worked hard all their lives, were proud of her: here she was doing so well, and she had not forgotten where she came from.

One evening about six months ago Joyce and I had dinner alone in her apartment. David was away at an academic conference, and the children were spending the night in Brooklyn with her parents. We talked about many things, and then at one point our conversation required checking a certain reference. Joyce said she had the book that would clear up the point, and led the way down the hall to her bedroom, where her desk and bookshelves were gathered. (David used the spare bedroom as a study.) As Joyce rummaged around the bookshelves looking for the book we needed, I glanced at her desk. To my surprise, it was an unholy mess—papers, books, pen, pencils, spread over its surface in hopeless disarray. An application form of some sort was tossed on top of the whole pile, and surrounding it were many sheets of yellow legal-size paper covered with columns of figures, scratched-out, rewritten, scratched out again, altogether unintelligible.

"Jesus!" I said. "How the hell do you work here? How do you find anything?"

Joyce turned from the books, followed my glance and blushed. "That's a grant application I'm trying to fill out. It requires my listing all the sources of my income, and I'm going crazy trying to do it."

"Why?" I asked innocently.

"Well," she said, her blush deepening, "I don't know what my income is."

Joyce sank into a chair beside the desk, looking suddenly, strangely distracted. For a moment she seemed to have difficulty speaking. Then she blurted out, "That's exactly what I mean. I don't know. I've never known. I don't really know how much I bring in. I just bring home my paycheck, sign it, and turn it over to David. And any other monies I get, I do the same with. Every week I draw what I need to get through the week . . . and, well, David takes care of all the rest."

"David takes care of all the rest?" I repeated idiotically.

Joyce nodded. I turned back toward the desk. Beneath one particularly messy pile of papers I spotted a rectangular leather-bound clip of paper. I picked it up. It looked like a rat had been chewing on it.

"What's this?" I asked in amazement.

"That's my checkbook," Joyce said, her face now beet-red.

"I don't get it," I said. "What goes with you and your money?"

"I don't know," she said. "I just can't deal with it."

"Deal with what?"

"Making money!"

I stared at her. I was not surprised by the words Joyce was speaking (how could I be?), but somehow I was surprised that it was she speaking them.

"I have never, never felt at ease with making money," Joyce said. I looked around the room. The implication of my gaze was obvious: We both knew that it was mainly her money that kept this establishment afloat. "Yes, yes," she said, "I know, when I think about it, that it's mainly my money that provides us with the life we lead, and we *do* lead it. And yet, it seems, somehow, impossible for me to take direct responsibility for it. I feel guilty for wanting money, guilty for making it, guilty toward David, guilty toward my parents, guilty toward other women, guilty toward every single person in this lousy exploitative society who *can't* make money."

It had not occurred to Joyce that she'd feel less guilty if she cleared up that desk, had a separate checking account, consciously shared in controlling the expenditures of the house, and made some rigorous decisions about the kind of material life she and her family were going to lead.

Joyce's guilt over making money is shared, I believe, by every morally sensitive man and woman in the world. Her ostrich-like response to that guilt is more common to women than to men. The guilt over making money is the guilt of having power and privilege in a world where so many are without either. The ostrich-like response is the behavior of those who have always associated themselves with the powerless and *now,* suddenly, without warning or preparation, find themselves in the other camp. The fear, anxiety, and denial attendant upon such a change is—how could it be otherwise—enormous. The unspoken (unexamined) question behind the ostrich-like position is: Will I turn out to be like all the rest? As long as I had no power I could smugly rail against the grasping character and low morals of those who did have it. Now that I am beginning to have some too, will I find I am as selfish and shallow as they are? Having lived so long as one of the oppressed, will I now so easily become one of the oppressors? Will I no longer make common cause with all those with whom I have shared a lifetime of real and imagined experience? Simply give up my place in the ranks of the victims, and move easily into the columns of the victimizers?

These questions are real, not imaginary, and they speak with urgency to some of the deepest notions of power and powerlessness that feminism has been steadily attempting to clarify. They reveal the confusion and ignorance with which we have all approached the complex Pandora's box so casually labeled "liberation." They demand that we think through, and act upon, distinctions it will take most of us a lifetime simply to define. They pose the necessity of understanding—and making real—the difference between power that is sought for the sake of independence and power that is used for the sake of social exploitation and personal betrayal. They force us to confront the sharpest definitions of self-control in contradistinction to the murk and panic of circumstantial control.

Joyce's irrational refusal to take full responsibility for the money she makes is a study in "willed" emotional ignorance, an ignorance with far-reaching consequences. To begin with, it speaks to the precariousness of her marriage. Having yelled, "Let me do it myself!," she now finds herself halfway out on the tightrope of independence, suddenly paralyzed with fear, pleading, "Put back the net! Put back the net!" David, out of his own complex needs, rushes to do so. In fact, they both know she doesn't need the net, and she will get to the end of the tightrope one way or another, but it is a fiction useful to them both, in their still-threatened marriage, that she does need it. Hence, she who can think so supremely well is unable to "think" about the money, and David "takes care of all the rest." They both fear the consequences of her independence; they do not really trust themselves to remain together once it is firmly established that she can bloody well stand on her own two feet. Her inability to deal with her own money is an instrument of self-deception, a convenient infantilism shared by two people who are not certain that in adult freedom they would freely choose to go on living together.

Secondly, Joyce fears that in facing the fact that she does earn good money she is cutting herself off from that which she has previously identified herself with: her working-class family, the helplessness of other women, the poor and deprived of the earth. If she goes on chewing up the checkbook and never knowing how much money there is in the bank, in some way she remains a disheveled, victim-identified person, and she need not face what in her depths constitutes a betrayal.

Thirdly, Joyce fears her own incipient greed. The accumulation of material goodness in her life has been steady. Her bourgeois appetites, unexamined, have gone unchecked. She has not even faced the fact yet that as her income has grown so has her taste for middle-class comforts. If she clears up the desk, takes a long, hard look at what has come in, and what has gone out, she will be forced to see that as the years have gone on she has wanted—and accumulated—*more*.

In short: Joyce without money was out of control, Joyce with money is out of control. Liberation, it seems, is more complicated than the mere absence or presence of money in a woman's life, and economic independence turns on the capacity to make conscious, controlled decisions about money as well as the capacity simply to make the money. Without that consciousness Joyce will be pulled about by the question of money as long as she lives, never free of it, never in control of it, and, I think, probably falling into the kind of self-hating helplessness that *really* corrupts.

What money-consciousness means for a middle-class professional woman with a social conscience is a question each woman must ask and answer for herself. There are no prescriptions, no charts and tables, no systematic measurements that will tell women how much money to make, how much to spend, and what attitudes to assume toward money. There is nothing but the pursuit of that consciousness in the belief that self-understanding will produce the self-imposed need to set natural, moral limits on money in one's life.

To say this in a world dominated by the obscenities of the capitalist system may seem reckless and self-absorbed, but I say it for the following reasons: What Marxists share with capitalists is a profound belief that we are all defined, utterly and entirely, by our functional circumstances in The System. And, indeed, no one could deny the truth of this insight; certainly, I would never deny it. Nevertheless, for me, the beauty of feminism is that it is a social and political movement that has redefined the power and obligation of the self: self-possession and self-regulation as a tool for social reform.

What would I have done if I'd discovered that I *really* lusted after that lamp and everything that went with it? Well, I think— I hope—I would have concluded that it is better to control rather than gratify that lust. For, in the final analysis, I do not think it legitimate to live a materially opulent middle-class life.

What it comes to is this: I do not wish to make $50,000 a year. Nor, for that matter, do I wish anyone else to make it. There is no way—none—for anyone in this society to make a great deal of money without exploiting other people. If I had my way, capitalism and the consumer society would end tomorrow; it produces nothing but greed and injustice. I would like to see a world in which material tastes and needs are kept to a minimum, and if we must continue to destroy and humiliate each other, let the metaphor for human aggression become something other than money, filthy money.

The idea that money brings power and independence is an

illusion. What money usually brings is the need for more money—and there is a shabby and pathetic *powerlessness* that comes with that need. The inability to risk new lives, new work, new styles of thought and experience, is more often than not tied to the bourgeois fear of reducing one's material standard of living. That is, indeed, to be owned by possessions, to be governed by a sense of property rather than by a sense of self, to forfeit human values in a large and frightening way. Where lies the "power" in that? Where lies the "independence" in such an ugly dependence?

On the other hand, I never again wish to be economically dependent or out of control. As a woman—as a feminist—I feel it incumbent on myself to take full and permanent responsibility for the care and feeding of myself; to make wise, controlled decisions about my money needs and face whatever realities are entailed in fulfilling those needs. The trick is to identify and control the need rather than be unaware of and controlled by the need.

So easy to speak those words! "Make wise, controlled decisions. . . ." Indeed! Like every other step on the road to liberation it is a long, wearying, sideways process. If I manage better than I once did—and I do—it's only fair to note that, during one particularly distracted week (as a matter of fact, the week when I was writing this piece), I made a $100 subtraction error in my checkbook, received news of a bad credit rating, and wrote a check on a check that had not yet cleared.

(July 1976)

Why Do These Men
Hate Women?

Last month Grove Press published a book called *Genius and Lust: A Journey Through the Major Writings of Henry Miller*, by Norman Mailer. The book was reviewed widely, with varying amounts of attention given to a fresh appraisal of Henry Miller. Richard Gilman's review in the *Village Voice* paid more attention to the relationship between Miller's writings and Norman Mailer's running commentary, recognizing accurately that the relationship between the two was what, in fact, the book was all about. The underlying tone of Gilman's review was: "As an *au courant* person, I know this book will drive the feminists up the wall but, gee, fellas, it's really pretty terrific stuff, anyway." That tone, together with the publication of the book, speaks to an attitude that, in 1976, remains essentially unchanged, insisting that certain truths about life and art are timeless; that, misogyny notwithstanding, the work of both these men remains hungry and alive, telling us something urgent about what it is to be human.

I find that insistence remarkable. I find it remarkable because it simply is not true. Certainly, in the case of Norman Mailer it is not true; nor is it true in the case of those American writers who most resemble Mailer in that misogyny is at the heart of their work. Not true at all. On the contrary: what *is* true is that misogyny is the characteristic mark of the arrested nature of their work, the regressiveness at the center of their books.

As for Henry Miller, what can one say? Miller has often been (and is again in these reviews) compared with Louis-Ferdinand Céline, the great French nihilist writing at the same time as

Miller—obsessing about Jews while Miller obsessed about women—and producing the same kind of mad, blazing, hate-filled beauty on the page. I used to think: I must be more of a woman than a Jew because I can read Céline but I can't read Miller. But the fact is that Céline is by far the greater of the two writers. In a curious way his larger talent turns on the all-inclusiveness of his nihilism. Céline's self-hatred is as great as his hatred of others; his own anguish is felt, his own mad pain descends into a swamp of loathing that hits and mingles with the general currents of self-hatred that were about to engulf Europe in the thirties, and it transforms his work into radiant poison.

With Miller it is an altogether other matter. In Miller, one feels a tone of separating self-regard at work: "You geeks, you cunts, you freaks and whores, I may look like all the rest of you but I'm not! I'm different, better, more sensitive. My lust is of a higher order. Its sheer giganticism sets me apart."

This difference between Céline and Miller is perhaps the difference between Europe and America; Céline knows better; *everyone* is down there in the pits. Miller really thinks he takes Bunyanesque steps across the world of human vermin. This belief is at the heart of his work; it is responsible for both his power and his severe limitations. It is also the essence of the adolescent psyche that has dominated the work of many American writers, Miller being only one of the most prominent. And there is, undeniably, something powerful and admirable in this spitting, hissing, yowling insistence, this American self-regard that will be goddamned fucked if it will simply take its properly world-weary place in the universe. Miller stands up there in Rabelaisian sprawl and yells into the black surround: "Goddamn you, world, I *exist!*" When it works, this is infantilism transformed, invested with mythic properties. But it often doesn't work and, when it doesn't, it is merely infantilism.

The natural state of the infantile psyche is one of self-absorption. In this state, other people are only projected images of the self's own need, its own fantasies, its own blood-congested urgencies. Above all, other people are projected images of its own fears: dreadful fears of mortality. These fears must, at all costs, be conquered, otherwise life is unlivable. It is a function of emotional infantilism that it imagines the way to conquer fear is to conquer the people who embody it.

In Henry Miller, those who must be conquered are, of course, women. And the lengths to which Miller goes to conquer these projected images of fear, hunger, and need know no bounds. The degradation in which he steeps himself and the unreality of his women are just short of insane.

Yet Miller's work carries with it the insistent power of this central life fever truly felt, truly expressed. This because Miller's work is profoundly of its time: a time when this lusting, enraged, adolescent ego hit a receptive nerve in American life and history. The time and the work found deep reverberations in each other. Each knew exactly as much about itself as the other did: no more, no less.

What Miller and the thirties knew about themselves and each other is no longer what writers and the seventies know. Therefore, those writers who continue to echo the misogyny of Henry Miller as though it contained a metaphysical knowledge of the self are arrested in their development, wildly off the map of cultural time, living inside a sensibility that is no longer instinct with the subterranean truths of world and being as most of us are experiencing them. These writers are isolated from our life, and they do not know it.

Norman Mailer is, of course, the most glaring example of such a writer. I have grown up with Norman Mailer's misogyny, and it did not always seem so dismaying to me as it does now. But it *was* not always so dismaying. Take a story like "The Time of Her Time"—as woman-hating a tale as anyone could wish for. Yet, most of us read it with as much amazement and complicitous laughter as outrage. This because Mailer's own sweating, lunging, disheveled, despairing sexual fantasies were so nakedly at work that he drew you into his anguish, made his dilemma one of general human appeal: you shared the condition; you were all helpless, ridiculous human beings together.

Two things have happened since "The Time of Her Time." One, my ability to "identify" with the Mailer protagonist has altered forever; I can no longer make common cause with the humanness of the men in Mailer's woman-objectifying melodramas. Two, Mailer has remained fixed in his literary mode of sexual antagonism which, even as the life within it evaporates decade by decade, he coldly, somewhat hysterically insists on raising to the level of religious ceremony.

Mailer has never understood that stories like "The Time of Her Time" can *only* be a function of emotional adolescence. He figured it worked for a lifetime for Miller and Hemingway, why not for him? He has not seen, and to this day does not see, that it worked for those two supreme American swaggerers only as long as the culture as a whole also subscribed to the same adolescent truths about men and women and experienced these truths as a metaphor for life. When the culture no longer did, and Miller and Hemingway themselves could not grow and mature, their writing lives were over, and they both declined into self-parody.

For Mailer, unlike Miller and Hemingway, it was to some extent over almost before it began. He did not grasp the importance of the thirty years' lapse between his time and theirs, and he descended into self-parody much earlier than either of the other two. That is why he never wrote the "great" book expected of him and, in all probability, never will. By the time he was writing *An American Dream,* he was lost to a psychological sense of things, which, more often than not, was turned in upon itself, not reflecting the truth of our lives at all, speaking to private wishes, private fears. This deluded sense of things has always, without exception, turned on the elaborate structure of his misogyny. It is in his misogyny that Mailer is most regressive, most at a distance from the creation of live literature.

Mailer's misogyny is trapped inside a mythic terminology that is presented as though it were cosmic truth. The essence of this mythology may be found in the following sentence from *The Prisoner of Sex:*

So do men look to destroy every quality in a woman which will give her the powers of a male, for she is in their eyes already armed with the power that she brought them forth, and that is a power beyond measure—the earliest etchings of memory go back to that woman between whose legs they were conceived, nurtured, and near-strangled in the hours of birth.

That, says Mailer in all of his books, is at the heart of what passes between human beings who are men and women. The human being who is a man can encounter the human being who is a woman in one way only: he must mount her, fuck her, suck her, penetrate and impale her, conquer and reduce her, for she is not simply another human being like himself but rather the embodiment of the mysterious heart—the universal elemental source—and it is only through that raging lust, in that Cosmic Fuck, that he can hope to close with the Mysteries of the Inner Space, thus reducing her powers and increasing his own. *That,* says Mailer, is the truth about men and women, and all the rest is totalitarian bullshit. And don't you ever forget it, you Shock Troops of the Liberation, you pathetic dumb-cunt broads (uh, excuse me, you Great Female Power of the Universe).

It is now abundantly clear that Mailer will probably go on speaking this sorrowful male-female nonsense, with no more wisdom than he had twenty-five years ago, until he is in his doddering seventies. A number of the passages in Mailer's commentary in *Genius and Lust* were taken word for word from *The Prisoner of Sex,* an essay Mailer wrote in 1971. Mailer reproduces those sentences five years later without the slightest trace of irony or self-consciousness, as though the sentiments behind them are exactly as true for him today as they were then. Here are some samples:

Miller captured something in the sexuality of men as it had never been seen before, precisely that it was man's sense of awe before woman, his dread of her position one step closer to eternity (for in that step were her powers) which made men detest women, revile them, humiliate them, defecate symbolically upon them, do everything to reduce them so that one might dare to enter them and take pleasure of them.

And, conversely, Miller

screams his barbaric yawp of utter adoration for the power and the glory and the grandeur of the female in the universe, and it is his genius to show that this power is ready to survive any context or abuse.

What is one to do with such writing? Who does Mailer imagine such language speaks to? Is it possible he thinks women will recognize any element of themselves—real or imagined—in these ludicrous and dehumanizing descriptions? And, I wonder, how many men are there left who recognize *them*selves in these descriptions? Is the sexual obsession that passes here for myth really central to our lives?

I, for one, say no. It seems to me that the writers with the least to say today are obsessed with a myth of male-female sexuality that daily presents itself as an ever more foolish, ever more falsifying construct. Worse: this myth now sounds downright fascistic. Racists, from the Ku Klux Klan to Hitler, used the same kind of mythifying rhetoric in order that they might oppress and destroy blacks and Jews: If women are not simply other human beings, if they are indeed possessed of frightening powers, then one stands in awe of them in order that one might strike them down. It is a classic mechanism of oppression, one that is *always* offered as an insight into cosmic truth.

Not only is the truth of our lives not to be found in this construct, but, more and more, there is less and less art to be found in it. Mailer himself says in his Miller commentary that what "separates the artist from everyone else who works at being one . . . is that the artist has risen precisely from therapy to art . . . the artist's ultimate interest is to put something together which is independent of the ego." Indeed. Mailer knows whereof he speaks. The struggle between therapy and art is spread generously across the pages of his work; it is a struggle he loses more often than he wins.

Within this context, *The Prisoner of Sex* is an important piece of work, a sad piece of work. The essay is divided into two parts: one, an enraged denunciation of the women's movement into which is woven Mailer's cosmic truth about men and women; two, a critical defense of the work of Henry Miller and D. H. Lawrence against what Mailer takes to be Kate Millett's distorting polemic in *Sexual Politics*.

The defense of Miller and Lawrence is eloquent: persuasively reasoned, beautifully written, the work of a fine truth-speaking mind. Especially in the case of Lawrence. Mailer makes live again Lawrence's great power: that devotion in him to the idea of salvation through the sexual tenderness between men and women that amounted to emotional genius. Never mind, says

Mailer, Lawrence's purple prose, the fascism of his "blood-consciousness," the mean fears of his theories of woman's submission and man's domination—look only to the beauty of his sense of men and women caught together in the richness and terror of being. If you lose that, if you strip that down, if you distort that for the sake of your politics, you lose the meaning of literature, you impoverish life immeasurably. In the writing of these passages Mailer speaks nobly.

In the denunciatory part of the essay he is speaking in his own voice, out of his own art, that art he thinks puts him squarely in the tradition of these writers he is defending. The failure is dismaying. Making full use of that ravening, glutted language that has become his hallmark, abusing and hating women at top speed, the work disintegrates entirely. There is no substance here; there is no wisdom; only a mechanical, driven rhetoric: the rhetoric of therapy rather than the language of art.

There are at least two other widely known writers in this country whose work is as stultified as Mailer's and whose chief symptom of stultification is woman hating: Philip Roth and Saul Bellow. Each of these writers is a man of great talent and intelligence; each of them also increasingly displays the kind of self-absorption that results in emotional stupidity. In the matter of creating art the presence of the last renders the first two as nothing.

Philip Roth began his writing career sixteen years ago with the publication of a collection of stories called *Goodbye, Columbus.* The stories were brilliant and deeply moving. They were filled with character, wisdom, and a luminous sense of the quest for a moral, feeling life. They were everything Tolstoy said a book should be. They made you "weep and laugh and love life more because of it."

Roth never again achieved the control over his work that those stories reflected. What has characterized his work since that time is panic. Sometimes this panic is wildly funny, sometimes viciously bitter, but always it prevents vision, control, transcendence. It is the panic of immature vanity: a writer's preoccupation with the question of self-worth becoming greater than his preoccupation with the world as it enters into him. This confusion, in art, is fatal and, indeed, Roth's books have suffered mightily for it. More and more, it has become apparent that Roth is writing, helplessly, about himself. Not drawing upon the materials of his life to create a fictional world: just talking about himself.

And what is the chief element of this obsessive, eaten-up-alive exercise in self-absorption? The hatred of women, nakedly, more desperately in possession of the writers. With each book one sees the horror of a writer who has failed to mature personally, has contrived unsuccessfully to make of that failure a modern myth, and recedes yearly into literary self-delusion. *Portnoy's Complaint* was startling, but *My Life as a Man* was frightening.

Portnoy's Complaint in Roth's career was the equivalent of "The Time of Her Time" in Mailer's. It was a work so full of wonderful human dishevelment, a work so clearly *about* panic rather than driven by it, that we could not but laugh and anguish together with the dubious Portnoy. The hateful caricatures of women in it were clearly a function of the neurosis of the character and, as such, engaged us, drew us in, demanded and gained our reluctant attention.

With *Portnoy* Roth approached the edge of genuine insight. With *My Life as a Man* he withdrew from that edge, back into emotional darkness. Here there is no distance between character and author. Here the hatred of women is not a function of character illumination but a statement of the author's swamped being. In *Portnoy* the mother and the Monkey are monstrous because Alex Portney experiences them as monstrous; in *My Life as a Man* the wife is monstrous because Roth is saying women are monstrous. When the wife is being beaten to death and she surrenders to the ecstasy of what is happening to her, losing control of language as though of her bladder, screaming, "Die me, die me!" Roth is clearly saying this repellent creature—and all those who resemble her—*deserves* to die.

And it is here—from this crucial lack of sympathy, this dehumanizing vileness—that the failure of this book flows. The unacknowledged misogyny of *My Life as a Man* leaks like a slow, inky poison all over its pages, obscuring artistic coherence, disintegrating moral intelligence, making of its true subject something so private and ugly as to be of virtually no use to those men and women who read books in order to love life more.

In his sixtieth year and on the eve of winning the Nobel Prize Saul Bellow wrote the most regressive novel of his distinguished career: *Humboldt's Gift*. Again, regression turned on misogyny. Again, regression could be traced back to an earlier novel in which misogyny was a function of character that had now, in the later novel, become a symptom of the author's self-absorption. The protagonist of *Humboldt* is the protagonist of *Herzog* ten years later. In the earlier novel, the distance between the author and his character created an energizing force that made you run madly with Moses Herzog, searching frantically for his life in the streets of New York, in the beds of women, in the writing of letters to the living and the dead. The women were dreadful caricatures but, still: they served felt life.

Humboldt's Gift, a sprawling, feverish work filled with the jet stream of Bellow's language brilliance, is purportedly about the inability to live a life of significance in contemporary America. For me, this was a supremely unrealized novel and, again, a work soaked through with the sef-absorption of the writer, not at all something put together independent of the ego. The protagonist, Charlie Citrine, is a thinly disguised Saul Bellow around whom is gathered an enormous cast of characters. None of them has independent life, each one is a projection of the fears, needs, and disappointments of a self-preoccupied writer claiming, unsuccessfully, that what is true for him is true.

Nowhere in this novel does the bilious quality of projected life—as opposed to felt life—come through more clearly than in the creation of the women. To begin with, the women are uniformly referred to as cunts, broads, chicks, and bimbos. Then, they are all either beautiful or "gorgeous." Then, they are all either thin, cold, intelligent, and castrating (these are always the wife) or they are dark, sensual, and mindless (these are the mistress). These characters are like papier-mâché grotesqueries; figures with little magnets affixed to the backs of them triggering fantasies of hunger and deprivation. The wife figure flashes: Touch me. I will evoke for you everything in life that is perpetually doing you in. The mistress figure flashes: Touch *me*. I will evoke for you everything in life that is perpetually holding out on you.

What we have in the work of these writers is not a vital relation to the forces of our moment but rather an infantile preoccupation with themselves. We have here what is fatal in writers: men who hate and fear the moment in which they are living, men who are in flight from their times, at a profound remove from the inner experience of their time and place, filled with a conservative longing for an inner truth that is no longer *the* truth.

The writer's sensibility is the heightened sensibility, and in it, indeed, lies the world discovered. But the difference between self-inspection and self-absorption is the difference between art and therapy. For me, much of the current work of Mailer, Roth, and Bellow is merely therapy, and at that, the worst, the most childish kind of therapy: not the kind that gets to the bottom of things but rather the kind that hardens its defenses, ritualizes human sacrifice, makes do with a primitive kind of bargaining about who's human and who's not. In the misogyny of these writers lies the deluded ancient dream of frightened men: if she is made less human, I will be made more human.

No great writer succumbs to these fears. No great writer sacrifices the humanity of half the world in order that the half identified with his protagonist may gain more life. One thinks of the women of Hardy, Stendhal, Lawrence, and one wants to weep with shame over the shabbiness and emotional cowardice of the best of American male writers. The Europeans struggled brilliantly to face down the fears of their age, the Americans have not. The Europeans identified need, the Americans wallow in it. Out of the struggle of the Europeans came wisdom and a true record of the life they were living through. Out of the fears of the Americans come lots of smarts but not much wisdom and, increasingly, a failure of the work to mature, to say something valuable to us about our world.

In short: When I read Hardy, Lawrence, or Stendhal, their words compel me because they are filled with live men *and* women, rich with dimension and autonomous being. When I read Mailer, Roth, and the later Bellow, not much lives except the self-absorption of an arrested psyche, the sullen vanities of disappointed men, the forfeited talents of writers who, incapable of struggling through into emotional maturity, have lost the ability to create a compelling fictive universe.

The inability of the writer to mature personally is more crucial in the second half of the twentieth century than it has been at any other time in modern history. Awareness of the self is more acutely at the heart of things than it has ever been before. On the foundation of self-awareness alone rest all our hopes for a new politics, a new society, a revitalized life. If we do not genuinely know ourselves, the void will now, at last, surely rise up to meet us.

(December 1976)

Agnes Smedley Reclaimed

One night in December 150 people gathered together in the upstairs dining room of a Chinese restaurant on Mott Street. They were there to consume a banquet meal, contribute to a worthy cause, and pay honor to the publication of a book with a very special history. The cause was the survival of the Feminist Press, the book was Agnes Smedley's *Portraits of Chinese Women in Revolution*. The people in the room were feminists, partisans of feminists, radicals old and new, people who had known Agnes Smedley in China and in the last years of her life in the United States, and a husband-wife pair of historians who wrote the introduction to *Portraits of Chinese Women* and are now writing Smedley's biography. The evening was an event in the sense that it embodied the dynamic relation between feminism and radicalism that has begun to seem as natural in the past decade as it often did in other, more remote times of political activism. That the Feminist Press should have resurrected the work of Agnes Smedley, making it available to a generation of readers who would otherwise never have known of its existence, seemed to me both moving and significant.

Agnes Smedley was born in 1892 in rural Missouri and died in 1950, a world-famous independent American radical whose name was linked with the 1920s Indian movement for independence and the Chinese Communist revolution. Raised in towns and villages all over the West, Smedley came out of the harsh primitivism of Western frontier life: the life of day laborers and itinerant workers, of mining camps, lumber mills, and river bums;

a life of raw poverty and isolation, of drinking, violence, and brutal appetites brutally satisfied. In short, the life of the nomadic, declassed American frontierspeople whose sweated labor built the railroads and highways of this country, settled its lands, mined its minerals, turned its trees into lumber, its raw materials into textiles.

Out of such discouraging circumstances, through an amazing force of will, brains, and hungriness of spirit, Agnes Smedley made herself into an extraordinary human being. She managed to break loose from the life into which she had been born, get herself somewhat educated, become a socialist and then a journalist. In her brief student days in the West she met Lala Rajpat Rai, a leading Indian revolutionary who urged into coherence her own latent radicalism. The cause of Indian independence became the cause of all the oppressed people whose histories she carried within her, and she gave herself to it from 1917 to 1928, first in New York, then in Germany (throughout the twenties Berlin was the center for Indian revolutionaries in exile).

In 1928—after much personal and political tumult—she fell out with the movement, suffered a nervous breakdown, and broke with the Indians. In 1929 she went to China, where she felt herself instantly—and for the rest of her life—at one with the land, its history, and its people. China, the Communists, and the spectacle of this mighty peasant country moving toward revolution stirred her more deeply than any other political experience ever had. (Just before she died in England she said, "As my heart and spirit have found no rest in any other land on earth except China, I wish my ashes to lie with the Chinese revolutionary dead." And they do. Her stone in the Peking cemetery reads, "Agnes Smedley, Friend of China.")

Smedley became one of the small but intensely devoted band of American partisans living and working in China during the twenties, thirties, and forties. She felt it her personal mission to make understandable to the West what was happening there. For more than ten years she remained in China, reporting continually for German and American newspapers and magazines. She was the only American who marched with the Red Army; she lived in the Communist capital of Yenan, knew Chou En-lai,

Mao Tse-tung, and almost every other well-known Chinese and Western person then in China, as well as scores of ordinary Chinese men and women.

In 1941 she returned to the United States in an attempt to put her life in order. Throughout the mid-1940s she lived in Yaddo, the writers' colony. In the late 1940s she came under attack in America as a "Red spy." The Communist Party, which had always regarded her as a maverick, did not come to her aid. Smedley's last years were filled with chaos, harassment, and political isolation. In 1950, in England on her way back to China, she died after undergoing an operation for stomach ulcers. Her books were removed from the library shelves of America, and her life and her work disappeared into historical oblivion.

Agnes Smedley left behind an autobiographical novel and seven books on India and China. All these books have been out of print for more than thirty years. The Feminist Press has returned Smedley to us by first reprinting her novel *Daughter of Earth* (in 1973), and now this collection of pieces, *Portraits of Chinese Women,* drawn from her many books on China.

Daughter of Earth is one of the most remarkable American autobiographies ever written. When it was first published in 1929 the critic in *New Republic* said, "It is a record of experience so authentic, so intense, that it burns itself into the mind of the reader, leaving him with a sense of wonder at the enduring quality of the human fabric, and with a deep resentment at human cruelty and injustice." When it was republished in 1973 another critic said, "It has a terrible beauty, and the women who discover and experience *Daughter of Earth* always discuss it as comrades who have traveled somewhere together." The book is now in its fifth printing. Since 1973 it has sold over 30,000 copies— without being widely reviewed—and it continues to sell on an average of 700 copies a month.

Thinly disguised as a novel, *Daughter of Earth* tells the story of Smedley's life, from birth to the moment she left Germany for China. The book is written with the same kind of crude, untutored power with which Jack London wrote. A tale of American disinheritance told from the inside out, it is essentially about

Smedley's struggle to come to spiritual consciousness in a world of unimaginable cruelty and deprivation.

Her parents, both gay and handsome when young, descended very quickly into the brutality to which their rootlessness, poverty, and illiteracy doomed them. The father drank, fought, told tall tales, and repeatedly abandoned his family in the classic Western wanderer's search for the main chance. The mother took in laundry, bore children endlessly, was old at twenty-five and dead before she was forty. The children grew up like wary animals, looking only to survive the violence and starvation— both spiritual and physical—that was their legacy.

An entire society is limned in the pages of this book: that society of sub-working-class America which bears the closest resemblance to the peasants of Asia and Europe. What makes the American difference is what Smedley herself embodies: the outraged democratic sense of self pushing up out of nowhere to demand its own life; the sense of right rather than of obligation which separates declassed Americans from peasant Europeans.

Because Smedley is a woman, that sense of right burns with white heat in the pages of *Daughter of Earth*. Above them all stood the iron law of their disfranchisement, but above the women stood the men, and that extra bitterness made Smedley see their condition with a hard, unyielding clarity that lasted all her life. Her feminist sense of things from earliest childhood is breathtaking in its directness.

One day her mother stood exhausted at the laundry tubs. Her father appeared in the doorway drunk and angry, a horse-whip in his hands. The mother looked up wearily and said to the daughter, "He's gonna hit me. If he hits me with that whip, I know I'll just drop down dead." The child hurled herself on the drunken man, clawing and scratching. But even as she did so she was thinking, "He's got the right to do this because she's his wife. . . . She's his *wife.*"

The idea that love and marriage for a woman was pure slavery haunted Smedley. It threw her own passionate nature into life-long conflict, ruined her early marriage to a decent man who loved her, and developed in her a protective abrasiveness that made her seem, in her own words, "a hard, thankless, graceless

girl." It was the price she paid for the hard-won independence
she prized above all else; it made her in her time a freak, an
"unnatural" woman to many who knew her, including the Indian
and Chinese revolutionaries among whom she lived and worked.

The power of *Daughter of Earth* lies in the erotic heat that
informs every page of the book, erotic in the original Greek
sense of life force. That vital energy burned hotly in Smedley;
it swept like a searchlight across the landscape of her experience,
and aroused her curiosity and sympathy for all it illuminated.

This same intensity informs *Portraits of Chinese Women in Revolution.* The language is spare, even homely, but the *tone* of the
language is so striking that it pulls us into the life and times
of its subjects as no other kind of writing can. And it makes
China and the meaning of the Communist revolutiion come alive
for a Westerner with an immediacy that is startling.

The pieces in *Portraits* were all written in the 1930s; most of
them appeared originally as newspaper and magazine articles.
They were written by a working journalist who wanted passionately to make her fellow Westerners "see" the harsh meaning
of Chinese lives and the promise the revolution held out for
those lives. What the pieces as a whole accomplish is exactly
that: through these women's lives we see vividly the flux and
turmoil, the despair and exultation of China. Above all, what
Smedley has captured brilliantly—and this is most important—
are the forces of the old and the new China struggling up in a
different configuration in each person she describes. It is the
thing that makes one understand the sometimes fluid, sometimes
lurching, slowly accumulating way in which a society is changed.
And there is particular power in seeing this process take place
through the lives of the women.

In the 1930s, every Chinese woman Agnes Smedley knew had
had her feet bound since childhood, and had been sold by her
family into either prostitution or marriage. Repeatedly Smedley
describes the feet and the sexual condition of the women.
Women her own age with feet three inches long, walking on
toes curled under them like hard little stones. Women who had
had mothers brave enough to unbind their feet at the age of
ten (if the father fortuitously died), as opposed to women whose

feet were unbound at thirty. What it meant for a Chinese woman to escape from her father or husband, cut her hair, take the bandages off her feet, and hobble along to join the Communists!

Beginning with such details, Smedley's portraits expand to sketch Chinese society as a whole, and before she is done the sheer enormity of that society is felt so keenly, and the massive undertaking of the Communist revolution is so sobering, one wonders how on earth any Westerner, at this moment in history, dares sit in judgment on the Chinese revolution.

For me, personally, it is a matter of great pride that Agnes Smedley's books are now being made available to new generations of American readers by the Feminist Press. One of the very best things to emerge from the women's liberation movement is the proliferation of feminist publishers. Distinguished among them is the Press. Founded in 1970 by a group of dedicated feminists, and located on the campus of SUNY Old Westbury, the Feminist Press is a nonprofit, tax-exempt educational and publishing corporation that has, by dint of ardent labor and slowly acquired expertise, made itself into a wholly admirable enterprise. The staff consists of eleven salaried individuals aided by one or two work-study students and innumerable volunteers who, in return for their unpaid labor, are taught a variety of publishing skills.

The Press publishes books in three areas: feminist biographies, reprints of lost or forgotten works by women writers, and non-sexist children's books. It is also involved in myriad educational projects aimed at helping elementary, high school, and college teachers change school curriculums, and at educating the mass of our society in general to the condition of women in America. Toward this end, the Press prints and distributes educational materials, publications widely used in women's-studies programs, and a large variety of books and pamphlets aimed at students and faculty alike at every educational level. It also keeps the files of the Clearinghouse of Women's Studies, a repository of information about women's-studies courses throughout the country.

The Press, supported by educational grants, struggles each year for its financial life. With all that, it produces paperback books that are physically beautiful and, increasingly, intellectually excellent. If it had done nothing more this year than publish Bell Chevigny's *The Woman and the Myth: Margaret Fuller's Life and Writings,* the Press would have more than justified its existence.

What has always seemed especially valuable to me about the Feminist Press is its reprint program. This program has returned to us not only Agnes Smedley but also the collected stories of Kate Chopin, Mary Freeman's *The Revolt of Mother,* Rebecca Harding Davis's *Life in the Iron Mills,* and Charlotte Gilman's *The Yellow Wallpaper.* These books are important documents not only in the history of women but in the history of our culture as well.

With each day that passes we become more acutely aware of the "lost" history of women: the deletions and distortions, the elliptical references and half-truths in the official histories, that have served to wipe out the complex role women have played in the development of American politics and culture. Book after book off the presses these days serves to show us who and what we have really been in this country. Some of what we learn is marvelous, some of it extremely painful. But the point is: it is *our history.* It tells us who and what we have been, and therefore who and what we may become. That is the purpose history serves; that is the meaning of having a past, cultural as well as individual.

For this reason alone, the reprints of the Feminist Press are worth their weight in gold. When I "found" Chopin, Gilman, and Smedley, I marveled. And I thought: Why have I not grown up with these books? Why have I never known of the existence of these women, this literature? How would the lives of the women of my generation been different if we had had these books during our growing years?

And there is more. Consider the contribution a woman like Agnes Smedley made to the history of radicalism in this country. Reading *Daughter of Earth* today, one sees clearly the intimate relation between the struggle of women to live free lives and the struggle over the last two centuries to salvage human consciousness from the relentless oppression of modern industrialism. The link between radicalism and feminism becomes undeniable.

It is all part of a vital rereading of the culture that contemporary feminism has stimulated. The publication of Agnes Smedley by the Feminist Press is a genuine contribution to that rereading.

(February 1977)

Margaret Fuller: The Woman and the Myth

Margaret Fuller—the nineteenth-century intellectual whose name we associate with American transcendentalism—was loved and respected by many people, but she was perceived by her contemporaries as a social and psychological embarrassment, a creature of formidable intellect and overwhelming arrogance, alternately ridiculous and grotesque in her assumption of masculine poses, a fit subject for female caricature by writers like Hawthorne and James. In short: a human oddity who spoke and wrote much that stirred the people around her but did so out of a life that, while stimulating, was on the whole incomprehensible and irritating.

For 126 years we have accepted the terms of description fashioned by the society that so perceived Margaret Fuller. Of the actual human being walled up inside the prison of such descriptions we have had no glimpse. Of the historical environment in which *she* saw herself living and of the way in which *she* perceived her life we have known nothing.

Now, under the impetus of feminist scholarship, Bell Gale Chevigny, a teacher of literature at SUNY, Purchase, has "rewritten" Fuller's life from the inside out, so to speak, and there emerges the portrait of an extraordinary human being whose experience places her at the direct center of the modern struggle to emerge, against prevailing social dictates, into conscious being. Rather than viewing Fuller as an atypical woman, Chevigny sees her as archetypal. "The problem of being Margaret Fuller," she writes, "was that of any woman who sought free self-development and an active life in a culture which could neither countenance or even conceive of such goals [and] made people locate the problem not in the culture but in the women themselves."

So begins a remarkable work designed to shake the kaleidoscope of historical truth, letting the pieces of fact rearrange themselves into a new illumination, a new and truer configuration of history, culture, and the meaning of a single significant life. What Chevigny has done is to put together an anthology composed of Fuller's writings, the writings of her contemporaries about her, and Chevigny's own long running commentary—the whole arranged in such a way that we come as close as possible to experiencing Fuller's life as she herself lived it. This approach, says Chevigny, is justified not only by the legitimate desire to resurrect a life potent with meaning for us today but also because "the complex and powerful effect Fuller had on thinking men and women is probably more revealing of American attitudes than the effect of any other woman in her century, and it cannot be deduced from her writings alone."

These are the "facts" of Fuller's life: Born in 1810, she was the first of Margaret and Timothy Fuller's many children. Timothy was a Harvard lawyer and Massachusetts politician whose political independence placed him on the social and political edge of Cambridge life. In his isolation, Timothy quickly recognized his eldest child's extraordinary intelligence and set himself the task of developing it in order that he might have the intellectual companionship he craved. Thus, at the age of six Margaret was reading Latin and Greek, at the age of eight Shakespeare. She grew up reading, reading, reading. Through her father she came into contact with the intellectuals of Harvard, and from earliest youth theirs was the world in which she moved.

By the 1830s she was a familiar of Emerson, Thoreau, Channing, and the entire intellectual circle that came to be known as the transcendentalists. Between 1830 and 1845 she conducted her famous Conversations with Women, edited and wrote for the transcendentalist magazine *The Dial*, translated "Eckermann's Conversations with Goethe," became the first woman journalist on Horace Greeley's New York *Tribune*, and published her book-length feminist tract "Woman in the Nineteenth Century."In 1846 she went to Europe, where she met Carlyle, Giuseppe Mazzini, Adam Mickiewicz, and George Sand. Galvanized by their ideas, she found herself compelled to join the revolution about to engulf the Continent. In 1847 she went to Italy, where she became a partisan of the revolution, reporting throughout the crucial years of 1848 and 1849 for the *Tribune*.

In Italy, also, she became the lover of Angelo Ossoli, an aristocratic Italian partisan, and bore him a child. In May of 1850, having just turned forty—hating to leave Italy, but driven by the need for money—she, Ossoli, and their child set sail for America. In July their ship was wrecked off the coast of Fire Island, and she died within fifty yards of the American shore.

Her friends and family were shocked by the events of her last years, and when they came to write her official life they bowdlerized the many papers and letters that illuminated the meaning of these events, thus burying Margaret Fuller's life along with Margaret Fuller.

The full restoration of the writings, letters, and journals, both by and about her, and as they are arranged and commented on by Chevigny, reveals a life shaped by a serious and slowly cohering quest for the self even as that self was being powerfully acted upon by the social and political thought of its time. Fuller's life, clearly, was lived in a debilitating state of conflict that has until now been either ignored or glossed over by the official histories. It is to the sources of this conflict that *The Woman and the Myth* addresses itelf.

To begin with there was the question of being a woman; to end with there was the question of modern political consciousness. In between there were such other questions as: the German romantic influence, Emerson's definition of the American destiny, and, most significant, the inability of this quintessential American woman to become either an American or a woman until she left America.

When Alexis de Tocqueville and Harriet Martineau visited America in the 1830s, one characteristic of American life struck them both forcibly: as unmarried girls American women had more freedom and independence of thought than Europeans had; as married women they lived in a state of submission more thorough than anything known to many European women. Fuller herself could not *see* what Tocqueville and Martineau saw, she could only be shaped by the conflict at the heart of their observation. To be free, independent, and intellectual meant not to be a natural American woman; not to be a woman meant to be something other than her full self. Thus, bursting with spiritual and intellectual vitality, she was condemned to act out a partial and deforming existence that stunted both her intellectual work and her emotional development.

From earliest childhood intellectual work was accompanied by ferocious migraine headaches and dreams of horses trampling on her head. (Of the ever-present migraine she once wrote self-mockingly: "It is but a bad head, as bad as if I were a great man!") She both loved and hated her father for having made her an intellectual, and at thirty she accused him of being derelict in his duty toward her as a father. (On this matter, Chevigny observes tartly, "The duty Timothy had shunned was showing his daughter what to do with what he had made her. . . . Instead, he abandoned her to a society in which she could only be useless and freakish.")

The act of writing paralyzed her—one remembers how Fuller has always been described as an astonishing conversationalist unable to transfer the quality of her talk to the written page—and she described her agony in a letter to a friend:

For all the tides of life that flow within me, I am dumb and ineffectual when it comes to casting my thought into a form. No old one suits me. If I could invent one, it seems to me the pleasure of creation would make it possible for me to write. What shall I do, dear friend? I want force to be either a genius or a character. One should be either private or public. I love best to be a woman; but womanhood is at present too straitly-bounded to give me scope. At hours, I live truly as a woman; at others, I should stifle; as, on the other hand, I should palsy, when I would play the artist.

This split within her was echoed in her conflicted relation to transcendentalism; again, a conflict never fully documented until now. Drawn to Emerson, Channing, and Company mainly because they were the only intellectuals to admit her to their circle, she was always at odds with the absolutism of self as Emerson pursued it, lured by the complex thought and literature of Europe as he was not, and—although she did not know this until she left New England—by the social and political world.

In Italy—in the midst of a social revolution out of which would emerge modern political consciousness—everything in Fuller came together with force and suddenness. It has been said that in Italy she became "a true woman," meaning that here she took a lover and became a mother. But it is abundantly clear now, from the letters and the *Tribune* dispatches, that these acts released her, not for love and motherhood, but—exactly as they have ever released men—for more integrated intellectual work and an even more acute sense of the importance of being in the world.

Her writings during this period are alive with a concentrated power and a clarity of insight they had not quite known before. This power and insight came, undeniably, from the conviction of mind and feeling, there on the page to be seen, that she and Italy and *America* were all "becoming" together. Even while the *Communist Manifesto* was being published in February of 1848 in London, Margaret Fuller in Italy was moving swiftly and comprehensively toward the idea that socialism was going to change the world forever, and in its growth was to be found the fulfillment of the American democratic promise. (Chevigny writes of Fuller's thought at this time: "Emerson's model of national growth was singular and organic; the nation and the reliant self unfold together. . . . Fuller's model was multiple and morally dialectic; nations change under the pressure of challenges posed them by other societies.") It now seems more than likely that, had she lived, Margaret Fuller would have become one of the first important American Marxists, and it is as such that she might have been remembered—rather than as the "handmaiden" to major transcendentalist talents.

What is profoundly important about this view of Fuller's life is that it recalls vividly the meaning of the lonely struggle conducted in cultural isolation, and the cumulative effect such struggles have had on the slowly growing notion that every human being has the right to a conscious and deliberate life.

This book is the work of a gifted teacher absorbed by a worthy subject, asking the kinds of questions no one asked fifteen or twenty years ago. As such, *The Woman and the Myth* is, genuinely, a work of moment.

(January 1977)

On Rereading
Virginia Woolf

Rereading the books of youth and early maturity, and feeling that one is reading them as though for the first time, is a common experience among contemporary feminists. The new consciousness is a kind of litmus paper; dip it into the most familiar of works and there suddenly stands revealed a new pattern, a previously hidden picture, a now decoded text.

I've been reading Virginia Woolf, and experiencing precisely such magic. It's not that I've not always known Woolf as a feminist (after all, *A Room of One's Own* is a fundamental text). It's rather that I've always thought of Woolf's feminist pieces as a single, separate part of her writings, not integral to the major body of her work: those brilliant novels we have always read as the imaginings of a nonsexual, upperclass writer of sensibility exploring, with an imperious intelligence, the solitariness of modern life.

Now, reading the novels once more, the litmus paper is dipped, and I see I was wrong. The feminist pieces *were* integral to the work. (I read and think: How is this possible? A blind man could have seen this. Why did you not see this?) How central to her work was the relation between men and women, how keen the emotional attention she paid to the trauma of identity any intelligent woman suffered, what metaphoric use she made of a woman's sexual withdrawal to say something important about human beings struggling to possess themselves! This last, for me, is most significant, the thing above all that makes me feel I am indeed reading Woolf for the first time.

214

Virginia Woolf's women have always been called "cold." (Their coldness, in fact, has often been central to a critical interpretation of her work.) Clarissa Dalloway was cold, Lily Briscoe was cold, countless others were cold. When I read *Mrs. Dalloway* in my twenties I thought, Why won't she love Peter? She's so cold! When I read *To the Lighthouse,* I thought of Lily Briscoe, Why won't she marry? She's so cold! They were all cold: sexually aloof, witholding, without warmth or sensuality.

Now I reread *Mrs. Dalloway* and *To the Lighthouse* and I find I myself saying calmly of Clarissa and Lily, "Why, its crystal clear. They're fighting for their lives. Given the terms of their struggle they have only one weapon at their disposal—sexual withdrawal." Clarissa does not marry Peter, whom she loves, because she feels suffocated, even in courtship, by the devouring quality of his blind male force. Marriage to him—precisely because she does love him—will smother her entirely. She marries Richard Dalloway—no emotional threat to that frail "I" at her noncohering center—and sleeps on a virginal cot for the rest of her life, sacrificing on terms that at least allow her to breathe. Lily Briscoe does not marry because she watches the overwhelming Mr. Ramsey tyrannize his wife and children. And ever she hears in her mind the voice of Charles Tansley—an arriviste caricature of Mr. Ramsey—repeating "women can't write, women can't paint," and it is a sound that makes "her whole being bow, like corn under a wind, and erect itself again from this abasement only with a great and rather painful effort."

Such sentences are at the heart of the dense, gathering silence that fills the pages of Virginia Woolf's novels; sentences in which we can almost see Woolf herself, her aristocratic head cocked, her lean body perfectly still, listening hard for the meaning: the meaning of the thing behind the appearances.

The meaning of the thing for Woolf was, always, what human beings do to one another: the frightening lack of sympathy that condemns each of us to unholy isolation. And nowhere, for her, was that lack of sympathy more painfully in evidence than between men and women.

Discovering the novels anew makes me wish to rediscover the woman, the life, the whole work anew. I dip back into the diaries, the letters, the essays, the things her friends said about her. She comes closer, closer.

In 1941, a year after her death, E. M. Forster delivered a eulogistic lecture on Virginia Woolf at Cambridge—the university whose library doors were locked against her throughout her lifetime. Amidst much love and praise, Forster spoke with bewilderment of her continuing feminism. It seemed old-fashioned to him. After all, he said, by the 1930s there wasn't that much to complain of, and still she kept grumbling. But Forster, a deeply civilized man, then added, "However, I speak as a man here, and an elderly one. The best judges of her feminism are neither elderly men nor even elderly women, but young women. If they think that it expresses an existent grievance, they are right."

I find myself wondering these days: What would Virginia Woolf make of it all if she could be here to see American feminism bursting across the 1970s? And I think—I am sure—she would be applauding. Despite everything—the vulgarity she would find deplorable, the bad writing that would make her flinch, the abusive language she would simply stare at—she'd be applauding.

Last week I was reading again her famous 1924 essay, "Mr. Bennett and Mrs. Brown." Writing in defense of modern literature, she says:

All human relations have shifted . . . and when human relations change there is at the same time a change in religion, conduct, politics, and literature. . . . At the present moment we are suffering not from decay, but from having no code of manners which writers and readers accept as a prelude to the more exciting intercourse of friendship. . . . Signs of this are everywhere apparent. Grammar is violated; syntax disintegrated. . . . The sincerity (of modern writers) is desperate, and their courage tremendous; it is only that they do not know which to use, a fork or their fingers.

Surely, she who urged women—however clumsily, with whatever difficulty—to write in their own voices would have seen the applicability of these words to contemporary feminism. She who created Lily Briscoe, not to marry but (after a day, a night,

and another day, with a symbolic ten years in between) to finish
her painting, would have looked on, her thin cheeks flushed
with pleasure, at all those struggling now to finish that painting.
And certainly, she who said generations of women must write,
write, write before a Judith Shakespeare would arise among us
would now nod her head in approval, her upper-class voice which
I always imagine with a thin rasp in it) crooning wickedly, "My
dears, it is a fertilizing proh-cess. And we all know, my dears,
what fertilizer is mainly composed of."

(1978)

Female Narcissism as a Metaphor in Literature

One of the great literary metaphors for human experience is maleness itself. In much of our literature men as men bear the burden of visionary perception. The emotional culture of men's lives—the maleness of experience—is used metaphorically. The bildungsroman—with its central image of a young man from the provinces going out into the world on a symbolic journey of self-discovery—is *the* literary model for maleness used as a metaphor for humanness itself.

By the same token, women as women have also been used in literature to say something important about what it is to be human. The emotional culture of women's lives—the *femaleness* of experience—has in the hands of many great writers assumed metaphoric proportions.

By the maleness and femaleness of experience I mean this: Given the obvious—namely, that the long cultural dictates of society have determined that, generally speaking, men live one kind of life and women another kind of life—certain emotional experiences common to all have nevertheless accumulated with force and depth in men, and others in women. These experiences we respectively associate with maleness or femaleness. "That is such a male experience," we will say, or conversely, "That is such a female experience."

For instance: Men as such know more about power, and women as such know more about powerlessness. Together, power and powerlessness are an interlocking two-part fundament permanently associated with the fears and desires of organized human life, shared by all, yet, in a mythic sense, divided between men and women.

The quest for power speaks to our deepest selves, tells us much about our lives, our history, the entire world-making enterprise. It has to do with a journey into mastery—over the self and others—that is an act of assertion, a piece of defiance in the face of death and nothingness. That journey is one we associate with men's lives, not women's. Thus, it is a given that when literature turns on the search for power it is male characters who will dominate, and it is the maleness of experience that will assume metaphoric dimension.

But let us imagine that a writer wishes to write about powerlessness—how it works, what it means, what portion of the human soul the condition speaks to and arises out of—wishes, in short, to write about the nether side of human existence, about fear rather than hunger, uncertainty rather than mastery. Would that writer so easily turn to the "maleness" of experience, or would he or she not more naturally swerve toward the "femaleness" of experience?

In Thomas Hardy, Edith Wharton, and Henry James we have three writers who, to lesser or greater degrees, were all keenly drawn to the idea of the divided psyche: the hesitations of the soul split between being and nonbeing, the complex rather than simple meanings of passivity, the struggle between repressive fears and sympathetic impulses, the awesome power of self-hatred. For these writers the femaleness of experience was a natural, and it was through the metaphoric properties with which many of their female characters are endowed that they—not always but often—arrived at ultimate illumination. In particular, it was mainly through their arresting usage of female narcissism that they spoke so acutely to these preoccupations.

Just as men and women "share" between them the bulk of human experiences so, of course, they—again, in a large, mythic sense—divide between them the psychological order and disorder that experience both causes and is symptomatic of. One of the great emotional disorders of human life is narcissism—that paradoxical condition of self-regard in which absorption with the self speaks to an absence of the self. To put it briefly:

It is a characteristic of infantilism that the external world is experienced solely as a source of gratification or deprivation. Ideally, as the infant matures and the adult self forms, that sense of things dissolves, the world is perceived more objectively, the adult takes his or her place in it, among other separate beings, and interacts with them in the only real experience. When the self fails to mature, it remains arrested in this early stage of development, and genuine engagement with the objective world is precluded. Hence: narcissism.

Now, while narcissism is certainly a shared characteristic, common to men and women alike, it is in women that it has, for obvious reasons, often flared most vividly—most primarily, as Freud might have said—and it is a state of inner being we frequently associate specifically with women; with, if you will, "the femaleness of experience." Sometimes, the term "female narcissism" is spoken as though it were one word.

It is an unhappy condition, narcissism, retrograde in its character and vile in its behavior patterns. Often, it is experienced as an enemy of life. Certainly, D. H. Lawrence saw it as such. His women are classics in female narcissism: strong-willed and life-destroying.

But in three great novels—*Jude the Obscure, The House of Mirth,* and *Portrait of a Lady*—Hardy, Wharton, and James endowed female narcissism with metaphoric properties and observed it, with psychological depth and extraordinary sympathy, in order to search out its deeper meanings: to show us how powerfully it speaks to the divided psyche within us all.

Jude the Obscure is set in a disinheriting time: the late nineteenth century, when the countryside is being abandoned and the towns are becoming industrial centers. Country people wander in search of work, alone now in a harsh time and place where everything is in flux and human beings are thrown back on themselves as though the world were beginning anew—but this time with no help from the earth.

Jude Fawley and Sue Bridehead, cousins who meet as adults in the town, are descended from country people who are both typical and atypical of their class. Like all other country people, the Fawleys are dour, silent, hard-working. Unlike all other country people they are also passionate, eccentric, artistic. The unexpected spiritual dimension that Jude and Sue inherit both sets them in their world and lifts them beyond it, makes them children of their time. Hungry to experience themselves, yet anchored to the social station birth has assigned them, they wander in loneliness through a moment filled with contradiction and illusory promise, their life together a heroic doomed attempt to declare the principle of inner being supreme.

Theirs is an extraordinary boldness, alive with courage and frailty, the parts mixed differently in each of them, the sum of it binding them together. From the first, Hardy establishes that they are "one," that they share and complement each other's spiritual makeup. Jude's strength is sensual, emotional: powerful in its capacity to make him yearn for the life within him. Sue's is spiritual, intellectual: triggered by an acute and moving sense of class injustice and of her own natural value.

An internal war is waged in each between the fear of history and the desire to ignore history. Together, they fortify each other against the anxieties crowding up inside them. But as their life goes forward, encompassing one melodramatic disaster after another, Sue steadily loses her nerve. In the end she dissolves into demented religiosity, her madness an act of aggression against her life with Jude. And although Jude can survive almost anything, he cannot survive the loss of Sue: as they have risen together, so they go down together.

There is a single crucial difference between the two of them, and it lies at the heart of their common tragedy. Jude has the emotional capacity to move forward through his life, and Sue does not. At every turn of the way, as his mind and senses absorb new evidence for the rightness of the life they have chosen to live, Jude acts upon what he "sees." Once an emotional truth has been internalized, he never goes back on it. There is in Jude an essential wholeness of self ready to receive his own experience; it is, ultimately, the source of his strength, the thing that makes him a noble creature able to endure so brilliantly that in him endurance becomes a form of victory.

Sue, on the other hand, intellectually quicker than Jude, is beset by fears so enormous that at every turn of the way she is torn in half, wrung out by anxieties that force her to double back on herself, never permitting her simply to act. Her superior intelligence—the intelligence that persuades Jude to a higher courage—is without the power to control the deeper dictates of her emotional terrors. These terrors derive from an essentially fragmented self; that fragmentation dissolves Sue's ability to possess her own experience; it corrodes her mind, blots out the world, makes concentration on anything but her own fears an impossibility.

Sue, with all her many, many virtues, is the embodiment of female narcissism. Nervous, mercurial, sensitive and willful, intent on her devotion to a higher spiritual principle, she is desperately self-involved; she cannot escape her worried preoccupation with her own worth for s single moment. Wanting only to do the morally right thing, wracked endlessly by self-doubt, she torments Jude with a behavior so driven and contradictory—and then so stricken with tearful remorse—that it eats away at them both, unraveling the fabric of their life together even as it is being woven. . . . And ever at the heart of Sue's impulsiveness and regret are the anxiety-ridden questions "Do you love me? Am I lovable? Am I desirable? Will you never forget that it is me, me, me here at your side, beneath you in bed, sharing your thoughts, necessary to your existence?"

Sue Bridehead is the true mother of Miriam in *Sons and Lovers*, even as Jude is father to Paul Morel. Both Sue and Miriam are strong-willed and spiritual, both Jude and Paul are intuitive and sexual. Sue and Miriam are both enslaved by humiliating fantasies of grandiosity, Jude and Paul are both excited by the dimensions of the actual self. Sue and Miriam are both consumed with the need to be desired, Jude and Paul eager to know the felt reality of desiring. In short: the women are characteristically infantile, the men characteristically adult.

But whereas Lawrence bitterly condemns Miriam, Hardy sympathizes intensely with Sue. To Lawrence, Paul Morel is life itself, and Miriam is the enemy stealing that life. To Hardy, Sue is not the "other," she is one half of the whole. She and Jude are, significantly, a single "one," brought down by internal conflict. The fate they ultimately share is that of a single being divided against itself.

The greatness of *Jude the Obscure* lies in the psychological depth and compassion with which Hardy imagines both Jude and Sue, and raises them to metaphoric heights. Jude's wholeness of self speaks to the longing for completion, Sue's lack of wholeness to the terror of completion. Together, they are the human condition—riven, conflicted, torn with irresolution, and finally, in a world where there is no help forthcoming from the outside, doomed by its own failure to cohere to a loneliness so great it amounts to death by emotional starvation.

In *The House of Mirth* Edith Wharton creates a piece of female narcissism that blooms in primitive radiance, like something bred in hothouse isolation for the special purpose of observing the organism in its most unadorned state.

The novel is set in the world of upper-class New York society at the turn of the century. It is a philistine world of mean and narrow restriction based on the raw accumulation of material wealth and strict adherence to a rigid set of rules that serves no real purpose beyond assuring its members of their exclusivity. Here art, education, and emotional freedom are unknown, looked upon with fear and distaste. Here men make money and exercise money power, and women display that money and set themselves as decorated creatures at the center of the display. The glitter is hard and joyless, a jeweled veneer surrounding an emptiness of mind, heart, and spirit.

Lily Bart, with all her virtues and limitations, is emblematic of this world. Her rise and fall is the "story" Wharton has to tell, her character the means through which the story will be told.

Lily is a woman of grace, intelligence, and immense beauty. Born into New York society, raised to take her place in it by virtue of birth, wealth, and beauty, she loses her assured position at an early age when her father goes bankrupt and then dies, leaving Lily and her mother penniless. Instantly catapulted to the outer edge of the gilded cage, the mother clings madly to its golden bars, clawing to regain her inner place. Eaten alive by her own bitterness, she grips the girl's arm as she is dying and says, "You're beautiful. You'll get it all back. You'll make it up. You're beautiful."

Lily grows up more spirited, more intelligent, more comprehending than her mother. She sees the shallowness and cruelty all about her, she knows there's more to life than this. Still, she is in thrall to the only world she has ever known. Still, she is more her mother than she is herself. Still, a voice within whispers fiercely, "I'm entitled. I'm beautiful."

The beauty is Lily's glittering weapon. She knows from earliest girlhood she must make final brilliant use of it to secure her position socially and gain for herself the wealth she *must* have. And for a very long time she does not doubt that she can and will do so. Beneath her very real gifts of mind and spirit lies the fixed emotional conviction that her beauty *is* her true birthright, her aristocratic claim upon the goods of life, her "entitlement" to the regal world unfairly snatched from her. At times, she knows better. But do what she will that voice within her keeps repeating, "You're entitled. You're beautiful. You were born to be adored." This voice commands her. It dominates her life, overrules her honesty, prevents growth, commits her to an infantile longing to redeem original loss.

Yet, time passes and Lily cannot bring herself to make the necessary marriage of convenience. Each time she approaches final success, at the ultimate moment, having used all her considerable powers of wit and allure to gain her desired ends, something in her suddenly turns away; when it is within her reach, she cannot stretch out her hand to pluck the fruit of her labor.

On the surface it would appear it is the best in Lily responsible for this curious exercise in self-defeat: her fine mind and honest spirit are sickened by the emotional shabbiness of what she is about to accomplish, the emptiness ahead appears as a great lid sealing down her life. And while this is true enough, the driving force behind her conflicted behavior lies elsewhere.

Lily's need for adoration is bottomless. Not only must she go on making men want to marry her, she must be in a position to have an endless supply of men wanting her. To marry is to choose one, thereby precluding all other choices. To have the ultimate triumph is, finally, to have only one triumph. That is not enough. The image of her beauty being newly adored is the need of her soul. It is food, nourishment for an impoverished being. The need is enormous, the hunger insatiable, the emptiness at its center wide and deep as the ocean, nothing and no one can ever fill it. Lily is indeed penniless; no amount of wealth can cure her poverty.

Lily's narcissism—the narcissism of a beautiful woman in a gilded world—is Wharton's great metaphor. It constitutes, for her, an emotional power greater than all the benign influences of reason and spirit. The world, the woman, the coldhearted self-adoration all reflect on one another. They shine into a yawning void: at the heart of things a fatal emptiness, a gaping absence, an emotional incoherence that flourishes in the open space of the hollow center. And behind that emptiness a truth more deadly even than the vacuum itself.

As the years pass, Lily's social position becomes ever more precarious. Her beauty begins to lose its brilliance; an edge of desperation hardens about her; in a world where all human beings are objects, and friendship is a function of circumstance, Lily becomes more and more an outsider: a single woman past a certain age is a curiosity rather than a delight. She is despised by those she had intimidated, manipulated where previously she had manipulated, and her waning beauty becomes a wellspring of poisoned regrets, stagnating in the bitterness of false promise.

At the penultimate moment, when one social disaster has piled onto another and the tightrope she has walked so long is clearly breaking beneath her, Lily is offered the last chance of rescue she will have. A weak and humiliated man—nevertheless rich and socially secure—begs her to marry him. They stand on a deserted road; each stares into the face of the other. Lily hears the offer, understands its meaning for her. She sees the man's naked need, she has experienced humiliation, they are alone under an empty sky, she is at last face to face with the knowledge she has fled all her life: her own power fills her with horror.

She recoils in a fear so great it is revulsion. Fear of herself, fear of her own power, fear of her very being. She wants to take the power so badly she can almost taste it. Her own hunger terrifies her. Suddenly, she experiences herself as rapacious; she senses the aggressive, infuriated animal within; she hates the man and she hates herself; she wants to smash the man; she has *always* wanted to smash the man. She feels then that which is at the heart of all political reaction: "We really *are* animals. Better not to become at all than to become and face that ultimate truth."

Lily's narcissism is a blind, a smokescreen behind which has always stood this fear of being. The emotional confusion between the natural exercise of her own power and the conviction that power is aggression is what produces the fury behind her self-absorption. The malice of narcissism stems from the rage of the thwarted self; the courage simply *to be* would have long ago dried up the flow of anger.

But this Lily cannot see. All she can see is that any exercise of power is of necessity an act of humiliating aggression against all others. She is persuaded that this is a fundamental truth, and life for her then becomes a circular horror. Because she *is* decent, and cannot find her way out of the moral dilemma, she commits suicide, dying, in fact, of her own unlived life, alone at the melodramatic end as only a true narcissist who has received quality adoration is finally alone.

Wharton's insight is brilliant, but hard-edged. It will be left for Henry James and Isabel Archer to penetrate deeper, with a profounder pity and richer understanding, into the heart of the matter.

If Lily Bart had been given the money she "needed," she would have become Isabel Archer. Lily is a primitive narcissist, Isabel a cultivated one. Lily's fate is melodramatic, Isabel's clearly self-inflicted. Edith Wharton thought no one could have freedom, Henry James knew no one wanted freedom.

Isabel Archer, like Lily Bart, is young, beautiful, intelligent, and—by social standards—penniless. Unlike Lily, however, Isabel does not want money, marriage, or social position. What Isabel wants is to *live*. She wants to experience the world and all things in it. Above all, she wants to experience herself.

Isabel's nature appeals. Sitting alone in a house in Albany, reading a book in a room sealed off from the street, she is rescued from her obscure state by Lydia Touchett, an eccentric aunt she hardly knows, carried off to Europe, installed in the Touchett's English country house, and set upon her destined course: she will receive everything she needs for the express purpose of discovering whether she in fact wants what she says she wants—to live fully and freely.

Isabel's ardency becomes a catalytic force; it sets in motion the longings and appetites of various people who are "reminded" by her of their own lost selves (after all, she claims she will do what they have all been unable to do themselves). Primarily, she reminds Ralph Touchett.

Ralph Touchett, Isabel's cousin, has everything—money, grace, education—everything but vitality (symbolized by his near-terminal tuberculosis). Ralph thinks Isabel can do what he could not do. He induces his father to leave her a fortune so that she may have the freedom to live for them both. When Mr. Touchett does so, it is as though scalpel is placed to flesh, and the exploratory operation begins.

Upon receiving the money, Isabel quails. Without fully understanding it, she is suddenly up against herself as she has never been before. She says to Ralph, "I try to care more about the world than about myself—but I always come back to myself. It's because I'm afraid. Yes, I am afraid. I can't tell you. A large fortune means freedom, and I am afraid of that. . . . I am not sure that it's not a greater happiness to be powerless."

With these words Isabel has spoken the deepest truth about herself: she does fear freedom, she does crave powerlessness, the spirited independence is bravado. And the next three hundred pages of *Portrait of a Lady* will become one of the most brilliant explorations in English literature of the meaning of that truth.

Isabel takes her money and travels. Her travels are a mockery. Unlike those of the young man on a journey of self-discovery in which event becomes transformed into experience, Isabel's travels are a round of meaningless exertions. She experiences nothing, feels nothing, learns nothing. The world remains a picture postcard without dimension or substance upon which she gazes with dull eyes. An invisible pane of glass stands between her and what she sees. She fails to connect; she cannot become engaged. She is in no emotional position to see that the failure is hers, not that of the world. She draws the inevitable conclusion: it is not that she cannot see but rather than there is nothing to see; it is not that she has no self with which to experience but rather that one can have experience only through another; it is not that she does not value her freedom but rather that it is far nobler to make of that freedom a gift to a higher being. (After all, she reasons, what better thing can a woman do than lay her rich, useless existence at the feet of a fine man?) She returns to Italy and marries Gilbert Osmond.

It is a characteristic of narcissism that all other human beings are experienced as either superior or inferior, as the narcissist sees everyone and everything in comparative terms, with the gratified or deprived self at the center of the comparison. It is also characteristic that the actual superiority or inferiority of a thing or a person is inevitably confused, as the narcissist is not responding to what actually *is* but only to the sensation of self-value that is aroused. Thus it is with Isabel and Osmond.

Isabel perceives Gilbert Osmond, an intensely Europeanized American, as the poetic principle come to life. For her, Osmond is the embodiment of the higher ideal, a man of sensitivity removed from the sordid business of getting and spending, living in that rarefied atmosphere where the goodness of beauty is endlessly contemplated. Osmond had told her he loved her; she had been flattered. Frightened by the glimpse of inner emptiness her year of traveling has given her, she now concludes that she must, after all, be a person of value if Osmond loves her.

In fact, Osmond is a man of evil vanity, inconsequential and artificial, terrifying in his need to manipulate others and to receive from them spiritual obedience; a man who has performed the supreme confidence trick of passing off his monumental self-absorption as a form of higher remove from the vulgarity of material life. Everyone in the world can see Osmond for what he is; everyone except Isabel. We watch with dread and with painful understanding (so deeply has James made us enter into her helpless self-deception) as Isabel places her person and her fortune in Osmond's hands, and marries herself forever to her own incapacity.

Very quickly, Osmond realizes that in Isabel he has not got a woman whose mind he can bend to his will (she is not independent but she *is* rebellious), whose being he can "collect" as he does his precious objects. He turns on her with a power of malevolence, and only then does Isabel realize exactly what it is she has done to herself. There follows a description of psychological bondage that occupies pages surely among the most frightening ever written in the English language.

The house in Rome where Osmond and Isabel live—filled as it is with Osmond's cold collected beauty, now a bitter reproach to Isabel—is a dark and desolate place in which they each wander alone, condemned to the isolation of their dreadful alliance. As James' description mounts, the house becomes a prison fortress: a chilling metaphor for the marriage in which they are both trapped. In Isabel's imagination the house, at last, seems to narrow to a towerlike room in which she sits alone and, from a window placed high up in the wall, Osmond's mind stares down at her in silent mockery. Isabel understands then, and we with her, the deeper reality: she has married the grotesque version of her own worst self. Osmond is her double, carried to an annihilating extreme. He is her own infantile vanity, her own emotional incapacity, the distorted mirror image of her own fear of life. He glitters with the evil of inner emptiness, the treachery of the voided self. For Osmond, human beings are objects. Now Isabel sees—to the black, fathomless bottom of such sight—that for her Osmond was also an object. As no one is real to him, so no one is real to her. For Isabel, whose whole conscious life has been predicated on her moral and spiritual superiority, this insight is paralyzing.

Osmond's narcissism is powerful, but it is Isabel's that is significant. For Isabel *is* lovely and intelligent and decent; she lacks only bravery. But that "only" is all the world. That failure of nerve has made her self-absorbed; that self-absorption precludes real experience; that preclusion induces terror of life; that terror is ultimately stronger than beauty, intelligence, decency.

Understanding everything, Isabel is yet helpless. Her fears bind her like chains, they are the prison from which there is no escape. All around her there are outstretched the hands of people who love her, who offer to help and protect her. Isabel listens silent, inert. What is there to say? They can never understand.

At the last, Caspar Goodwood—that fine American innocent who has loved her throughout—grasps her in his arms and kisses her passionately. "Come back to America," he implores her, "where there is no past, only the open future." Isabel is fiercely aroused by the kiss. She knows the arousal is life itself, the risk of real experience, the world flung open to her again. But she is more afraid than she is aroused. She flees Goodwood as though *he* is the danger, and returns to the safety of her prison.

For Isabel there is no future, only the past, the past within, the past we first observed when we found her sitting in her father's house in Albany, in a room sealed off from the street, reading. She has never really left that house in Albany. The prison fortress she shares with Osmond is an emotional re-creation of that sealed-off room. The dark silence of the house in Rome is the silence surrounding her entombed self, the self that never emerged from childhood. The house itself, adorned by the elaborateness of European art and beauty, is a brilliant parallel to Isabel's own adornment of beauty, spirit, intelligence, and at the center of both house and woman the silent, flickering, smothered self, moving and awful in its inability to become.

Henry James—for whom the abyss began at the edge of the writing desk—understood the complexity of narcissism, and behind it the fear of one's own life, perhaps better than any other writer in this century. He understood it because he shared it, he felt it moving inside himself. He knew intimately the fear of acting, and its consequences: what it meant *not to act.* He did not despise what he knew, he stood in awe of it. He watched its workings with a depth of concentration unparalleled in modern literature.

Above all, James watched narcissism take metaphoric shape in the lives of women. He lived in their drawing rooms. He knew that those rooms—where he and they did, indeed, withdraw—contained symbolic weight. He knew *why* there collected in women's lives rather than in men's the exquisite nervelessness, the radiant self-absorption. He understood deeply what a breeding ground for Hamlet's illness were the cultural lives of women, and for him it was the real thing. He knew the sorrow and mockery of divided male and female disorder. He knew what a lie it was. He created Isabel Archer to reveal the lie. For Isabel is indeed a superior creature, so supremely realized she is beyond pity, and dismissal is unthinkable. James forces us to look, with silence and dread, upon her meaning. As an intelligent woman in an inactive state, she is by way of ritual sacrificed to the fears of the race itself: the common helplessness before the imprisoning past, the inability to break free, to become, to act.

(1978)

Index